THE CONTRACT GUIDE

DPIC's RISK MANAGEMENT HANDBOOK FOR ARCHITECTS AND ENGINEERS

by Sheila A. Dixon
and Richard D. Crowell

Different by Design®

The Professional Liability
Specialist of the
Orion Capital Companies

DPIC Companies, Inc.
P.O. Box DPIC
2959 Monterey-Salinas Highway
Monterey, California 93940
800/227-4284

©1987, 1993 DPIC Companies, Inc.
Monterey, California
Revised edition; formerly titled *DPIC Companies' Guide to Better Contracts*

ISBN 0-932056-06-7
Library of Congress Catalog Card Number 93-71220

 Printed on recycled paper.

ACKNOWLEDGMENTS

No book can reach publication without the help and advice of many people whose names do not appear on the cover. This is especially true of DPIC's *Contract Guide*.

When the *DPIC Companies' Guide to Better Contracts* was published in 1987, it was based extensively on the *ASFE Contract Reference Guide*, 2nd Edition. Both books were developed by John Bachner of Bachner Communications. This book builds upon his very solid foundation. For that foundation, the authors of this edition are supremely grateful.

In writing the Guide, we called upon the expertise of many professionals. In particular, special thanks go to engineer/attorney Dan Smith of CH2M Hill and Larry Segrue, FAIA, who gave us valuable input for both the business and legal discussions. David Hatem, Esq., of Burns and Levinson provided independent legal review as well as very welcome assistance. Susan Tsantiris, Esq., of Orion Capital Companies' law division contributed an in-house review and answers to endless questions. Our thanks also go to the many members of PLAN — the Professional Liability Agents Network — who were always at the ready with advice and comments.

At DPIC Companies, the regional claims managers, headed by Senior Vice President Elliott Gleason, and the Monterey claims staff all deserve our gratitude for timely critique and help. At the home office, Russ Chaney, Senior Vice President of Policyholder Services, oversaw the project from its inception, and President Peter Hawes lent his support, direction and counsel.

Ruth Menmuir, who edited interminable drafts, and Cris Dawson and Lark Simmons who designed the book, each merit our thanks.

Finally, our heartfelt appreciation to the DPIC Communications Department — Vice President Patricia Marshall, Manager Paula Crisler, Editor Tom Owens and Word Processing Supervisor Dorothy Doudy — for undertaking the monumental task of the final editing and production of this book.

Notice to Readers

TABLE OF CONTENTS

Table of Contents

FOREWORD

It will come as no surprise to most design professionals that since the publication of *DPIC Companies' Guide to Better Contracts* in 1987, the liability crisis has not only intensified, it has reached epic proportions. During the last decade, tort litigation costs increased from $40 billion to more than $120 billion. In the United States — which claims 70 percent of the world's lawyers — we can count on millions of new lawsuits each year.

The tort liability system in this country is not merely out of control; it has broken down. Instead of providing rational compensation to victims, all too often the system compels defendants who may be scarcely liable — sometimes completely blameless — to pay substantial settlements simply to avoid the costs of further litigation and potential judgments against them.

While there has been some response in the shape of tort reform agendas in the medical community, there is little encouraging news from the construction industry. In all but a few states, joint and several liability is still the rule. Even the "winner" in most lawsuits pays enormous legal fees, not to mention the costs in frustration, interrupted work and lost staff time.

More than ever, design professionals need a strategy for dealing with the liability crisis, a strategy that serves one all important goal: **Avoid litigation!** To help you achieve this goal, DPIC suggests focusing on three objectives:

1) **Eliminate liability illiteracy in your firm.** Teach your employees the effect of everyday business practices on your exposure to litigation. Engineering and architectural schools don't teach much about the real world problems of low bidding contractors, failed expectations and lawsuits. So it falls to you to undertake your own education program in loss prevention practices. That's where DPIC comes in. This Guide, along with *DPIC's Lessons in Professional Liability*, alerts you to the contractual pitfalls and professional practices that cause most disputes.

2) **Avoid unnecessary litigation by implementing alternative dispute resolution provisions in contractual agreements.** Inserting ADR provisions in all of your contracts has enormous potential. Since its founding, DPIC has been committed to early intervention when claim problems arise. We've found that many disputes can be resolved fairly, quickly and inexpensively by resorting to formal mediation and other ADR techniques before attempting litigation. In this Guide, we recommend that every professional service contract you sign call for consideration of nonbinding mediation as a first step in dispute resolution.

3) **Refuse to accept unlimited liability for your services**. Work for a limitation of liability (LoL) clause in your contracts that caps the amount of liability you assume if there is a problem on the project. This won't be easy. While our hope is that you can obtain such a clause in every contract, there is still resistance to the concept from some owners, contractors and even design professionals. But the tide has turned. More and more architects and engineers are successfully negotiating LoL clauses.

There is another very effective way you can limit your liability: **develop and implement carefully-written agreements** with your client that, while equitable, assume only the risk that is rightfully yours. The best loss prevention step of all is to avoid litigious clients. The contract formation and negotiation process offers you an excellent opportunity to size up your clients' potential for litigiousness and their attitudes on risk allocation. To help you, we've updated DPIC's contract handbook. Just as the design professions have grown and changed, so has this Guide.

We've been busy updating the Guide since 1987. We've talked to architects, engineers, prime consultants, subconsultants (and, yes, even contractors) to learn more about the risks of the real world in which they practice. We've asked lawyers, judges, arbitrators, mediators and risk managers to help us better understand the realities of the tort system. We've studied our claims files to keep abreast of dispute trends in the construction industry. We've culled the choicest elements of industry contracts and adapted them. We've distilled the best legal advice available and worked to make it understandable and usable. But most of all, we've listened and learned from our family of DPIC insureds.

The result, we believe, is a more comprehensive, more practical Guide to understanding and creating design professional contracts. While there are many elements of the original Guide we insisted on preserving (and updating where necessary), we've added a number of new topics to better reflect today's design professions. We think this new edition will be even more useful for primes, subconsultants, architects and engineers alike.

We hope *The Contract Guide* will become a mainstay of your loss prevention library.

Peter B. Hawes, CPCU
President and Chief Executive Officer
DPIC Companies, Inc.

HOW TO USE THIS BOOK

A key element in managing professional liability risk is the development and negotiation of your professional services contracts. In this Guide, we discuss a number of contract provisions you may encounter when working with your clients. These are the provisions that can prove most troublesome and that surface most frequently when we examine the causes of disputes and claims.

You'll find this Guide a useful reference in a number of common, but contrasting, approaches to contract formation. You may have developed your own standard contract language. It may have evolved over the years, as you've borrowed the best (or worst) provisions from other sources or long-completed projects. Or you may use a preprinted form someone recommended or that a colleague has used with evident success. And you used it successfully, too — for a while. But when you needed it most — perhaps because of a potential claim — you've learned that a boilerplate contract doesn't hold up as you'd hoped. You realize you must take stock and develop an agreement that will better protect your practice.

On the other hand, perhaps your agreement has served its purpose, more or less, caused no real difficulty and at least is a document your clients sign willingly enough. But be careful! Having a claim-free record doesn't mean your contract is all that it should be. The very real risk of a lawsuit that confronts even the most careful architect or engineer means that you must do everything possible to prevent claims. And that means having a well-worded, reasonably protective agreement for every project.

No matter how confident you may be in your standard contract language, we recommend that you sit down with your attorney and compare the provisions in your current contract with the ones in this Guide. (Pay particular attention to those we've flagged as **Deal Makers** or **Deal Breakers**. See *Exhibits 1a* and *1b*.) Then, using the suggestions in this book as a starting point, strengthen the wording of your contract as appropriate.

Some clients prefer to use their own contract forms. Often these client-developed agreements attempt to shift a great deal of the client's risk onto your shoulders. Again, you should carefully review these documents (using your lawyer's help as needed), compare the provisions with those offered here and make any modifications necessary to protect yourself. With the help of this Guide, you'll learn to recognize onerous language and unacceptable provisions often hidden in client-written contracts and be able to suggest equitable allocation of risk.

Perhaps you prefer to rely on the standard contract forms developed by professional societies. That's fine as a starting point. But remember that those forms are consensus documents meant to be acceptable to architects and engineers, primes and subconsultants, owners and contractors. To obtain the endorsements of all these groups and to reflect the broadest range of projects and practices in the industry, some negotiation was inevitable during contract development. These standard contracts may need to be adapted to your particular situation. Talk to your attorney and look carefully at each potential project. Also work with your attorney to supplement standard contract forms with some of the ideas embraced in this Guide, perhaps by strengthening some protective provisions and adding clauses such as Limitation of Liability and Dispute Resolution to every contract you sign. To help you, we've developed a checklist to use with the standard contracts. (See *Appendix I*.) You may want to develop your own checklist of additional clauses.

Not all the clauses in this Guide are meant to be included in one agreement. Nor would all the clauses comprise a complete contract. In many instances, you could combine two or more clauses into one. We present them — alphabetically — for your reference and guidance only; they need to be tailored to fit your practice, the circumstances of your projects and the rest of your contract.

We have tried to keep the clause language as precise and unambiguous as possible. Sometimes this makes the provisions longer than usual, but that is infinitely preferable to leaving a clause open to interpretation. You'll also want to keep this in mind when reviewing client-developed provisions. If the language isn't clear and unequivocal to you, it won't be clear to a jury. If your client says, "What that means is thus-and-so," ask your client to rewrite the provision to say just that.

The discussions that accompany each clause are explanatory and may provide you with effective "ammunition" to help educate your clients. It is important to note that when your clients are other design professionals, they should seek similar indemnifications or other protections or concessions from the owner. Encourage them to become more familiar with their own liability exposures, perhaps by obtaining a Guide such as this.

Any and all statements presented in this Guide, including those pertaining to fees and client dealings, are based on generally accepted concepts of risk management and prudent business behavior. In all cases, your fees, client selection measures and related practices are your business and your business only.

Recognize, also, that this publication is a general guide and should be used in conjunction with specific guidance from competent legal counsel experienced in the design and construction industry and familiar with the laws in your state or the state whose laws will govern your contract.

An Introduction to Professional Services Contracts

A contract is a legally enforceable agreement that sets forth the obligations of each party to the other. If any party to a contract breaches these obligations, he or she can face legal sanctions. In the construction industry, a well-written professional services contract is one that outlines a precise understanding of the duties and responsibilities of each party to the process — the client, the design professionals and the contractors — leaving as little room as possible for interpretation.

Contract Terminology

There are many legal terms used to describe certain aspects of contracts. In working with contracts, you will most likely encounter some of the following commonly used legal terms:

An *oral contract* is one that is based on the spoken word, and a *written contract* is one that is in writing. Both may be binding and thus enforceable; it's just more difficult to prove the precise terms of an oral agreement.

An *enforceable contract* is one that has all the elements necessary to bind the parties; that is, to place the parties under legal obligation to perform their contractual duties. A party who reneges on performing his or her contractual duties *breaches* the contract. The party injured by that breach may find it necessary to seek *judicial relief*. In granting relief, the *trier of fact* (a judge or a jury) may assess damages against the breaching party or may require that party to complete the contract as originally agreed. The cost of obtaining judicial relief usually must be borne by the party seeking it, unless the contract specifies otherwise. (See the section on *Attorneys' Fees*.)

A contract is *void* when one of the elements required to bind it is missing. This doesn't mean you are without recourse if, after performing $10,000 worth of work, you learn that the contract is void. It may be possible to seek at least partial payment for the services you performed.

When a contract is *voidable*, either party has the legal right to call it void. One party may exercise this right because the other party used fraud, duress, disparate bargaining power or some other means to encourage acceptance of the contract, thus making its enforcement contrary to public policy. If one party made a mistake, such as mislocating a decimal point in the fee, this, too, could make the contract voidable.

An *unenforceable* contract is similar to a voidable one, in that something about it makes it legally impossible to enforce. For example, a contract with a public owner for a project that was approved but was not funded is unenforceable.

Contract Elements

For a contract to be considered *binding*, it must comprise several elements. These include *agreement* (offer and acceptance), *consideration, legal form, competent parties* and *legal purpose.*

Agreement exists when one party makes an offer and the other party accepts. An *offer* is just that: one party's tender or proposal to perform an act or service in return for some form of consideration. The offer may be unequivocal or, more commonly, made with reservations. The offer will be considered outstanding and valid until its acceptance or rejection or withdrawal by the party making it. Withdrawal is automatic when a reservation states that the offer will expire if not acted on within a certain period. *Acceptance* means the favorable approval or reception of the offer by the party to whom the offer is made.

Consideration is the inducement to enter into the contract — a promise to do or give something of value to bind the contract. For instance, the architect promises to prepare plans and the client promises to pay the fee. The amount of the consideration doesn't have to be substantial, so long as it is bargained for and agreed to by the parties.

Legal form refers to the contract being enforceable if it is not against public policy. It is not uncommon for certain elements of an agreement to violate law or interpretations of law (for example, a usurious rate of interest). In some jurisdictions, only the offending clause is struck; in others, the entire contract is considered void or unenforceable. To help prevent the latter action, contracts should include *severability* provisions. (See the *Severability and Survival* section of this book.)

A contract must be executed by *competent parties*, individuals who are sane and, when representing business entities, have the authority to bind or make commitments for those entities. Most contracts include a brief provision that states that the individuals signing the contract must attest that they are legally empowered to act for their firms.

A contract must be for a *legal purpose.* A contract to undertake illegal activity is not enforceable in courts of law. "Illegal activity" may be more subtle than supposed. For example, unlicensed persons claiming to be architects or engineers may find that they are unable to enforce contracts because their offer to perform such work without a license is illegal.

CONTRACT FORMATION

PROPOSALS

Contract formation frequently begins when a client requests submission of a proposal. In a normal situation, the design professional becomes familiar with the extent and nature of the client's needs and the site. He or she will then prepare the first element of the proposal, a *scope of services*, or *workscope*, for the project. On some projects the client or the architect or engineer may unilaterally prepare the workscope without consulting the other party. (See **Client-Developed Proposals** in this section.)

Terms and conditions, the second element of the proposal, describe business understandings relating to the services to be rendered, mutual responsibilities, time schedules, payment terms, limitations of liability and so on. Most architectural and engineering firms have developed standard terms and conditions that they submit as part of their proposals. All the clauses discussed in this Guide relate to terms and conditions that address specific issues.

Cost or *fee,* the third element of the proposal, can vary in its presentation. It may simply list the hours staff members are likely to expend in implementing services and their hourly rates, and the cost of direct reimbursable items. Or it may establish a flat fee for accomplishing the workscope, or it may utilize/draw upon any number of other methods of determining the fee to be charged for the services. Whatever the approach, cost proposals should normally contain a standard schedule of fees and costs that will be charged should additional services be required during the project.

CLIENT-DEVELOPED PROPOSALS

Sometimes a client will develop his or her own proposal format for a project — commonly called a request for proposal (RFP) — that includes a workscope, terms and conditions and a fill-in-the-blanks-type fee proposal. In such a case, you should be particularly wary of any unilaterally-developed scope of services. Remember that it has been prepared by the client, who of necessity has made assumptions about your needs and preferences and the requirements of your profession. This can increase misunderstandings and may encourage submissions of unrealistically low fees. You must review such RFPs closely before responding to them. If modifications are needed, speak with the client before making them. It may be possible to submit an altered proposal that will better serve the interests of you both.

In some instances, a client will ask for competitively priced proposals — or competitive bidding. Many design professionals consider this form of procurement unprofessional and refuse to participate in the competition without the normal professional interaction with the client. The format used is essentially the same as that discussed above, but here the architect or engineer is required to develop a unilateral workscope. Ideally you would submit the same workscope that you would have recommended were competitors' fees not a factor. More often than not, however, there is pressure to keep the fee (and thus the workscope) to a minimum in order to get the job. There is great risk in undertaking jobs with a minimal scope of services. If you decide to pursue such projects, you must delineate the workscope precisely to help prevent misunderstandings about the services being offered or excluded. (See *Excluded Services* and *Scope of Services*.)

NEGOTIATION

The proposals you submit to clients are usually subject to discussion, a process called *contract negotiation*. This term can be misleading, however, since "negotiation" often connotes dollar issues only. While dollar issues may be involved, discussions also address the scope of services, which is customarily fine-tuned through additional interaction with the client and the other design professionals.

Once a final scope of services has been agreed to, you and the client move to a discussion of terms and conditions. Risk assessment and allocation are vital elements of this process. The client may not agree to everything contained in your standard terms and conditions and may seek alternative and/or additional conditions. You, in turn, may or may not be willing to accept certain terms and conditions sought by your client.

In some cases, the proposal modifications required are so extensive that your standard terms and conditions must be wholly rewritten. In other cases, they can be amended with an *addendum* that identifies additional conditions to which the parties agree.

CONTRACT FORMATS

PROFESSIONAL ASSOCIATION STANDARD CONTRACTS

Many architects and engineers rely on standard professional service agreements and construction contract forms developed by The American Institute of Architects, the Engineers Joint Contract Documents Committee or other professional organizations. These forms represent a good starting point (but only a starting point) when negotiating an agreement. Carefully researched and compiled, these standard forms nevertheless require tailoring to each particular project. Because these documents are written as general-purpose contracts and represent a consensus of the groups who developed the forms, you should adapt and strengthen the terms and conditions where necessary to suit your own practice and particular/specific project. For instance, this Guide recommends several modifications, such as inserting a Mediation provision in every professional services contract you sign. (See *Dispute Resolution*.) Because the standard forms are carefully integrated and coordinated with other agreements used on a project, any change — minor or otherwise — may need to be reflected in other clauses and documents. For this reason, you should obtain competent legal advice when modifying the standard association forms to ensure the integrity of the final documents.

DESIGN PROFESSIONAL-DEVELOPED CONTRACTS

Many architectural and engineering firms have developed their own contract forms over the years. Often, these documents have evolved from many different sources. These design firms have found that it is a simple matter to customize their contracts, using word processing to tailor each to fit individual projects. You may want to develop an agreement for your practice, but do-it-yourself contract writers need to be especially careful. Your agreement could be missing important protections or be worded incautiously or inconsistently. It is crucial to review these documents periodically with a knowledgeable attorney and, with the help of this Guide, modify and strengthen your agreement.

CLIENT-DEVELOPED CONTRACTS

The need for legal review may be even more important when dealing with clients — such as government entities and major corporations — who insist on using contracts they have developed. Certain terms of such contracts are often one-sided and seek to transfer client liability to the architect or engineer. Some design professionals will agree to these terms because they fear that attempting to modify them will cause an important client to seek a more amenable consultant. This is precisely the type of contract that often needs the most modification, since it could otherwise force you to accept a severe liability exposure you are powerless to control. As difficult as it sometimes may be to change the attitudes of major clients, it is even more difficult to win disputes with them after you have signed an onerous contract limiting your defenses. What's more, some client-drawn terms may undermine your insurance carrier's ability to defend you, fall outside certain conditions of your insurance coverage or affect your ability to obtain insurance in the future. (See *Insurance*.)

In some instances, a client-developed contract will be nothing more than a standard purchase order, used to procure all types of labor and materials. A purchase order is not an appropriate professional services agreement and the client should be so informed. Sometimes, the client will agree to delete all the offending boilerplate terms — often in fine print on the back of the form — by crossing them out and initialing the deletions. You can then execute the front of the form (to satisfy "corporate policy" requirements), append your standard terms and conditions pages and incorporate this into an acceptable agreement.

Some clients attempt to use a modified general construction contract for design professional services. These are typified by language that refers to you as "contractor" and clauses that require a performance bond and/or retainage. Such forms are also inappropriate and can lead to serious misinterpretations. If you can't persuade the client to use a more suitable professional services contract form, then you must drastically modify the contract to reflect a design professional's services. (See *Contractual Reference to the Design Professional*, *Performance Bonds* and *Retainage*.)

CONTRACT STRUCTURE

No matter what type of contract is involved, the scope of services, terms and conditions and fee proposal may be included in one continuous document. Or the workscope and fee proposal may be appended to and referenced in the terms and conditions. Certain other material may also be appended to the document, and thus become part of the agreement. Note that documents don't have to be physically appended to a contract to be part of it. Rather, other contracts or portions of them can be *incorporated by reference*. (See **Incorporation by Reference**.)

Note, too, that a contract can grow in size, over time, as agreements are modified or expanded through addenda. Unless specifically stated otherwise, each addendum is subject to the same terms and conditions as other parts of the agreement.

ORAL AGREEMENTS

You've probably heard about the "good old days" when all that was required was a spoken word, an understanding and a handshake. Today, oral agreements can still be binding, but it's almost always a mistake to rely on one for performance of professional services. The world we live in and the civil justice system that governs business dealings have become highly complex. Architects and engineers are responsible and thus liable not only to their clients but also, in most jurisdictions, to any other party who foreseeably could be damaged or injured because of their services. Should a dispute of this type arise, each of the parties involved will be required to recall what was said months or years before. Even the best-intentioned people may have trouble remembering details and, when it comes to monetary issues, many have difficulty remembering their good intentions.

Despite these problems, some design professionals begin work on small assignments based only on an oral go-ahead from the client. Nevertheless, within a day or two they will present a written proposal for client acceptance. This approach is not for everyone. It is meant only as an accommodation to long-time clients for whom the design professionals have frequently worked in the past and who often have signed their standard agreements before. Most architects and engineers agree that it would be foolhardy to take such an approach when a major, complex or risk-prone project is involved, or when there is an insufficient track record or pre-existing relationship with the client. In fact, oral agreements with many public owners will not be enforceable. When you're tempted to rely on a handshake and a good memory, remember the old adage: oral contracts aren't worth the paper they're written on.

THE BENEFITS OF A WRITTEN AGREEMENT

Although some of the benefits both parties derive from forming and having a written contract are obvious, it is important to review them in more detail. The most significant are mutual understanding, establishing your own rules, sizing up your client and identifying and allocating risk.

Mutual understanding. The process of developing a scope of services and the terms and conditions by which the parties will operate requires each party to communicate its views of the issues being addressed. As a result, each party derives better understanding of the other's concerns. And better understanding promotes better contracts and more satisfying relationships.

Establishing your own rules. When a contract is silent on certain issues, the law may infer or imply certain terms to address those issues. For example, when a contract does not specify how a dispute will be resolved, litigation generally is required or can be instituted by either party. But parties to a contract can agree to use some other dispute resolution mechanism instead of the civil courts. Similarly, parties to a contract can agree that neither will sue the other for consequential damages, or that the period during which either can initiate a claim is shorter than otherwise required by the applicable statute of repose or limitations. The ability to establish one's own rules does not permit measures that are against public policy or are illegal. Nevertheless, the contracting parties' own rules can eliminate or at least lessen problems that could otherwise arise. (See *Consequential Damages* and *Statutes of Respose or Limitation*.)

Sizing up. It is important to understand your client's attitudes and motivations because some are likely to lead to problems. The process of contract formation allows you to assess the entities or individuals with whom you are dealing and to determine whether you want to work with them. Beware of clients who have little compunction about sacrificing quality or shifting their own liabilities to others. Exercise great care in selecting your clients, just as they select you.

Identifying and allocating risk. It's easier to evaluate a client's attitudes and motivations when the subject of risk is brought up at the outset of the relationship. Astute design professionals believe that the process of contract formation should include a candid discussion of risks. This helps assure that risk-reduction and risk-handling mechanisms are incorporated in the workscope as well as in the terms and conditions of the contract.

An open discussion of risk is essential, and the process of contract formation provides a ready opportunity for it. Informed clients are more apt to accept a scope of services that will reduce needless liability problems and other exposures. They also are more likely to agree to fair and reasonable terms and conditions and the allocation of risks to the party best able to control them.

DEALING WITH RISK

Whenever you accept a project, you also accept risks. The most common risk is the necessity of defending an allegedly negligent act. The impact of such a risk can be severe, particularly because you owe a duty of care to more than your client. If your negligent act damages others who foreseeably could have been damaged, you generally are liable to them, too. They do not need a contract with you to file a claim — and win.

You can manage risk in a number of ways:

1. You can help minimize or reduce risk by offering more extensive or more comprehensive services. A quality-oriented client will authorize such services. Many clients have learned the hard way that the most complete professional service is the least expensive in the long term. In order to assess client attitudes and to reduce risk, many design professionals always propose a full scope of design and construction phase services in their initial proposals. (See *Construction Observation* and *Scope of Services*.)

2. You can transfer some of your risk by obtaining professional liability insurance. Do not overestimate its comprehensiveness, however. And remember, many claims and costs of legal defense are likely to be paid by you under your deductible. Nor will insurance compensate you for lost staff time and productivity in defending a claim. (See *Insurance*.)

3. You can educate your clients about their responsibilities regarding risks that are within their control (such as the reuse of your plans). You can then use your contract's terms and conditions to require your clients to cover any costs you might otherwise have to bear. Fair and reasonable clients will accept a form of risk allocation called an *indemnity*. (See *Indemnities*.)

4.   You can identify potential problems that both you and your client are powerless to prevent. Inform the client about these risks and the options available for dealing with them. Assuming they are not major, you may be willing to accept them. If you do, however, it may be appropriate to charge an additional fee that recognizes your increased liability. Alternatively, your client can either retain the risk (typically through an indemnification) or transfer it (via insurance). A combination of these two approaches is possible by relying on a *limitation of liability* agreement. (See *Limitation of Liability*.)

5.   You can identify those risks that are so significant you cannot possibly accept them, such as risks stemming from hazardous materials (including asbestos). Let clients know that they must retain such risks (through indemnities) if you are to provide services on the project. (See *Environmental and Health Hazards*.)

6.   You can use your contract to close certain loopholes that could otherwise become traps. For example, you could list services you have explained and offered to the client, but the client has declined. This could prevent attempts to hold you liable for failing to perform an optional service the client decided to forgo. (See *Excluded Services*.)

7.   You can establish conditions in the contract reducing certain risks that other-wise would exist by virtue of law. For example, you and your client can specify a dispute resolution mechanism that is more effective than litigation, reduce the impact of a statute of limitations and restrict either party's ability to sue the other for consequential damages. (See *Consequential Damages, Dispute Resolution* and *Statutes of Repose or Limitation*.)

8.   You can reduce risk overall by developing a contract that precisely states the intent of both parties. Such an agreement helps prevent misunderstandings and makes provisions easily understood by a judge or jury. This alone may discourage a plaintiff's pursuit of an otherwise marginal claim.

Reducing your exposure to risk depends to a large extent on your contract formation efforts. Your clients should be made aware of risks as well as techniques for dealing with them. If they are adamant about not taking prudent measures, not compensating you adequately to accept risk or not accepting reasonable risks themselves, then the ultimate risk reduction method must be considered: walk away from the project!

NEGOTIATING A CONTRACT

Although many believe contract negotiation is an adversarial procedure, it isn't — nor should it be. You are expected to serve as the client's trusted professional advisor, and the contract negotiation phase of your relationship gives you an opportunity to demonstrate your professionalism. To do so, enter discussions with a clear understanding of your bottom line on risk. Recognize the important interplay between your fee proposal, general conditions and scope of services so you are in a position to give and take. Before you enter into negotiation, know your walk-away position on every issue.

If the client's budget is so restrictive that you have to reduce the scope of your services, your risk is increased. You may be able to counteract this increased risk through certain provisions in your terms and conditions, assuming the scope is not reduced to such an extent that it creates a public safety concern.

If the client is unwilling to accept certain defensive provisions in your terms and conditions, can you charge a higher fee to fund the heightened risk? Can you expand the technical services offered, thereby reducing the unknowns and risks arising from them and eliminating your need for defensive provisions?

Be candid and objective in discussing these issues with your client. Good clients who are aware of your concerns and who want you to solve their problems will work with you to develop fair and equitable agreements. Candor and objectivity very often establish the foundation on which lasting relationships are built.

Several books have been written about negotiating contracts, and seminars are frequently given on the subject. (Refer to the *Bibliography* for a few suggested resources.) These and similar materials are invaluable to anyone who needs to develop expertise in negotiation techniques.

DEAL MAKER AND DEAL BREAKER CONTRACT PROVISIONS

Some contract clauses are so important that if your client will not agree to include them, you must consider walking away from the project. In this Guide, we call these provisions **Deal Makers**. Conversely, some clients will try to impose on you certain clauses that are so onerous or unfair that you must never agree to them. We call these provisions **Deal Breakers**.

There are several important provisions that, depending on how they are written, can be either Deal Makers or Deal Breakers. For example, a clause that asks your client to indemnify you for claims arising from hazardous materials discovered on his or her own property is a Deal Maker. On the other hand, a clause that asks you to indemnify your client under the same circumstance would be a Deal Breaker.

This Guide identifies some of the clauses we consider Deal Makers or Deal Breakers. However, because no two firms are alike and because each project is different, with varying degrees of risk, fees and workscope, you must carefully weigh and develop your own list — your own bottom line on risk — and then use it in your negotiations. (For a suggested list of Deal Maker and Deal Breaker provisions, see *Exhibits 1a and 1b*.)

No matter who the client may be, always be prepared to say no, respectfully declining the engagement if you cannot develop acceptable terms. Serious losses have befallen many design professionals who have given up too much in order to obtain a contract.

Recognize that even if you terminate negotiations, you will not necessarily lose the job. Often, clients with whom you are unable to come to terms will be sufficiently impressed by your professionalism to rethink their own position. On the other hand, you may never hear from a client again. And that may be the best loss prevention measure of all.

EXHIBIT 1A

DEAL MAKERS

Certain contract clauses are so important to the protection of your firm that they must be included in each contract you sign. We call these clauses **Deal Makers.** If your client won't agree to these vital provisions, you may want to decline the project. Your practice and your clients are different from those of other firms, and you may find that your level of acceptable risk varies from project to project. As a starting point, here's our list of suggested Deal Makers:

Attorneys' Fees
Construction Observation
Delays
Dispute Resolution
Environmental and Health Hazards
Jobsite Safety
Limitation of Liability
Scope of Services
Statutes of Repose or Limitation
Termination

Of course, not every clause will apply to every project. What's more, depending on the circumstances of a particular project, other important clauses in this Guide may become Deal Makers. Here are some suggested Deal Makers to consider if your project includes these risks or elements:

Asbestos (See *Environmental and Health Hazards*, Part Four)
Condominiums
Fast Track Projects
Preliminary Site Assessments
Renovation/Remodeling

Review the list of topics in this Guide. Many are project specific (such as Prototype Designs or Value Engineering) and may constitute Deal Makers on a particular project. It is important to determine your bottom line on risk — the point beyond which you must never venture — and develop your own list of must-have Deal Makers.

EXHIBIT 1B

DEAL BREAKERS

A **Deal Breaker** is a client-written clause that is so onerous that you must insist it be deleted from all contracts. If your client refuses to delete or substantially modify such a clause, seriously consider refusing the project. One such clause is Liquidated Damages. Another Deal Breaker is a client-drawn Warranty clause that requires you to guarantee a technical result or condition.

Many provisions may be either Deal Makers or Deal Breakers. For instance, a badly-worded indemnity that is not limited to your negligence is a Deal Breaker and must be deleted or modified substantially. On the other hand, a well-worded insurable indemnity may be acceptable to you. A mutual indemnity or one in which your client indemnifies you is desirable.

Depending on how they are worded, the following clauses can be either Deal Makers or Deal Breakers:

Assignment
Certifications, Guarantees and Warranties
Indemnities
Insurance
Opinion of Probable Construction Cost
Stop Work Authority

AMERICANS WITH DISABILITIES ACT (ADA)

The Americans with Disabilities Act, most of which became effective in January 1992, is federal legislation aimed at providing disabled Americans with equal opportunity in employment through reasonable access to commercial and public facilities. Affecting one-sixth of the American populace, the ADA defines disability as a "physical or mental impairment that substantially limits one or more of the major life activities of an individual."

That the ADA greatly affects the design professions is evident. Less clear, however, are the precise obligations imposed upon architects and engineers. The Act is not another new set of building codes. Instead, it is civil rights legislation that carries with it the full weight of the United States Justice Department. Anyone who believes he or she has been discriminated against can file a complaint with an appropriate federal agency or file a civil lawsuit in Federal District Court against anyone who owns, leases or operates a facility. The court can levy stiff penalties against a building owner or operator and can order the facilities be made accessible.

Of greatest concern to design professionals, Title III of the ADA mandates the removal of architectural and communications barriers in all existing public accommodations — if the changes are "readily achievable." The vague guidelines to the Act define this as "easily accomplished and able to be carried out without much difficulty or expense." What is "readily achievable" will, we are told, be determined on a case-by-case basis by weighing the nature and cost of the modifications against the financial resources of the facility, as well as a variety of other factors. In other words, designers can expect conflicting interpretations of the Act.

The law applies to new and existing public accommodations. This includes places that are privately owned and operated but serve the public. For example, restaurants, theaters, stores, professional offices, other service establishments, galleries, lodgings and places of recreation are all considered public accommodations. The ADA does not apply to single or multifamily housing.

The Act affects design professionals in several ways. First, architects and engineers should evaluate their own offices to make certain they conform to ADA guidelines. Second, building owners undoubtedly will ask designers to help them determine their conformance with the ADA and to make recommendations as to modifications that may be required. Third, designs for alterations or new construction must comply with the ADA. Finally, architects and engineers will need to familiarize themselves with what could be significant changes — depending on where they practice — to state and local codes as they are brought up to ADA standards.

The Problem

Because the ADA is civil rights legislation and not a building code, it will be the courts, not the legislators, who emerge as the true authors of the Act. The problem isn't the underlying concept of the Act itself (which many feel is long overdue) but instead the lack of clear-cut direction. Congress has passed a bill so fuzzy in its language, that the actual guidelines can only be determined through the painful and less predictable process of administrative interpretation and litigation.

What this means to you and your peers is that there is — and will continue to be — much uncertainty and confusion surrounding the requirements under the ADA. Until a body of published interpretations, regulations and case law evolves, your obligations and the extent of your liability will not be established. It is unclear, for instance, whether you, the designer, could be named directly in a lawsuit. If so, you could be subject to civil rights prosecution should something you designed be involved in a charge of discrimination by a disabled person. On the other hand, if you cannot be directly named, your client can — and probably will — seek damages from you should a complaint be filed against him or her. But the difference between direct and indirect action against you could be significant: a direct civil rights action against you seeking fines and penalties is not insurable under most professional liability policies written today.

The United States Attorney General will certify state and local building codes for compliance with the ADA. While compliance with local building codes gives you some protection, it is not altogether airtight. A building designed and constructed in compliance with state codes could nevertheless be found in violation of the ADA, and variances and interpretations by local building officials are not binding for ADA purposes.

The new requirements for building owners and operators also could mean new business opportunities for designers. But be careful: this new work carries with it potential risk. Because compliance with requirements imposed on existing facilities will require analysis of facilities and development of alternative proposals for construction, building owners will seek your assistance. They will want to know how much needed changes will cost them. They may request recommendations for phased implementation. They (and, perhaps, their lenders) may want certifications or warranties that their buildings are in compliance with the ADA. Finally, they may want your assurance of indemnity from any ADA-related action against them.

THE SOLUTION

The most important point to keep in mind — and underscore to your client — is that compliance with the Americans with Disabilities Act is a legal and economic problem, not an architectural or engineering issue. If a client requests your inspection of a property for ADA conformance, you must limit your services to evaluation of the property's noncompliance and the development of a range of possible solutions. You must not, however, provide recommendations on which modifications are "readily achievable. . . in light of the resources available." Nor should you help decide the priority or phasing of those measures. These are questions that must be answered by the owner and the owner's attorney and accountant. You are not licensed or insured to provide legal or accounting advice to your clients. (Refer to *Opinion of Probable Construction Cost* for a related discussion.) Ironically, attorneys and accountants may seek you out for your opinions as a design professional. Tread carefully here: you will want to insist on solid contractual protection.

Familiarize yourself with the provisions of the ADA and make certain your client understands its implications; both of you have new requirements to uphold. Explain why you cannot certify or guarantee that something is in compliance with the ADA.

Since compliance with the ADA will be determined on a case-by-case basis, you cannot know whether your design or recommended modifications are in compliance. Accordingly, we recommend you always address the ADA in your contract with a clause that explains these limitations. Furthermore, you should delete any language that requires you to comply with "all laws, codes, standards and regulations." (Refer to *Codes and Standards Compliance* for a discussion and an alternative clause, if necessary.) Also, delete any provision that requires you to provide a certification, guarantee or warranty that a building is in compliance with the ADA. (See *Certifications, Guarantees and Warranties* and *Lenders' Requirements*.)

ADA Compliance in Existing Buildings

Since the ADA was effective in January 1992 for existing public buildings, many such facilities have already been inspected for compliance. However, if you are called upon by a client to perform a compliance assessment, here is a sample clause you may use when providing review of existing buildings:

ADA Compliance

The Americans with Disabilities Act (ADA) requires the removal of architectural barriers in existing facilities where such removal is readily achievable. The Client acknowledges that the definition of "readily achievable" contained in the ADA is flexible and subject to interpretation on a case-by-case basis. The requirements of the ADA will therefore be subject to various and possibly contradictory interpretations. The Design Professional will use his or her reasonable professional efforts and judgment to interpret applicable ADA requirements and to advise the Client as to the modifications to the Client's facility that may be required to comply with the ADA. Such interpretation and advice will be based on what is known about ADA interpretations at the time this service is rendered. The Design Professional, however, cannot and does not warrant or guarantee that the Client's facility will fully comply with interpretations of ADA requirements by regulatory bodies or court decisions.

This clause and all other clauses herein are intended as examples only and should be reviewed and modified by competent legal counsel to reflect variations in applicable local law and the specific circumstances of your contract.

ADA Compliance in Alterations Projects

Alterations to buildings must provide for accessibility to "the maximum extent feasible" if the costs for accessibility are not disproportionate to the overall cost of the alteration. This could be up to as much as 20 percent of the alteration budget, according to one Justice Department "clarification." Alterations to primary work areas include required accessible paths of travel to restrooms, telephones and drinking fountains that serve each area. Consider the following suggested contract provision:

ADA Compliance

The Americans with Disabilities Act (ADA) provides that alterations to a facility must be made in such a manner that, to the maximum extent feasible, the altered portions of the facility are readily accessible to and by individuals with disabilities. The Client acknowledges that the requirements of the ADA will be subject to various and possibly contradictory interpretations. The Design Professional, therefore, will use his or her reasonable professional efforts and judgment to interpret applicable ADA requirements and other federal, state and local laws, rules, codes ordinances and regulations as they apply to the project. The Design Professional, however, cannot and does not warrant or guarantee that the Client's project will comply with all interpretations of the ADA requirements and/or the requirements of other federal, state and local laws, rules, codes, ordinances and regulations as they apply to the project.

This clause and all other clauses herein are intended as examples only and should be reviewed and modified by competent legal counsel to reflect variations in applicable local law and the specific circumstances of your contract.

If you and your attorney decide to use such a clause, make certain it agrees with any other provision you have regarding code and standards compliance.

ADA COMPLIANCE ON NEW CONSTRUCTION

New construction must comply with the ADA. Here again, you should attempt to provide for contradictory interpretations of the ADA in your contract and be sure to coordinate such a clause with any other provision concerning codes and standards compliance. Consider the following language:

ADA COMPLIANCE

The Americans with Disabilities Act (ADA) provides that it is a violation of the ADA to design and construct a facility for first occupancy later than January 26, 1993, that does not meet the accessibility and usability requirements of the ADA except where an entity can demonstrate that it is structurally impractical to meet such requirements. The Client acknowledges that the requirements of the ADA will be subject to various and possibly contradictory interpretations. The Design Professional, therefore, will use his or her reasonable professional efforts to interpret applicable ADA requirements and other federal, state and local laws, rules, codes, ordinances and regulations as they apply to the project. The Design Professional, however, cannot and does not warrant or guarantee that the Client's project will comply with interpretations of ADA requirements and/or requirements of other federal, state and local laws, rules, codes, ordinances and regulations as they apply to the project.

This clause and all other clauses herein are intended as examples only and should be reviewed and modified by competent legal counsel to reflect variations in applicable local law and the specific circumstances of your contract.

Alternatively, you may prefer a more comprehensive provision that puts more emphasis on your client's obligations:

It is recognized that the Client faces certain obligations under the Americans with Disabilities Act (ADA) that could affect the design of this project. It is further recognized that the ADA is federal civil rights legislation that is not part of, or known to be compatible with, state or local law, codes, and regulations governing construction. Consequently, the Design Professional will be unable to make recommendations or professional determinations that will ensure compliance with the ADA or guarantee that all design decisions will conform to the ADA standard of "reasonable accommodation." The Design Professional strongly advises the Client to obtain appropriate legal counsel with respect to compliance with the ADA.

The Design Professional will endeavor to design for accessibility by the disabled in conformance with any applicable provisions in or references by applicable state or local building codes. The Design Professional further agrees to include in the design such provisions for the disabled as the Client may request in response to the ADA, provided such requests are timely made, technically achievable, and in conformance with all other pertinent codes and regulations.

The Client will determine the full extent of his or her obligations under the ADA. The Client shall communicate design requests regarding compliance with the ADA to the Design Professional in writing at the appropriate times during the project to allow for incorporation of such requests without requiring revisions after the completion of a given design phase, i.e., schematics, design development, construction documents.

Whenever you are contemplating ADA-related services, pay particular attention to your loss prevention practices. Be careful in your client selection. Make certain your client understands his or her obligations under the ADA — and your limitations. Check and recheck plans and specifications and, if you are performing a building review for ADA compliance, be extremely circumspect in your wording in any report of your findings.

SEE ALSO:

Bibliography
Certifications, Guarantees and Warranties
Codes and Standards Compliance
Lenders' Requirements
Opinion of Probable Construction Cost
Renovation/Remodeling
Standard of Care

ARBITRATION

Arbitration is perhaps the best known formal dispute resolution alternative to litigation. It can take several forms; it can be voluntary or mandatory, binding or non-binding, specialized or expedited, one of several variations of mediation-arbitration — or even a method called "baseball."

The focus here is on binding arbitration as it is sometimes used in design professional contracts. This is a formal dispute resolution technique in which the opposing parties present their cases before one or more neutral individuals who are empowered to render a binding and court-enforceable decision. Although this procedure was originally intended to offer significant benefits over litigation by providing a forum in which disputes could be resolved without spending large amounts of time and money, today this is not always the case.

THE PROBLEM

Many standard contracts (including AIA documents) contain an arbitration clause that calls for mandatory binding arbitration if there is a dispute. Under this type of contract, you must submit disputes to arbitration even if circumstances suggest that other dispute resolution methods would be more appropriate in resolving the conflict.

You should be aware that although arbitration may be an effective dispute resolution tool in some limited situations, there are several drawbacks to the process that can render it an unsatisfactory and sometimes disastrous remedy.

First, arbitration does not generally permit joinder (naming other involved parties), although most construction claims involve many different parties. Because of this, it may be necessary to submit to multiple arbitration proceedings to resolve the conflict. As a result, the procedure can cost you as much money and time as litigation.

Second, unless specifically provided for in your contract, discovery proceedings are not generally allowed in arbitration. This means you may not be able to obtain documents and other information that could be vital to your case. You cannot subpoena documents, and you cannot require sworn testimony (depositions) from witnesses.

Third, arbitration does not follow the rules of evidence found in civil litigation, and this can result in proceedings that may or may not be focused on relevant issues. Arbitrators can refuse to accept documentary evidence, for example, and even permit hearsay.

Fourth, arbitrators are not required to apply legal principles or even the terms of your contract in reaching their decisions. In fact, they are generally not required to state the grounds or reasons for their decisions.

Fifth — and this is a major drawback — it is difficult to obtain knowledgeable, qualified arbitrators through some arbitration services.

Finally, unless arbitrators are found guilty of bias, prejudice or fraud, you cannot appeal their decisions.

In spite of these limitations, there are some occasions in which you may wish to use arbitration or some form of tailored arbitration as a problem-solving forum and in which the above drawbacks do not come into play. For instance, small, two-party disputes may lend themselves to arbitration. Consider a fee dispute with your client. Typically, claims by design professionals for unpaid fees result in cross claims for huge amounts by the client. However, if fee disputes are decided by mandatory arbitration, such cross claims may be forestalled. Claims involving relatively small sums also lend themselves to arbitration. Some firms stipulate in their agreements that they will arbitrate disputes involving less than $10,000 or $20,000, while others will arbitrate disputes up to $50,000. You and your attorney need to weigh the consequences. If the conflict does not involve more than two parties and the evidence is readily available to you, arbitration may be the right method. If, however, there is a chance other parties might be brought in, or if the amount involved is significant, then you, your attorney and your insurer will want to look at other dispute resolution methods.

The Solution

When faced with a standard, preprinted contract that calls for mandatory, binding arbitration, your best course is to delete the clause and replace it with a paragraph that calls for some form of mediation as the first step in resolving a dispute. (See *Dispute Resolution* for discussion and suggested contract language.) However, if your client is adamant about retaining the arbitration clause, then insist on changing the language from "shall be decided by arbitration. . ." to "may, with the consent of both parties, be decided. . . ." Regardless of the modifications you make, we recommend that you always make a concerted effort to add a provision for mediation as the first step in dispute resolution.

Some design firms prefer to specify in their contract that certain types of disputes or disputes involving less than a specified dollar amount are to be settled by mandatory binding arbitration. If you and your attorney believe arbitration might be an acceptable solution for some simple disputes involving small sums, you will want to insert such a provision in your contract. Again, make certain you have provided for mediation elsewhere in your contract as a first step in conflict resolution, as well as provided for options for other dispute resolution techniques.

ARBITRATION

In the event the parties to this Agreement are unable to reach a settlement of any dispute arising out of the services under this Agreement, involving an amount of less than $ _____ , in accordance with Paragraph _____ (Dispute Resolution), then such disputes shall be settled by binding arbitration by an arbitrator to be mutually agreed upon by the parties, and shall proceed in accordance with the rules of {insert appropriate reference to a specific arbitration service's set of rules, such as the Construction Industry Arbitration Rules of the American Arbitration Association or the Center for Public Resources' Rules} **then pertaining. If the parties cannot agree on a single arbitrator, then the arbitrator(s) shall be selected in accordance with the above-referenced rules.**

This clause and all other clauses herein are intended as examples only and should be reviewed and modified by competent legal counsel to reflect variations in applicable local law and the specific circumstances of your contract.

Be sure to check with your attorney or your insurer's claims staff regarding the set of rules you should reference. They may have a set they prefer to use.

Instead of specifying a dollar limit, you could change the language to limit arbitration to certain kinds of issues, such as fee disputes.

Because appeal is so difficult, it is important that you retain the right to some control over the selection of arbitrators, no matter what set of rules you select. Work with your attorney to choose wording that either gives you and your client mutual agreement over an arbitrator or specify a set of rules that gives you some measure of veto.

Note, too, that while lack of joinder is a drawback in normal arbitration rules, courts in a few jurisdictions may force you to be joined or consolidated in disputes between other parties (typically among owners, contractors, subcontractors and suppliers). Usually, it is not in your best interest to be joined in such disputes. For this reason, AIA has a "no-joinder" clause to attempt to prevent such unwanted joinder or consolidation. You and your attorney may want to consider such a clause. (Refer to AIA B141, Paragraph 7.3, 1987 Edition.)

Remember, arbitration is only one option in the array of dispute resolution techniques available. As with any tool, it works well when used correctly and for the right task. Even if your contract does not call for arbitration, it is a means that is always available to you and your client, even if only to focus on the solvable issues in a dispute before proceeding — if all else fails — to litigation.

SEE ALSO:

Dispute Resolution

ASSIGNMENT

An assignment clause in a contract may give one or both parties the ability to transfer their rights under the contract or forbid such a transfer. The difference is important. If a client can assign the rights to a design professional's services to another party, the designer could be forced to work for someone with whom the designer has never bargained and for whom the designer may prefer not to work at all.

THE PROBLEM

If your contract gives your client the unilateral right to assign the contract to others, or if it requires that you "sign all necessary documents requested by client's lender" or that you "will cooperate with the lender in all respects," you may not be able to resist the client's efforts to assign or sell your remaining obligations under contract as if you were mere merchandise. Such an assignment could be triggered by the sale of the project or a default by your client to the lender. Unless you have protected yourself, either by prohibiting assignment without mutual consent or by providing for your compensation for any increased costs caused by the assignment, you could be asking for trouble. Instead of dealing with the experienced client with whom you originally contracted, you could find yourself suddenly working for the client's lender and trying to explain the details of the project to a freshly-scrubbed MBA whose previous construction experience amounts to building a treehouse in the backyard. Worse, you might inherit a new client with insufficient funds to pay your fees. Even if you are willing to continue working with someone new, you will need more time to bring him or her up to speed, and you will face added construction phase services and meetings — all of which should be compensated for as Additional Services. (See *Scope of Services*.)

If your contract contains no assignment clause — in other words, the contract is silent on the issue — there may be a presumption that your client has the right to "sell you" and all remaining rights under contract. A more obvious problem is the overreaching client who wants a provision that gives him or her the right to assign, but prohibits you from doing the same. This client may be thinking about selling the project — along with your construction phase services — for a fixed price (presumably the balance of your compensation) despite increased costs to you. A client's insistence on such a unilateral provision is a good indication of how fair a client will be.

Another scenario poses a fairly common problem. Your client sends you a routine document Friday afternoon to be signed and returned by the end of the day. Closer examination reveals the form to be an assignment of your plans and specifications to your client's lender upon default by your client. All you have to do, your client tells you, is sign on the dotted line so the loan can go through. If you have already agreed in your contract to sign any lender documents or to cooperate in all respects with the lender, you may have to agree to this assignment provision, although such a step dramatically increases your liability exposure. (See *Lenders' Requirements* for further discussion.)

THE SOLUTION

Have a strong, affirmative and mutual clause that prohibits either party from assigning rights to another. Such a clause could read:

ASSIGNMENT

Neither party to this Agreement shall transfer, sublet or assign any rights under or interest in this Agreement (including but not limited to monies that are due or monies that may be due) without the prior written consent of the other party.

This clause and all other clauses herein are intended as examples only and should be reviewed and modified by competent legal counsel to reflect variations in applicable local law and the specific circumstances of your contract.

Note that a strict interpretation of this clause could restrict your use of subconsultants. Therefore, also include a provision in your contract that enables you to subcontract. (Refer to *Right to Retain Subconsultants* for further discussion and a sample clause.)

As for the assignment of plans and specifications to the lender, you should delete any open-ended provision that requires you to "cooperate with any lender in every way" or "sign all forms required by a lender." Unless you have agreed to such a clause, you are under no legal obligation to comply with such a demand. Despite the lender's insistence that this is standard operating procedure, and your client's worry that the fate of his or her loan may be hanging in the balance, you must not give a lender unqualified ownership rights to your plans and specifications. (Refer to the related discussion in *Ownership of Instruments of Service*.) If you've protected your legal flanks from unreasonable assignment documents, you may be willing to execute reasonable lender documents that have been purged of risk-prone provisions and that give you some basic protections. Supposedly unalterable standard lender forms (or forms from anyone who wants to take over the balance of your contract by assignment) can be modified, if necessary, to reflect the following requirements in the event of assignment:

1. Require the lender to pay immediately any unpaid fees due you by the defaulting client.

2. Require the lender to retain you through completion of construction phase services, or agree to indemnify you against misuse of or changes to your plans and specifications. (Refer to *Indemnities, Supplanting Another Design Professional* and *Unauthorized Changes to Plans* for more information.)

3. Require the lender to acknowledge your plans and specifications to be instruments of service.

4. Specify that the lender not reassign the rights to your plans and specifications to anyone without your prior written consent.

5. Require the lender to accept all the terms of your agreement with your client.

An alternative is a provision that would give you the opportunity to approve in advance any documents you will be asked to sign during the project. You can insist they be appended to the contract before you sign it, and, if they are not attached (and these may well include certain lender requirements), you could demand adequate time to review and make any necessary modifications so as not to be subjected to the typical "Friday afternoon" pressure.

SEE ALSO:

ATTORNEYS' FEES

In the absence of some agreement to the contrary, each party to a lawsuit usually must pay for his or her own expenses, including attorneys' fees, court costs, expert witness fees and other related expenses. This holds true despite the outcome of the lawsuit. While there are jurisdictions that have enacted attorney fee-shifting statutes, these tend to favor the plaintiff in actions brought against "bad guys," such as violators of EPA regulations, for instance, or landlords who refuse to release security deposits.

But what of the design professional who is suddenly named in a lawsuit of little merit? Very often, merely the threat of the huge expense of a legal squabble is enough to make a designer throw in the towel and offer to settle — even if he or she is not at fault.

THE PROBLEM

It's a sorry commentary on our times, but it is not uncommon for unprincipled project owners to use threats of lawsuits against design professionals to reduce fees they owe designers. These clients view a lawsuit against you — or even a threat of a lawsuit — as an effective means of getting a "discount." They know that if you are forced to pursue them to get your last invoice paid, your legal fees would likely be higher than the invoice and often not worth the trouble.

If your client sues you claiming negligence, your defense costs could be astronomical. You might spend several years and thousands of dollars just to prove you weren't in the wrong. Insurance helps, of course, but you still bear the burden for your deductible and your time spent. It is an unfortunate fact of life that defending a lawsuit, no matter how frivolous or irresponsible, is costly, time-consuming and detracts from your ability to do productive work. That is why it is so tempting to cave into clients who threaten a lawsuit and pay them or write off your fee just to make the lawsuit go away.

If your contract is silent on this, you are probably responsible for your own legal fees even if you "win." But even worse than not having a provision is having a client asking you to agree to an attorneys'-fees clause that is one-way, that gives only your client the right to recoup attorneys' fees.

THE SOLUTION

The solution seems simple: delete any unilateral attorneys'-fees provisions and include in every contract a clause stating that the prevailing party is entitled to recoup his or her legal expenses from the loser. To be fair, such a clause should work both ways. While in some states, any clause that is unilateral — one-sided — would be interpreted as mutual, it is not true in all jurisdictions. You should not depend on the courts to interpret this in your favor.

But will your client agree to such a clause? Or does your client expect a one-sided attorneys'-fees clause — tilted in his or her favor? Your client's reaction is a good litmus test of the caliber of person you are dealing with.

Here is a sample clause you might consider:

ATTORNEYS' FEES

In the event of any litigation arising from or related to the services provided under this Agreement, the prevailing party will be entitled to recovery of all reasonable costs incurred, including staff time, court costs, attorneys' fees and other related expenses.

This clause and all other clauses herein are intended as examples only and should be reviewed and modified by competent legal counsel to reflect variations in applicable local law and the specific circumstances of your contract.

You might try going a step further. One way to deter frivolous negligence lawsuits is to require a Certificate of Merit in your contract. This means your client would agree by contract that, prior to bringing any lawsuit against you, the client would obtain a statement called a Certificate of Merit from another independent design consultant practicing in the same discipline and in the same geographic area as you. In it, the certifier would simply state that he or she had reviewed the facts of the claim and, in the certifier's opinion, the claimant's allegations have merit. Such a measure does two things: First, it might discourage an owner from suing you without justification. Second, if the owner does obtain such a certificate, it tells you that there is at least one member of your profession who believes the case against you is worthwhile and may be prepared to testify to that in court. Consider the following provision:

CERTIFICATE OF MERIT

The Client shall make no claim for professional negligence, either directly or in a third party claim, against the Design Professional unless the Client has first provided the Design Professional with a written certification executed by an independent design professional currently practicing in the same discipline as the Design Professional and licensed in the State of _____. This certification shall: a) contain the name and license number of the certifier; b) specify each and every act or omission that the certifier contends is a violation of the standard of care expected of a Design Professional performing professional services under similar circumstances; and c) state in complete detail the basis for the certifier's opinion that each such act or omission constitutes such a violation. This certificate shall be provided to the Design Professional not less than thirty (30) calendar days prior to the presentation of any claim or the institution of any arbitration or judicial proceeding.

This clause and all other clauses herein are intended as examples only and should be reviewed and modified by competent legal counsel to reflect variations in applicable local law and the specific circumstances of your contract.

Note that a few states have enacted Certificate of Merit laws that afford varying levels of protection and with varying degrees of success. Check with your attorney and professional society to find out if your jurisdiction has such a statute. If so, be sure to coordinate the above clause with the statute.

SEE ALSO:

Dispute Resolution
Limitation of Liability

AUTHORIZED REPRESENTATIVES

A design professional will often need to communicate with clients in order to make a report or get an immediate decision.

THE PROBLEM

Clear, effective and timely communication among authorized representatives of the various participants in a design project is crucial. If your client or a key client representative is unavailable, a decision may have to be delayed, and problems could result or be aggravated. On the other hand, if you make a decision for a client without his or her approval, you may incur a potential liability exposure that could create serious problems.

THE SOLUTION

Consider including in your agreement, under Client Responsibilities, a listing of the client's representatives who are authorized to make decisions on the client's behalf. Your client may even want to specify individuals who are authorized to make decisions at certain levels (for example, to approve change orders up to specified dollar amounts). This should be acceptable, as long as you are reasonably assured you can reach someone at all times. The agreement should also include your client's responsibility to keep the list current.

PROJECT REPRESENTATIVES

The Client shall designate representatives who are authorized to make all decisions on the Client's behalf when requested to do so by the Design Professional. The following designated Client representatives are authorized to make such decisions and shall be available on an on-call basis as required by the Design Professional and shall be called in the order listed herein:

Name _____   Work telephone _____
                          Home telephone _____
                          FAX telephone _____

Name _____   Work telephone _____
                          Home telephone _____
                          FAX telephone _____

The Client shall furnish a revised listing to the Design Professional when any changes affecting this listing are made.

This clause and all other clauses herein are intended as examples only and should be reviewed and modified by competent legal counsel to reflect variations in applicable local law and the specific circumstances of your contract.

Alternatively, you may state that the listing of authorized representatives is shown on a certain Schedule and appended to the contract.

Should you need to make such a contact, it is important to keep a complete record of who was called and when, who was not available and what the substance of the call was. To help prevent misunderstandings and reinforce documentation, send a letter to your client listing the contacts you attempted and outlining the substance of the calls — including any decisions made by the client's representative. Also send a copy to the person with whom you spoke, to give that person a chance to review and comment on your report.

SEE ALSO:

Assignment
Notices

BETTERMENT

In law, the concept of *unjust enrichment* or *betterment* means that a person who is damaged because of another's mistake should be entitled to recoup losses caused by that mistake, but not benefit because of it.

To illustrate, let's use a simple example: An architect of a post office omitted from her plans the restrooms for postal employees. It was not until the construction of the post office was nearly complete that someone finally noticed the glaring omission. Clearly, it had to be rectified, and the government demanded the bathrooms be installed at the architect's expense.

But what were the architect's obligations? Bathrooms had always been required, the contractor would have included the cost in the contract sum and the government would have paid for them if they had been installed in the first place. Because the post office was nearly complete, however, the restrooms would now cost more to install. There may be demolition costs, materials and labor may be more expensive, concrete would have to be sawed through, drains brought in, plumbing installed — and the portable bathrooms rented once again. What's more, the contractor may be entitled to profit and overhead on the resulting change orders.

Under the concept of betterment, courts would generally hold that the architect is responsible for the costs over and above what it would have cost had the bathroom been designed and specified correctly in the first place. This extra cost is known as the *premium* that must be paid to add the omitted item out of sequence. The government would still be responsible for the basic cost of labor and materials to install the restrooms — up to the amount it would have cost had it been done in the proper sequence during the original construction.

THE PROBLEM

Your client, when confronted with an unexpected bill for several thousands of dollars for something you neglected to specify, is going to blame you. If you make a mistake, the client may expect you to pay whatever it takes to make it right — the excluded item should come out of your pocket. If tempers were cooler, you could explain that your client would have had to pay for the item anyway, had it been in the plans. But he or she isn't going to want to hear a lesson on the legal concept of betterment just then. Unless you have paved the way for just such an eventuality, both in talks with your client and in a contract paragraph that makes your expectations crystal clear, this is exactly the kind of situation that can escalate to litigation.

THE SOLUTION

The best solution is to explain the concept to your client when you are drafting the agreement. Your goal is to avoid any misunderstandings should problems occur and have your client simply acknowledge that he or she understands the concept of betterment. Then, when you present a contract clause that reflects that understanding, your client will know what he or she can expect if a glitch arises. Here is a sample clause:

BETTERMENT

If, due to the Design Professional's error, any required item or component of the project is omitted from the Design Professional's construction documents, the Design Professional shall not be responsible for paying the cost to add such item or component to the extent that such item or component would have been otherwise necessary to the project or otherwise adds value or betterment to the project. In no event will the Design Professional be responsible for any cost or expense that provides betterment, upgrade or enhancement of the project.

This clause and all other clauses herein are intended as examples only and should be reviewed and modified by competent legal counsel to reflect variations in applicable local law and the specific circumstances of your contract.

You can avert many a crisis by talking to your client and educating him or her on the possible pitfalls of the construction process. Such a discussion may present the perfect opportunity to suggest that your client plan on a contingency fund for unexpected costs related to design. (See *Contingency Fund* for information and a sample clause.)

SEE ALSO:

Codes and Standards Compliance
Contingency Fund
Defects in Service
Standard of Care

BILLING AND PAYMENT

The method by which payment to the architect or engineer will be calculated usually is set forth in the contract or in the fee proposal. The more precise design professionals are in defining the details of how and when that payment is to be made, the better the likelihood of prompt payment later with fewer fee-related disputes.

THE PROBLEM

Money issues are frequently the source of disputes and claims, including those that may seem to stem from other causes. Poorly written contracts that do not precisely define when you should be paid, what the penalties are for late payment, and what your rights are in the event of nonpayment invite collection problems. They also encourage liability claims, as clients attempt to avoid paying you by alleging negligence or design error. The worst — and most ironic — scenario finds you forced to sue to collect your fees from a client, only to have him or her countersue you, with little or no basis, as a legal maneuver to avoid payment.

THE SOLUTION

Professionalism rarely offends good clients. Without compromising your client relationships or your professional stature, you can follow sound business practices and get paid for your services. You must use the tools — legal and contractual — available to you and do so in a consistent, impartial manner. Retainage, interest, collection costs, suspension, lien rights, litigation — all are implements you can use. The timely advice of your attorney on how each of these can help and how they can be provided for in your contracts will be invaluable to your firm's financial health.

Consider the following sample contract provisions as tools of the collection trade. These can be linked together to make as strong a provision as you wish to negotiate into your contract.

SAMPLE BILLING AND PAYMENT PROVISIONS

RETAINAGE. The Client shall make an initial payment of ____
dollars ($___) (retainer) upon execution of this Agreement. This
retainer shall be held by the Design Professional and applied
against the final invoice. Invoices shall be submitted by the
Design Professional {monthly, bimonthly, etc.}, are due upon
presentation and shall be considered PAST DUE if not paid
within ___(___) calendar days of the invoice date.

INTEREST. If payment is not received by the Design Professional within ___(___) calendar days of the invoice date, the
Client shall pay as interest an additional charge of one-and-
one-half (1.5) percent (or the maximum allowable by law, whichever is lower) of the PAST DUE amount per month. Payment
thereafter shall first be applied to accrued interest and then to
the unpaid principal.

COLLECTION COSTS. In the event legal action is necessary to
enforce the payment provisions of this Agreement, the Design
Professional shall be entitled to collect from the Client any
judgment or settlement sums due, reasonable attorneys' fees,
court costs and expenses incurred by the Design Professional in
connection therewith and, in addition, the reasonable value of
the Design Professional's time and expenses spent in connection with such collection action, computed at the Design
Professional's prevailing fee schedule and expense policies.

SUSPENSION OF SERVICES. If the Client fails to make payments when due or otherwise is in breach of this Agreement,
the Design Professional may suspend performance of services
upon five (5) calendar days' notice to the Client. The Design
Professional shall have no liability whatsoever to the Client for
any costs or damages as a result of such suspension caused by
any breach of this Agreement by the Client.

TERMINATION OF SERVICES. If the Client fails to make payment to the Design Professional in accordance with the payment terms herein, this shall constitute a material breach of this Agreement and shall be cause for termination by the Design Professional.

SET-OFFS, BACKCHARGES, DISCOUNTS. Payment of invoices is in no case subject to unilateral discounting or set-offs by the Client, and payment is due regardless of suspension or termination of this Agreement by either party.

This clause and all other clauses herein are intended as examples only and should be reviewed and modified by competent legal counsel to reflect variations in applicable local law and the specific circumstances of your contract.

If your client objects to these provisions, you may question his or her intent to pay you or to pay on time. Carefully weigh such risks before you take on the project or finalize your fee.

Still another measure you might consider is a provision that states your client's payment will be taken to mean that he or she is satisfied with your services and is unaware of any defect. (See *Defects in Service* for more information.) Consider the following example:

Payment of any invoice by the Client to the Design Professional shall be taken to mean that the Client is satisfied with the Design Professional's services and is not aware of any deficiencies in those services.

If your client insists on language to permit withholding fees for any disputed invoiced amounts, you might use language similar to the following:

> If the Client objects to any portion of an invoice, the Client shall so notify the Design Professional in writing within ___(__) calendar days of receipt of the invoice. The Client shall identify the specific cause of the disagreement and shall pay when due that portion of the invoice not in dispute. Interest as stated above shall be paid by the Client on all disputed invoiced amounts resolved in the Design Professional's favor and unpaid for more than ___(__) calendar days after date of submission.

Finally, you should discuss with your attorney the availability of lien rights for design professionals in your jurisdiction and, if available, the procedures and documents necessary to institute and enforce such rights. Usually, lien rights must be established within a very short time of providing services, so check with your attorney early if you want to preserve these rights.

By using appropriate contract language that has "teeth" and by following a consistent, well-designed billing and collection system, you can minimize the risks of write-offs and slow pay accounts as well as threats of retaliatory liability claims.

SEE ALSO:

Attorneys' Fees
Contingency Fund
Defects in Service
Ownership of Instruments of Service
Retainage
Suspension of Services
Termination

BURIED UTILITIES

Sometimes a client will want the design professional to locate underground utilities, lay out boring locations, or retain (subcontract with) another firm to provide these services. The client may then ask for a contractual provision that requires the design professional to accept responsibility for any damage done to underground improvements during the boring, testing or excavation on the site.

THE PROBLEM

Soils drilling or excavation operations that damage buried utilities or other underground improvements can result in substantial costs and liability claims. Normally, an independent consulting soils engineer will lay out boring locations for the drilling crew or boring subcontractor. Sometimes, as a cost-saving device, a client will ask you, as prime design professional, to provide those services instead. Such services are very high risk. Existing plans may not show underground locations accurately or may not locate them at all. Consider the consequential damages involved if an electrical line that serves a factory is cut during grading and production is lost, all because the line was located incorrectly on your plans or in the field. (See *Consequential Damages*.)

THE SOLUTION

Avoid accepting responsibility for high risk work that should be performed by others. When geotechnical services are necessary, all parties are best served if the owner selects and contracts directly with a competent soils engineer. If you become involved in geotechnical engineering, even indirectly through subcontracting, or if construction from your plans will involve grading, excavation or soils boring, you need appropriate contractual protection. Require your client to accept responsibility for furnishing you information on the location of underground utilities and structures and to accept the risk of damages — except for damages caused by your negligent use of the information furnished. You and your attorney may want to consider the following provision:

BURIED UTILITIES

The Client will furnish to the Design Professional information identifying the type and location of underground improvements. The Design Professional (or his or her authorized subconsultant) will prepare a plan that shows the locations intended for subsurface penetrations with respect to assumed locations of underground improvements. The Client will approve of the locations of subsurface penetrations prior to their being made. The Client agrees, to the fullest extent permitted by law, to waive all claims and causes of action against the Design Professional and anyone for whom the Design Professional may be legally liable, for damages to underground improvements that result from subsurface penetration locations depicted by the Design Professional.

The Client further agrees, to the fullest extent permitted by law, to indemnify and hold the Design Professional and his or her subconsultants harmless from any damage, liability or cost, including reasonable attorneys' fees and defense costs, for any property damage, injury or economic loss arising or allegedly arising from subsurface penetrations in locations authorized by the Client or from inaccuracy of information provided to the Design Professional by the Client, except for damages caused by the sole negligence of the Design Professional in his or her use of Client furnished information.

This clause and all other clauses herein are intended as examples only and should be reviewed and modified by competent legal counsel to reflect variations in applicable local law and the specific circumstances of your contract.

An indemnity is important, particularly because consequential damages could run into the millions. However, the indemnification could be placed in other clauses, such as Information Provided by Others or Consequential Damages. You also could combine those clauses with a single indemnity. The concept of having the client approve the location of borings and other penetrations may be unique, but many engineers have had success with this approach. It gives the client the last look and makes it crystal clear that it is the client who should bear the risk.

Your client may object to approving the location of the subsurface penetrations when he or she provides the original information. You could, as an alternative, offer to identify the location of underground improvements as an additional service — for an additional fee. Note that in some states this could be construed as engaging in the practice of geotechnical engineering. If you offer this service, in addition to being indemnified, be sure you are technically qualified, properly licensed and insured for such work. If you don't meet all these criteria, then subcontract it to a qualified geotechnical firm who does. The provision might then read:

> **The Design Professional and/or his or her authorized subconsultant will conduct the research that in his or her professional opinion is necessary and will prepare a plan indicating the locations intended for subsurface penetrations with respect to assumed locations of underground improvements. Such services by the Design Professional or his or her subconsultant will be performed in a manner consistent with the ordinary standard of care. The Client recognizes that the research may not identify all underground improvements and that the information upon which the Design Professional relies may contain errors or may not be complete. The Client agrees, to the fullest extent permitted by law, to waive all claims and causes of action against the Design Professional and anyone for whom the Design Professional may be legally liable, for damages to underground improvements resulting from subsurface penetration locations established by the Design Professional.**
>
> **The Client further agrees, to the fullest extent permitted by law, to indemnify and hold the Design Professional and/or his or her subconsultants harmless from any and all damage, liability or cost, including reasonable attorneys' fees and defense costs,**

for any property damage, injury or economic loss arising or allegedly arising from errors or inaccuracy of information contained in plans prepared by the Design Professional and/or his or her subconsultants, except for damages caused by the sole negligence or the willful misconduct of the Design Professional.

SEE ALSO:

Consequential Damages
Indemnities
Information Provided by Others
Subconsultants

CADD

In just a matter of a few years, the use of computers has become commonplace in architecture and engineering. Almost every design firm in North America now has some computer-aided design and drafting (CADD) capability and the typical firm now uses CADD on nearly three-quarters of its projects. These firms understand that computers can reduce the risk of conflicts, errors and omissions, improve communications between members of the design team, and enhance design and analysis capabilities. What many may not realize, however, is that along with these advantages comes a whole new array of CADD-related liability issues they must consider.

The Problem

Increasingly, project owners demand your plans in an electronic format. Some may want the disks for archival purposes or for space planning. And some may think documents on disk will be useful for facility maintenance of their project. Others may want your plans and specifications for future remodeling or expansion. Still others may regard your plans on disk as record documents or "as builts" and hope to rely on them without realizing they have the same limitations as hard copy "as builts." (See *Record Documents* for a related discussion.)

Then there are owners who may have other ideas for use of your disks. Unless you have protected your designs by contract and copyright, they could be reused — without your knowledge or consent — for another project. Some clients may decide to make a few little changes to your plans; it takes but a few strokes of a key to alter your design — and magnify your liability.

Furthermore, if you and your client have not agreed in advance to CADD specifications — exactly what hardware and software is to be used, as well as detailed computer design elements and just how much of the design documents are to be delivered on CADD — you may find yourself having to purchase new hardware or software and hurriedly training personnel or changing or duplicating work already completed in order to comply with a client's demands.

On the other hand, sometimes the client wishes to provide information to you on disk. Absent a clear understanding with your client, this can result in a great deal of extra work for you, as well as certain liability implications. You could find yourself having to purchase expensive hardware or translation software. Worse, the data may not be readable or in a format you can use, or you may have little or no support from the person who prepared the information.

Another source of concern is the software itself. The proliferation of available CADD programming is astonishing; it sometimes seems everyone with a computer is generating applications programs. Unfortunately, defects in purchased software packages may not be detected until your project is complete or a structure has failed. What's more, unfamiliarity with these very sophisticated programs can cause real problems. Changes to the software by your in-house computer whiz or inadequate training of your staff also can result in design errors — for which you can be held responsible. In addition, some design firms are developing their own software and making it available to the public. They may not be aware that these programs, without proper safeguards in place, subject their firms to claims of strict liability for failures resulting from defects in the software.

You also risk assuming liability if you function as a "service bureau" — running calculations for another designer — either for a fee or even as a favor to a colleague. Every design professional has heard the horror story about the structural engineer who agreed to run some calculations on a wall for her friend, a civil engineer. As the data was printed out, the structural made a small circle around a figure and noted that the civil should double-check it. When the wall failed, the circle and note were discovered on the documents. Because the structural had no written contract absolving her of responsibility, she was included in the resulting lawsuit.

THE SOLUTION

Find out why your client wants your CADD files. It is possible he or she may not need the design on electronic format, or at least not all of it. Perhaps your client doesn't understand that a requirement for all design work to be performed on CADD may well result in increased design costs. If he or she wants the disks for facility maintenance or future repair work, explain that information magnetically stored is easily damaged and its accuracy cannot be depended upon for very long. What's more, maintenance rarely requires all the drawings in a construction set. Instead, you could offer to generate a set on disk especially for maintenance as an additional service. If your client wants the data for archival purposes, again you should describe the limitations of relying on computer disks. Information stored on disks requires certain operating systems and software that may be obsolete in the not-so-distant future.

Your client may have perfectly appropriate reasons for wanting copies of some or all your CADD files, however. If so, you must take certain precautions in order to protect yourself against the reuse and misuse of that information. Many architects and engineers protect themselves by stating in their Scope of Services or Ownership of Instruments of Service clause that the hard copy is the actual contract deliverable and that any copies on disk or tape are for the client's convenience only.

It is a good idea to add a CADD clause to your contract. The following provision describes your construction documents — including computer files — as instruments of your service, and asserts that you will retain ownership. It is also important to be very clear about the CADD specifications, either in your Scope of Services or an addendum to the contract. List in detail the requirements for compatibility for CADD hardware and software. You will also want to specify a short acceptance period of one or two months, after which you cannot be held responsible for deterioration or modification of the disks. Finally, such a clause should also include a waiver and indemnity for claims resulting from unauthorized reuse of the CADD files or unauthorized changes made by the client or others. (See *Unauthorized Changes to Plans*.) Consider this example:

DELIVERY OF CADD FILES

In accepting and utilizing any drawings or other data on any form of electronic media generated and provided by the Design Professional, the Client covenants and agrees that all such drawings and data are instruments of service of the Design Professional, who shall be deemed the author of the drawings and data, and shall retain all common law, statutory law and other rights, including copyrights. The Client and the Design Professional agree that any CADD files prepared by either party shall conform to the specifications listed in Exhibit ___. The electronic files submitted by the Design Professional to the

Client are submitted for an acceptance period of ____ days. Any defects the Client discovers during this period will be reported to the Design Professional and will be corrected as part of the Design Professional's Basic Scope of Services. Correction of defects detected and reported after the acceptance period will be compensated for as Additional Services.

The Client further agrees not to use these drawings and data, in whole or in part, for any purpose or project other than the project which is the subject of this Agreement. The Client agrees to waive all claims against the Design Professional resulting in any way from any unauthorized changes or reuse of the drawings and data for any other project by anyone other than the Design Professional.

In addition, the Client agrees, to the fullest extent permitted by law, to indemnify and hold the Design Professional harmless from any damage, liability or cost, including reasonable attorneys' fees and costs of defense, arising from any changes made by anyone other than the Design Professional or from any reuse of the drawings and data without the prior written consent of the Design Professional.

Under no circumstances shall transfer of the drawings and other instruments of service on electronic media for use by the Client be deemed a sale by the Design Professional, and the Design Professional makes no warranties, either express or implied, of merchantability and fitness for any particular purpose.

This clause and all other clauses herein are intended as examples only and should be reviewed and modified by competent legal counsel to reflect variations in applicable local law and the specific circumstances of your contract.

There is little you can do to protect your electronic files from unauthorized modification by a client. Because of this, many design professionals remove all mention of their firm (title blocks, logos, proprietary symbols and other identifying marks) from every document on the disks before turning them over to their clients.

In spite of all your efforts, should your client insist on ownership of your documents on disk, tie the transfer of ownership to payment in full of your fees. In this case, your clause should again refer to such materials as instruments of your service and disavow any warranty of merchantability and fitness for any particular purpose. Again, insist on a waiver and indemnity for unauthorized changes and reuse of the data. Consider this provision:

CADD Documents

The Client and the Design Professional agree that any CADD documents prepared by either party shall conform to the specifications listed in Exhibit ___. The electronic files submitted by the Design Professional to the Client are submitted for an acceptance period of ____ days. Any defects the Client discovers during this period will be reported to the Design Professional and will be corrected as part of the Design Professional's Basic Scope of Services. Corrections of defects detected and reported after the acceptance period will be compensated for as Additional Services.

The Client acknowledges the Design Professional's plans and specifications, including all documents on electronic media, as instruments of professional service. Nevertheless, the plans and specifications prepared under this Agreement shall become the property of the Client upon completion of the services and payment in full of all monies due to the Design Professional. The Client shall not reuse or make or permit to be made any modification to the plans and specifications without the prior written authorization of the Design Professional. The Client agrees to waive any claim against the Design Professional arising from any unauthorized reuse or modification of the plans and specifications.

In addition, the Client agrees, to the fullest extent permitted by law, to indemnify and hold the Design Professional harmless from any damage, liability or cost, including reasonable attorneys' fees and costs of defense, arising from any reuse or modification of the plans and specifications by the Client or any person or entity which acquires or obtains the plans and specifications from or through the Client without the prior written

authorization of the Design Professional. The Design Professional makes no warranties, either express or implied, of merchantability and fitness for any particular purpose. In no event shall the Design Professional be liable for any loss of profit or any damages.

If your client is to provide information to you on disk, be certain you have a strong clause in your contract that protects you if erroneous data is supplied to you. (See *Information Provided by Others*.) You will also want to be very clear about CADD specifications, the scope of the information on disk, who is responsible for the content and condition of the disks and the source of the data.

Even if the commercial software you are using is found to have "bugs," in most cases you will still be held responsible for the accuracy of your completed designs. To minimize your liability for computer-related problems, you must be able to show that you exercised the proper care in researching, selecting, testing, training for and using your software and databases. If you have documented such steps, a court may find you performed to the standard of care even though there was a failure because of defects in the software. Therefore, establish sound CADD procedures in your firm and follow them. Keep informed of improvements in computer technology. Thoroughly investigate any new software package before you buy it, making sure it's applicable to the kinds of projects your firm designs, and negotiate with software vendors for as much contractual assurance and training support as possible. In general, you will want to rely on time-tested software that has been thoroughly checked in-house against a design with a known result. Insist that your staff be thoroughly trained in the use of any software. Never assume that simply because something is computer generated, it is correct. Make sure an experienced staff member checks any work produced by computer before incorporating it into the design.

If you are generating applications programs for sale or license to clients, other design professionals or the public, it is important to get the advice of an attorney who is knowledgeable in the design professions as well as in copyrights and licensing. He or she may advise you to set up a separate business entity to market the programs in order to protect your design practice from liability for any defects in the software.

Lastly, it is probably best to avoid running calculations on your computers for other firms. The fee is rarely large enough to make it worth your while, and you may be taking on substantial liability. Even when you have a written contract complete with waivers and indemnities, if something goes wrong, you still have to spend time and money extricating yourself from the legal mess created by someone else.

SEE ALSO:

Bibliography
Copyrights
Ownership of Instruments of Service
Record Documents
Unauthorized Changes to Plans

CERTIFICATIONS, GUARANTEES AND WARRANTIES

Architects and engineers are often asked to certify, warrant or guarantee that something has been accomplished or that certain conditions exist. Such certification requirements may come in a client-drafted contract, from the owner's lender or from a governmental agency. Although certifications, guarantees and warranties are commonplace in a constructor's contract, they have no place in a design professional's agreement.

THE PROBLEM

By definition, the words certify, warrant or guarantee mean to assure the total accuracy of something or to confirm that a standard has been met absolutely. Legally, these words and their derivatives are virtually interchangeable. Therefore, if you certify or warrant something, you have sworn that something is unequivocally true or correct or perfect.

If you must, you can certify known facts, such as your name, for instance, and your professional license number. You can certify that you visited a jobsite on a certain date and that you made certain observations during that visit. What you must not do, however, is guarantee something you cannot positively know. This also means avoiding the use of extreme or absolute wording, such as all or every. For instance, you cannot certify that a contractor has correctly placed all the rebar in a slab or footing. Even if you were looking over the contractor's shoulder day and night, you couldn't absolutely guarantee that the contractor had done the job perfectly. Similarly, you cannot warrant that a site is free of all toxic materials, even if your Preliminary Site Assessment uncovered no indications of hazardous materials. No matter how thorough you were, you could not have observed or tested every cubic inch of that site. (See *Environmental and Health Hazards* for more information.) You cannot certify that a building complies with the ADA, since that is a legal determination, not an architectural or engineering finding. (See *Americans with Disabilities Act.*) Nor can you certify that a building was constructed in strict accordance with your plans and specifications. You simply do not know that every detail the contractor built conforms to your design.

By certifying or warranting something, you are assuming a level of liability well beyond the standard of care required by law. And that extraordinary liability is not insurable. As a design professional, all you need do is conform to the standard of care as practiced by your peers. And that's what your professional liability insurance covers. By certifying something, you raise that standard of care. If you are certifying someone else's work, you may be assuming that person's liability too. Under the law, you do not have to guarantee your work or the work of others. (See *Standard of Care* for more information.)

When you certify or warrant or guarantee that something is perfect, you also hand your client an effective weapon to use against you. The smallest error — even if caused by someone else — could produce a new cause of action for breach of warranty, which is somewhat easier to prove than professional negligence. For the same reasons, beware of the "sure" words: *insure, ensure* or *assure*. Once again, if you ensure something is true, you might be setting yourself up for a breach of contract and/or a breach of warranty claim. Even the innocent-sounding words *state* or *declare* ("I hereby state that the building was constructed in conformance with. . . " for instance) may be interpreted as a warranty. It is important to remember that your professional liability insurance is not intended to cover breach of contract or breach of warranty, the assumption of someone else's liability, or a promise to perform to a higher standard of care than required by law. (See *Insurance* and *Non-Negligent Services* for more information.) What's more, claims against you involving alleged breaches of contract or warranty may be subjected to a longer statute of limitations period than would be applicable to claims involving merely negligent services.

The Solution

There are several possible solutions available to you. Discuss them with your attorney and work out a strategy that protects you and is acceptable to your client.

If your client has drafted a contract that requires you to certify, guarantee or warrant anything, delete those provisions. Explain why you cannot and should not be expected to expand your liability and jeopardize your insurance coverage. We consider a client's requirement for inappropriate certifications, warranties and guarantees to be a **Deal Breaker.** If you cannot delete or change the clause to your satisfaction, consider walking away from the project.

A more aggressive approach is to add a clause to your contract that prevents your client from requiring certifications proposed by anyone. The following wording would protect you from an attempt to withhold your fees because of your refusal to certify something:

CERTIFICATIONS, GUARANTEES
AND WARRANTIES

The Design Professional shall not be required to sign any documents, no matter by whom requested, that would result in the Design Professional's having to certify, guarantee or warrant the existence of conditions whose existence the Design Professional cannot ascertain. The Client also agrees not to make resolution of any dispute with the Design Professional or payment of any amount due to the Design Professional in any way contingent upon the Design Professional's signing any such certification.

This clause and all other clauses herein are intended as examples only and should be reviewed and modified by competent legal counsel to reflect variations in applicable local law and the specific circumstances of your contract.

A different strategy is to include a contract provision that prohibits any action that would jeopardize your professional liability insurance coverage. This also would protect you from being forced to sign any documents for the client's lender without your review and consent. (To avoid duplication or conflict, coordinate the following clause with any Lenders' Requirements provision in your agreement.)

The Design Professional shall not be required to execute any documents subsequent to the signing of this Agreement that in any way might, in the sole judgment of the Design Professional, increase the Design Professional's risk or the availability or cost of his or her professional or general liability insurance.

If your contract gives you the right to refuse to sign certification documents that are unreasonable or too risky, you are then in a position to substitute acceptable language. For instance, you can "certify" facts you know to be true. But, if you cannot promise something with absolute certainty, indicate that your declaration is "in my professional opinion" or that your statement is true "to the best of my information, knowledge and belief." This clearly takes the onus off a certification form and keeps it from being a warranty or guarantee. After all, as a design professional, you are trained and paid to render professional opinions. In the event your client or a lender thrusts a certification form in front of you for your signature, you can modify the form sufficiently to be insurable by making the following deletions and additions (underlined):

ARCHITECT'S/ENGINEER'S OPINION

I hereby certify that I am a licensed architect in the State of _____. ~~I further certify~~ To the best of my knowledge, information and belief, the building was constructed in ~~strict~~ general conformance with the plans and specifications, and ~~I hereby state~~ in my professional opinion, is in compliance with ~~all~~ applicable laws, codes and ordinances.

This clause and all other clauses herein are intended as examples only and should be reviewed and modified by competent legal counsel to reflect variations in applicable local law and the specific circumstances of your contract.

Some public agencies, lenders or owners may insist that the wording on their forms is non-negotiable and must be signed "as is." Most, however, are willing to listen to reasonable explanations of why you cannot "certify" or "warrant" something.

Finally, the EPA and several states have defined "certification" by law to give some protection to design professionals. This may not apply to your jurisdiction or project, however, and you should not depend on such protection. Check with knowledgeable local counsel. It is far safer to define these terms in the body of your contract to mean precisely what you intend them to mean. It is always a good idea to include a Definitions section in your contract in any case, in which you carefully explain the meaning of "certify" or "declare" or "state." (See *Definitions*.)

SEE ALSO:

Americans with Disabilities Act
Codes and Standards Compliance
Definitions
Environmental and Health Hazards

Insurance
Lenders' Requirements
Non-Negligent Services
Standard of Care

CHANGED CONDITIONS

Conditions that become apparent during the course of a project may differ significantly from those assumed to exist when the workscope was first developed. These new conditions may require substantial additional design services (with a correspondingly higher fee), may increase construction costs, may greatly increase the architect's or engineer's risk, or even necessitate services that the designer cannot provide.

In construction contracts, owners and contractors usually address the possibility of encountering differing site conditions by incorporating remedy-granting provisions. The same does not always hold true for design service contracts.

THE PROBLEM

Some clients seem to believe that if you agree to a specific workscope, this obligates you to "do" the project. If difficulties arise, they are your problem, not your client's.

Discovery of asbestos or PCBs in a renovation project; new codes, laws or regulations instituted after the contract is executed; an adverse development in the financial condition of the client; a switch of key client personnel involved in the project; a radical change in the nature or use of the project — all are examples of changed conditions that would adversely affect you and might cause you to re-evaluate fees, terms, or even continuing involvement with the project. Unless the possibility of changed circumstances is broached with your client beforehand, the situation could easily result in misunderstandings — and litigation.

THE SOLUTION

Since a contract cannot possibly contemplate all potential changed conditions, it is important to establish a means of identifying them as they occur. This means should be vested in your professional judgment. The following clause may be effective in providing for changed conditions:

CHANGED CONDITIONS

The Client shall rely on the Design Professional's judgment as to the continued adequacy of this agreement in light of occurrences or discoveries that were not originally contemplated by or known to the Design Professional. Should the Design Professional call for contract renegotiation, the Design Professional shall identify the changed conditions necessitating renegotiation and the Design Professional and the Client shall promptly and in good faith enter into renegotiation of this Agreement. If terms cannot be agreed to, the parties agree that either party has the absolute right to terminate this Agreement.

This clause and all other clauses herein are intended as examples only and should be reviewed and modified by competent legal counsel to reflect variations in applicable local law and the specific circumstances of your contract.

If the client is reluctant to give you blanket license to call for renegotiation, explain that no design professional wants to alienate a good client or stop working on a project that is both challenging and profitable, and that you have no incentive to do so. Show your client that your contract has (or should have) a Termination clause which ideally gives both of you the right to terminate the contract in any case — with or without cause. (See *Termination* for specific language.) However, if it helps your client, you could change the wording to include reference to your fee schedule for additional services:

. . . enter into renegotiation of this Agreement. In establishing fees for the new work to be performed, the Design Professional shall utilize the same fee schedule as already agreed upon, as shown in Exhibit____. If terms . . .

If your client is unwilling to provide a Changed Conditions clause, ask what his or her response would be to certain eventualities that may occur, such as the examples given earlier, or other situations that pertain to your project. If the reactions are what you would hope for, determine if this understanding can be committed to writing. Irrespective of the answer, examine the contract Termination clause closely, and make sure you have a way out should it become necessary.

SEE ALSO:

Codes and Standards Compliance
Environmental and Health Hazards
Excluded Services
Renovation/Remodeling
Scope of Services
Suspension of Services
Termination

Claims Arbiter Service

A client will sometimes attempt to require a prime design professional to interpret and render decisions on questions of performance or obligations of both the contractor and the client.

The Problem

Serving as an arbiter may well expedite resolution of certain issues, but it can also make you vulnerable to claims and lawsuits — or at least require you to spend a considerable amount of time in reaching decisions or defending those already made.

The Solution

The best solution is to avoid service as a claims arbiter altogether. (See *Excluded Services*.) Failing that, protect yourself with appropriate language in your agreement with your client, and require the owner (presumably your client) to insert similar provisions in his or her agreement with the contractor.

CLAIMS ARBITER SERVICE

On written request of either the Client or the Contractor, the Design Professional shall interpret and decide matters concerning performance of the Client and the Contractor under requirements of the Contract Documents. The Client will pay the Design Professional for these services in accordance with the Additional Services provisions herein. Decisions of the Design Professional shall be consistent with the intent of the Contract Documents and shall be made with reasonable promptness. The Design Professional shall endeavor to secure faithful performance by both the Client and Contractor and shall not show partiality to either. The Design Professional shall not be liable to either the Client or the Contractor for results of interpretations or decisions the Design Professional has rendered in good faith. The Client agrees, to the fullest extent permitted by law, to indemnify and hold the Design Professional harmless from any claim, cost (including reasonable attorneys' fees and costs of defense) or liability for injury or loss arising or allegedly arising from the Design Professional's service as a claim arbiter.

This clause and all other clauses herein are intended as examples only and should be reviewed and modified by competent legal counsel to reflect variations in applicable local law and the specific circumstances of your contract.

SEE ALSO:

Confidential Communications
Excluded Services
Public Responsibility
Scope of Services

CODES AND STANDARDS COMPLIANCE

Many client-drafted agreements require the design professional to comply with all laws, codes, standards and regulations. Although such an innocent-sounding clause may appear simply to state the obvious, it is a loaded, dangerous and perhaps unattainable requirement.

THE PROBLEM

The fundamental difficulty with such a provision is the word *all*. Thousands of laws, codes and regulations that relate to construction are on the books; all are subject to change, and some are open to interpretation. It is not unusual to find that a given regulation may conflict with another, and this places you in the untenable position of needing to comply with two differing requirements. If you can only adhere to one — and you have agreed in your contract to comply with all requirements — you may find yourself unable to fulfill a contractual obligation.

As a design professional, you are already required to comply with codes, laws and regulations. Failure to design to the standards set by local building codes is negligence per se. In fact, designing to code is the very least you must do. Under certain circumstances, merely designing to minimum code requirements may be negligent if the standard of care dictates a design that exceeds code. (Refer to *Standard of Care* for discussion.)

There are other issues to consider: Who pays for design changes needed to reflect a new code or regulation (ADA or OSHA, for instance) put in force during the course of a project? If the project is suspended at any stage of development for an extended time, who pays for any design changes necessitated by new regulations when the project comes back on line? If your contract does not provide for such eventualities (through a comprehensive Scope of Services, a Codes and Standards Compliance or Delay clause, or even a strong Changed Conditions provision), you may find yourself providing extensive redesign services to bring projects up to new code — and without compensation.

THE SOLUTION

Perhaps the best solution is to delete your client's compliance clause from the contract and, instead, carefully delineate your obligations in the Scope of Services. You also will want to select an appropriate cutoff date that states when your responsibility to adhere to new codes and/or regulations ends. A fair cutoff date might be on submission of your plans and specifications to the appropriate building authorities. Any design changes necessary after that date should be considered Additional Services, to be billed for accordingly.

Bear in mind that any renovation, alteration or preservation work calls for heightened caution regarding codes. Because these projects are so complex, the number of applicable codes and regulations may be greater than usual. This can expand your research efforts and generally make it more difficult to preserve the structure's design integrity while adhering to code. You may well find yourself working more closely with appropriate government officials and suggesting alternative materials and methods to comply with the intent — if not the letter — of the code. All these factors increase your risk and underscore the need for a cautious contractual approach. (See *Renovation/Remodeling*.)

If your client seems set on his or her contract clause, your best bet is to delete the word *all* and insert a finite cutoff date for redesign as part of your workscope. For example:

CODES AND STANDARDS COMPLIANCE

The Design Professional shall put forth reasonable professional efforts to comply with codes, regulations, laws. . . in effect as of the date of {submission to building authorities, the execution of this Agreement or other appropriate date}.

This clause and all other clauses herein are intended as examples only and should be reviewed and modified by competent legal counsel to reflect variations in applicable local law and the specific circumstances of your contract.

An alternative approach might be to accept the word *all* but tie your efforts to the standard of care, such as:

The Design Professional shall exercise usual and customary professional care in his or her efforts to comply with all codes, regulations, laws… in effect as of the date of _____.

Help your client realize the potential for conflict between codes at various levels and recognize that in any case you already have a professional obligation to comply with codes and regulations. He or she may well be sympathetic to your concerns and readily accept your request to delete or change the clause.

SEE ALSO:

Americans with Disabilities Act
Changed Conditions
Delays
Renovation/Remodeling
Scope of Services
Standard of Care
Suspension of Services

CONDOMINIUMS

Condominiums are far and away the most liability prone projects architects and engineers design. The problem is so significant that in one industry study by the University of California, a third of all condominium projects reported construction defects — and nearly 40 percent of those had major flaws. Almost 14 percent of the owners had filed lawsuits against their developers and another 12 percent had threatened suit. As too many designers have learned, suits against developers have an unfortunate tendency to envelop all the design professionals on a project.

There are several reasons why condominiums have such a high claims history. Condominium developers are frequently over leveraged and may give quality little consideration. Often the design team isn't given the chance to provide construction phase services; construction observation may be on call at the developer's discretion or eliminated altogether to save money. In addition, the potential occupants are frequently first-time home buyers, older people with limited resources or perhaps less sophisticated consumers. They believe the advertisements, promotional material and marketing tactics that tend to promise much more than their dollars can realistically buy.

Then there are the condominium homeowners' associations, whose directors set the budget for maintenance of the common areas and building exteriors. Perhaps because the money must come from their own pockets, associations tend to be reluctant to set dues high enough to cover all the necessary upkeep. The result is poor maintenance, deferred maintenance or no maintenance at all.

Homeowners' associations also provide ready vehicles for class action suits. Condominium boards often are targets of aggressive law firms who market their legal services by directly soliciting the homeowner associations. These firms promise recovery from the developers, contractors and designers for everything from leaky windows, to cracked sidewalks, to inadequate HVAC systems. Even the threat of such a suit can be enough to make some defendants throw in the towel and make a settlement, simply because the cost of defense is so high.

Sometimes, of course, the contractors and developers are nowhere to be found several years later when a claim is filed. Contractors can bankrupt their organizations and disappear; developers frequently set up a corporation for developing a single project and later dissolve it. The only (or most vulnerable) deep pocket remaining to face the lawyers and the condominium association is the design professional.

The frequency of claims against condominium designers is so high that, for a time, almost no professional liability insurer would cover architects or engineers who designed condominiums. When insurance again became available, designers found it expensive, difficult to obtain and with no assurance that it would be available in the future.

IF YOUR DESIGN COULD BE CONVERTED INTO CONDOMINIUMS

If an apartment building you design is converted — perhaps years from now — to a condominium, you unwittingly inherit the liability and risk just as if you had designed the project as a condominium in the first place. You might not even be aware of the conversion until a claim is presented.

THE PROBLEM

Where you once owed a duty of care to your client, you may now owe that same duty to 500 owners if an apartment complex you designed has "gone condo." Because you did not enter into agreements with these new condominium owners, you have no contractual protection of any kind. The contractor may have disappeared, the original developer is gone, and you weren't consulted and didn't participate in the conversion of your design. What's more, your liability may be further extended because the codes and regulations governing condominiums differ from those for a rental project.

THE SOLUTION

Frankly, there is limited protection available in this situation. Nevertheless, we recommend you add a clause to any agreement for a project that could conceivably be converted to condominiums in the future. Such a clause would provide that your client (presumably the original developer) indemnify you in the event of a conversion:

CONDOMINIUM CONVERSION

The Client does not now foresee that this project will be converted into condominiums. Because the Design Professional did not design this project for condominium ownership, the Client agrees that, if the Client decides to convert the project into condominiums in the future, the Client will, to the fullest extent permitted by law, indemnify and hold harmless the Design Professional and the Design Professional's officers, partners, employees and subconsultants from any and all claims, losses, damages and costs, including reasonable attorneys' fees and defense costs, arising or allegedly arising in any manner whatsoever due to the conversion to condominium ownership, except for the sole negligence or willful misconduct of the Design Professional.

This clause and all other clauses herein are intended as examples only and should be reviewed and modified by competent legal counsel to reflect variations in applicable local law and the specific circumstances of your contract.

This provision may offer you limited protection if your client still owns the project when it is converted. If there has been a change of ownership, that protection probably disappears. Even if your client still owns the building, however, any indemnity is only as good as your client's financial resources. If a million dollar settlement is beyond the client's means, you will still be at risk.

Of course, it is important to talk to your attorney about any proposed indemnity language to ensure it is consistent with local laws and as enforceable as you can make it. (See *Indemnities* for more information.)

IF YOU DESIGN CONDOMINIUMS

In some ways, knowingly designing a condominium project has advantages over a surprise conversion. At least you are aware of the risks and liability pitfalls and can structure your agreement and loss prevention practices accordingly.

THE PROBLEM

You know that condominium projects are liability minefields. Your problem, therefore, is to devise a strategy to maximize your loss prevention measures and contractual safeguards in order to minimize your exposure to claims. Even with the most carefully chosen preventive steps and the most protective contract terms, you must recognize that condominium projects still represent a high-risk undertaking.

THE SOLUTION

Assuming you are still determined to work on condominiums, your first concern ought to be selectivity — to decide which projects and clients you are willing to gamble on. Your client should also be concerned about the high-risk nature of condominiums. His or her liability (and yours) can extend for many years after substantial completion of the project. Therefore, work with carefully chosen clients to assure quality projects. In fact, your choice of client may be the single most important factor in a successful and trouble-free venture. Look for a client who has experience in condominium projects, is sufficiently financed and is not litigation-prone. Then ask yourself, "Is the reward enough to merit the risk?" If the answer is yes, try to anticipate and minimize problems early on by employing every loss prevention technique you can. You may want to suggest a project peer review, for instance, and a constructibility review. Condominium projects may be excellent candidates for partnering agreements, too. (Refer to the *Bibliography* for details on how to get more information on partnering.) You also should stress the importance of construction administration. (See *Exhibit 2* for a list of specific loss prevention recommendations.)

You might want to propose that the client purchase project insurance, if it is available. Your client should understand that your professional liability rates probably will increase over the next several years if you work on his or her condominium project, and it is appropriate that the owner assume some of those costs. Furthermore, project insurance is a way to protect your claims record with your insurance company. In any event, suggesting a project policy may be a good way to "smoke out" a litigation-prone client. (See *Insurance* for more information.)

In addition to the must-have contract clauses listed in Exhibit 3, we recommend three contractual concepts that separately may be helpful and, taken together, might give you substantial protection.

First, you should have a strong indemnity in your contract that requires your client — if he or she is still in existence and financially viable — to protect you from third party claims. Have your attorney help you draw up the broadest, most enforceable language possible. As a starting point, consider the following language:

CONDOMINIUMS

The Client acknowledges the risks to the Design Professional inherent in condominium projects and the disparity between the Design Professional's fee and the Design Professional's potential liability for problems or alleged problems with such condominium projects. Therefore, the Client agrees, to the fullest extent permitted by law, to indemnify and hold the Design Professional and the Design Professional's officers, partners, employees and subconsultants harmless from any and all claims, liabilities, losses and costs, including reasonable attorneys' fees and costs of defense, arising or allegedly arising from the services performed under this Agreement, except for the Design Professional's sole negligence or willful misconduct.

This clause and all other clauses herein are intended as examples only and should be reviewed and modified by competent legal counsel to reflect variations in applicable local law and the specific circumstances of your contract.

Two other creative contractual solutions have appeared in recent years. The first is the development of a maintenance manual as part of the scope of basic services. All design consultants on the project would develop, as part of their scope of services, written recommendations for the required minimum maintenance of their particular component of the project, such as the decking, plumbing, lighting, HVAC, roofing, sidewalks and so on. These recommendations would then be compiled into a maintenance manual for the project. Your client would agree to write into the by-laws of the condominium homeowners' association a requirement that the recommended maintenance be the responsibility of the association. The by-laws would require periodic inspection of each component by a qualified outside inspection service, which would report its findings and maintenance recommendations to the homeowners' association. Each purchaser would receive a copy of the maintenance manual at the time of purchase and would acknowledge understanding of the responsibility of the homeowners' association to have the necessary maintenance performed. A clause to accomplish this might read:

MAINTENANCE MANUAL

The Client agrees that the by-laws of the Homeowners' Association established for this project will contain a requirement that the Association will have performed the inspections recommended in the Maintenance Manual. The Client further warrants the by-laws will contain provisions requiring the Homeowners' Association to have performed all necessary maintenance when recommended as a result of these inspections. The by-laws shall also contain an appropriate waiver and indemnity in favor of the Client, the Design Professional and his or her subconsultants and the Contractor if the maintenance recommendations are not performed.

This clause and all other clauses herein are intended as examples only and should be reviewed and modified by competent legal counsel to reflect variations in applicable local law and the specific circumstances of your contract.

Another clause sometimes employed in an attempt to cut off claims at their source — the homeowners' association or individual owners — is *ADR by Covenant*. This is a relatively simple idea, developed by the ASFE: Professional Firms Practicing in the Geosciences, that provides in your agreement with the developer/client that he or she prepare and record a covenant on the deed to the parcel of land being developed. This covenant would then "run with the land" in any future sales and would bind all future owners of the condominium unit. The covenant would provide that any dispute between the homeowners and the original developer or the developer's design professionals or contractors must be submitted first to mandatory, nonbinding mediation. Attempting mediation of a dispute before resorting to litigation can resolve many conflicts quickly and inexpensively. (See *Dispute Resolution* for more information. Also refer to the *Bibliography* for details on how to obtain information on ADR by Covenant.)

Some condominium developers follow another innovative approach to resolving disputes with disgruntled buyers. The developer can include an option in the deed restrictions to repurchase units for the initial price plus a certain percentage increase per year. Because such an offer demonstrates confidence in the project, some developers have made it a part of their sales program. Although this may not be an item to include in your contract, any quality developer who has made this offer should certainly be at the top of your "preferred client" list.

Whatever solution (or solutions) you and your attorney decide upon, your agreement must be carefully crafted to include several other must-have provisions. These clauses should be considered **Deal Makers.** Remember, condominium design is so risky, if you cannot obtain adequate protection in your contract, you should consider walking away from the project. (See *Exhibit 3* for a list of important provisions for condominium projects.)

EXHIBIT 2

CONDOMINIUM PROJECTS LOSS PREVENTION POINTS

- Look closely at the developer. Is there adequate financing? Is there commitment to quality? Has he or she developed other condominium projects and with what results? Is he or she likely to be around in the future? What are the contractor selection criteria? Will the developer build the project with his or her own forces or act as a "paper developer"?

- Investigate the availability of project insurance and propose that the owner provide coverage for the design team. Make sure your subconsultants are well insured.

- Find out how the developer plans to market the project. Will the advertising be realistic? Will your name be used?

- Request a project peer review and a constructibility review of the design.

- Make sure there is an adequate contingency fund for the project that will apply to design defects.

- Carefully document all meetings and conversations pertaining to the project. In particular, note any recommendations you make that are not followed by the owner.

- Insist on providing full-service construction observation and administration. Watch for any substitutions requested by the developer or contractor. Document your objections.

- Develop a maintenance manual, have it incorporated into the homeowners' association by-laws and require that homeowners be educated about their responsibilities for upkeep and following the stated recommendations. Make the provisions of the manual binding upon the homeowners' association.

- Require that the developer have each purchaser inspect the unit and common areas for defects and have the purchaser sign some type of certificate of satisfaction.

Exhibit 3

Must-Have Clauses for Condominium Projects

Attorneys' Fees

Construction Observation

Contingency Fund

Corporate Protection

Defects in Service

Dispute Resolution

Environmental and Health Hazards

Indemnities

Interpretation

Jobsite Safety

Limitation of Liability

Opinion of Probable Construction Cost

Ownership of Instruments of Service

Severability and Survival

Standard of Care

Statutes of Repose or Limitation

Termination

Unauthorized Changes to Plans

SEE ALSO:

CONFIDENTIAL COMMUNICATIONS

Architects and engineers are expected to serve as their clients' professional advisors, candidly relating their observations, opinions and recommendations about the work of others. Such candor, however, can lead to problems if these remarks reflect negatively on another party.

THE PROBLEM

Like many architects and engineers, you may find yourself advising your clients on the qualifications and performance of others. For example, you may suggest that a certain contractor be excluded from a list of prequalified firms, a low bidder not be relied upon because of a poor performance in the past, materials be rejected because of unacceptable test results, or a contractor be replaced because of incompetence.

However, you should be aware that contractors and suppliers have been known to file — or threaten to file — libel or slander suits against design professionals in an attempt to either influence such reports to their clients or obtain damages from the design professionals if their clients act upon the reports.

THE SOLUTION

Be highly selective about the words you choose in reporting anything that could have a negative financial impact on another party. Report facts as facts, objectively, without embellishment or emotion; report opinions as opinions, carefully noted as such, and do your best to document everything you say. Make sure others in your firm do the same. By taking this approach, you will make it difficult for the affected party to win a libel or slander suit against you, as well as the punitive damages which are also sometimes claimed. Remember, the best defense to a defamation action is the truth.

Educate your client. Explain that the risks involved can be minimized through reliance on negotiated contractor selection — or at least prequalification of contractors. Your client must also recognize that you cannot act as an effective advisor if you face the threat of a lawsuit every time you state or imply something negative about someone.

The best solution may be a contract clause through which clients agree to indemnify you for a slander or libel action brought against you by other parties and about whose qualifications, performance or reputation you are required to render opinions and reports. Consider this example:

CONFIDENTIAL COMMUNICATIONS

The Design Professional may be required to report on the past or current qualifications and/or performance of others engaged or being considered for engagement directly or indirectly by the Client, and to render opinions and advice in that regard. Those about whom reports and opinions are rendered may as a consequence initiate claims of libel or slander against the Design Professional. To help create an atmosphere in which the Design Professional feels free to express himself or herself candidly in the interest of the Client, the Client agrees, to the fullest extent permitted by law, to indemnify and hold the Design Professional harmless from any claim, liability or cost (including reasonable attorneys' fees and costs of defense) for injury or loss arising or allegedly arising from the professional opinions and reports rendered by the Design Professional to the Client or the Client's agents.

This clause and all other clauses herein are intended as examples only and should be reviewed and modified by competent legal counsel to reflect variations in applicable local law and the specific circumstances of your contract.

SEE ALSO:

Claims Arbiter Service
Confidentiality
Construction Observation
Indemnities

CONFIDENTIALITY

On occasion, a client may want a strict contract provision that requires the design professional to keep confidential the nature of and data related to the project.

THE PROBLEM

Depending on how tightly it is worded, a client-drafted confidentiality provision may cause you difficulties. First, if the clause is too strict, it could prevent sharing vital information with subconsultants or even your own employees — clearly not the intent of the provision. Second, if you find yourself the target of a third-party claim, the act of providing information necessary to your defense could be deemed a breach of contract.

Such a clause may also create a conflict between your contractual obligations to the client and certain laws and regulations. For instance, if you obey the law by reporting the discovery of hazardous materials, you may be breaching your contract with your client. But if you abide by the contract and don't report your findings, you may violate the law. As discussed in Public Responsibility, your professional duty of care goes beyond that owed to the client. (Refer to that section for further discussion.)

THE SOLUTION

Delete, if you can, any Confidentiality clause from your contract and rely on provisions discussed in Public Responsibility. However, if your client insists on some confidentiality wording, you will need to be clear on certain points, such as government requirements and sharing information with employees and subconsultants. Such a clause, revised from a client-drafted version, might read:

CONFIDENTIALITY

The Design Professional agrees to keep confidential and not to disclose to any person or entity, other than the Design Professional's employees, subconsultants and the general contractor and subcontractors, if appropriate, any data and information not previously known to and generated by the Design Professional or furnished to the Design Professional and marked CONFIDENTIAL by the Client. These provisions shall not apply to information in whatever form that comes into the public domain, nor shall it restrict the Design Professional from giving notices required by law or complying with an order to provide information or data when such order is issued by a court, administrative agency or other authority with proper jurisdiction, or if it is reasonably necessary for the Design Professional to defend himself or herself from any suit or claim.

This clause and all other clauses herein are intended as examples only and should be reviewed and modified by competent legal counsel to reflect variations in applicable local law and the specific circumstances of your contract.

There are times you may want your client to treat material you provide as proprietary, too. In that case, consider adding additional language, such as:

The Client agrees that the technical methods, techniques and pricing information contained in any proposal submitted by the Design Professional pertaining to this project or in this Agreement or any addendum thereto, are to be considered confidential and proprietary, and shall not be released or otherwise made available to any third party without the express written consent of the Design Professional.

In addition, you might want to mark the technical and price sections of your proposal and/or agreement CONFIDENTIAL.

SEE ALSO:

Confidential Communications
Environmental and Health Hazards
Ownership of Instruments of Service
Public Responsibility

72

CONSEQUENTIAL DAMAGES

Consequential damages are expenses — such as the loss of profit or the loss of use of a facility — that are the indirect result of an alleged failure by the design professional. For instance, imagine that delays by an architect in reviewing shop drawings ultimately caused a toy store to be completed too late for the Christmas season. Or consider the costs involved if a minor error by an engineer resulted in a system failure that interrupted factory production for a month.

THE PROBLEM

If you are to be held responsible for consequential damages, you could be sued for damages wholly out of proportion to your fee or even to the cost of repairing the actual damage. Even if you have (and you should) a Limitation of Liability clause in your contract, you could still be held responsible for the entire negotiated limit of liability, despite the size of your fee or the price tag on the actual damage. Today, in equipment sales and many other commercial contracts, waivers for consequential damages are becoming the norm. Certainly, your professional practice deserves equal protection.

THE SOLUTION

Delete any language in a client-drafted contract that would make you responsible for consequential damages. But don't stop there. If your contract remains silent on the issue, you can still be sued for such damages. You need to go a step further and add a provision that makes certain neither you nor your client will be held responsible for consequential damages because of alleged failures of the other party. Such language could read:

CONSEQUENTIAL DAMAGES

Notwithstanding any other provision of the Agreement, neither party shall be liable to the other for any consequential damages incurred due to the fault of the other party, regardless of the nature of this fault or whether it was committed by the Client or the Design Professional, their employees, agents, subconsultants or subcontractors. Consequential damages include, but are not limited to, loss of use and loss of profit.

This clause and all other clauses herein are intended as examples only and should be reviewed and modified by competent legal counsel to reflect variations in applicable local law and the specific circumstances of your contract.

Besides using a specific clause such as the one above, it is always advisable to include a Limitation of Liability provision in your contract. (See *Limitation of Liability* for discussion.) As noted earlier, however, having this negotiated limit of liability should not discourage you from seeking additional protection against liability for consequential damages. Talk to your attorney. You'll want to make certain the clauses are coordinated and enforceable in your jurisdiction.

You may well find that your private sector clients are used to discussing consequential damage issues. Many want this protection when they are the seller, so requesting the same protection for yourself is rarely offensive to a sophisticated client. He or she should appreciate that you are willing to assume responsibility for your work in reasonable measure, but you will not accept unlimited liability or liability grossly out of proportion to your fee.

SEE ALSO:

Delays
Environmental and Health Hazards
Limitation of Liability
Timeliness of Performance

CONSTRUCTION OBSERVATION

Construction observation is a powerful weapon in the design professional's loss prevention arsenal. A full construction phase workscope that includes submittal review, review of payment applications and resolution of disputes between the owner and contractor is important. But only by visiting the project at appropriate intervals can the architect or engineer see if it is progressing in general conformance with the contract documents and according to his or her design concept. Project observation allows the designer to answer questions or clarify and interpret documents for the contractors on the spot, and may enable him or her to identify trouble spots early on — less costly by far than fixing problems after the project is built.

If construction observation is so important, why isn't it done on every project? There are a number of reasons. First, some owners regard construction observation as costly and unnecessary. If the owner cares little about the quality of the project, he or she may view construction observation as a needless front-end expense and ignore the high repair costs that might follow. This is typically the client who builds on "spec" and is primarily interested in the build-it-and-get-out-fast dollar. Another type of client, only slightly more quality-conscious, may hire a project or construction manager, believing a design professional's observation of the project is redundant. Yet another sort of client is the inexperienced owner, who thinks that a completed set of plans and specifications is a perfect product, like the directions for assembling a toy erector set. If the contractor just follows the plans, the client reasons, the result will be a perfect structure. That these plans may contain errors or ambiguities or may need interpretation during construction doesn't occur to this client.

For all these reasons, it may seem obvious that architects and engineers should have been educating their clients on the merits of full construction observation. But the design professions had begun to retreat from construction phase responsibilities in the 1970s because they felt these services were too risky. This impression may have come from the layperson's misuse of the words *inspect* and *supervise* to describe a designer's services. (See **Inspection** for discussion.) Both terms suggested that the designer was responsible for a great deal more than was intended and, accordingly, architects and engineers were blamed for anything and everything that could go wrong on a construction site.

THE PROBLEM

Some clients seem to want things both ways. They are unwilling to pay the fee you need to perform construction observation, but they want you to take full responsibility for the problems created by not doing it. Or they may hire someone else to do the observation more cheaply. They don't understand that another designer, unfamiliar with your design concept or the assumptions you made in preparing your plans, is less likely to recognize problems.

On the other hand, if you are not performing construction observation because you think it will increase your exposure to risk, think again. When you design a project, you assume the associated liability, whether or not you visit the project. In avoiding observation, you forfeit the opportunity to satisfy yourself that construction is proceeding as it should. No matter how detailed or near perfect your plans are, even the best contractor can't build from them without some degree of interpretation. It is far better to protect your interests and those of your client by ensuring that the clarification and interpretation is provided by you.

Even if your client does agree to full construction observation services, some client-written contracts contain onerous language that needs judicious editing. For instance, a client contract may state that the purpose of construction observation is to "guard the owner against all defects" or to "assure complete conformance with the construction documents." Both terms can be construed as warranties or guarantees. Agreeing to such overstated provisions furnishes your client with an additional cause of action against you (for breach of warranty) and jeopardizes your professional liability insurance coverage.

Also troublesome are limited services agreements in which you are asked to provide only partial construction phase services. Your client may ask you to provide project observation on an on-call basis, meaning your services may or may not be requested. You might not be asked to visit the project often enough to perform adequate observation. Certainly, there is no assurance that you will be called upon at critical stages in the work. (See *Design Without Construction Phase Services* for more information.)

Finally, when construction observation is performed, some designers assign less-experienced people who may not have adequate training in proper field procedures. Perhaps worse, sometimes people are sent to observe construction outside their own fields of expertise — a structural engineer, for example, to look over a mechanical system. A related problem arises when subconsultants are not retained to observe construction of their design work. (See *Subconsultants*.)

THE SOLUTION

We believe that every design services contract should include full construction phase services as a Basic Service. Your agreement should clearly show the scope of these services, stating what it is you will and will not do during the construction phase, and describe the purpose of these services. (Key loss prevention points are listed in *Exhibit 4*.)

The best approach may be to offer your client expanded construction phase services — exhaustive, continuous project field representative services — as a first option. (The AIA contract document B352 is a good starting point in developing such a workscope.) This provides the client with a choice: accept expanded services and increase the odds of discovering defects in the work, or accept reduced basic services and the uncertainty that goes with observation at "appropriate intervals" only. It is important that you explain the trade-offs between levels of service and quality and fee — and insist that your client make the decision.

If your client chooses the basic level of construction phase services, document your offer of expanded services and the client's refusal. The following sample provision addresses these ideas:

CONSTRUCTION OBSERVATION

The Design Professional shall visit the project at appropriate intervals during construction to become generally familiar with the progress and quality of the contractors' work and to determine if the work is proceeding in general accordance with the Contract Documents. The Client has not retained the Design Professional to make detailed inspections or to provide exhaustive or continuous project review and observation services. The Design Professional does not guarantee the performance of, and shall have no responsibility for, the acts or omissions of any contractor, subcontractor, supplier or any other entity furnishing materials or performing any work on the project.

If the Client desires more extensive project observation or full-time project representation, the Client shall request such services be provided by the Design Professional as Additional Services in accordance with the terms of this Agreement.

This clause and all other clauses herein are intended as examples only and should be reviewed and modified by competent legal counsel to reflect variations in applicable local law and the specific circumstances of your contract.

If you are considering performing construction observation or other construction phase services on a project designed by another architect or engineer, we urge you to discuss the significant risks with your attorney and professional liability insurance specialist. (See *Supplanting Another Design Professional* and *Information Provided by Others*.) Should you decide to proceed, you may be able to protect yourself somewhat by adding to the above paragraph:

CONSTRUCTION PHASE SERVICES WITHOUT DESIGN

It is further understood and agreed that because the Design Professional did not prepare the Contract Documents for the project, the Client waives all claims against the Design Professional arising from or in any way connected with errors, omissions, conflicts or ambiguities in the Contract Documents prepared by others.

In addition, the Client agrees, to the fullest extent permitted by law, to indemnify and hold the Design Professional harmless from any damage, liability or cost, including reasonable attorneys' fees and defense costs, arising from any errors or omissions contained in the plans, specifications or other Contract Documents prepared by others, except for the sole negligence or willful misconduct of the Design Professional.

This clause and all other clauses herein are intended as examples only and should be reviewed and modified by competent legal counsel to reflect variations in applicable local law and the specific circumstances of your contract.

It is also important that the General Conditions of the construction contract reflect your duties and responsibilities accurately. If you will not perform construction phase services, make certain the General Conditions state this fact too, to avoid confusion and inadvertent assumption of liability.

It is crucial that you avoid the words *inspect* and *supervise* in your contract and workscope and all your correspondence, notes and logs. Unfortunately, a layperson may believe that an "inspector" will uncover each and every error, unsafe condition and violation of law. (See **Inspection** for more information.) The term *supervise* may imply control of the contractor, his or her employees and the jobsite — all of which would have serious liability implications. If your client is determined to use these words, you should insist on defining them in a Definitions section of your contract. (Refer to **Definitions**.)

Another word you should avoid when describing the frequency of your project visits is *periodic*. The dictionary defines the word to mean "at regular intervals." Unless you intend to visit regularly once a day or once a week — even if your presence is not required — don't subject yourself to such a condition.

To keep from making any inadvertent warranty or guarantee in your contract, delete phrases like *guard the owner against defect*s or similar language. Even attempts to soften provisions by adding *attempt* or *endeavor to guard the owner* are somewhat risky. Will a jury think your "endeavor" was enough if a construction defect resulted in serious damages, injury or death? (Refer to **Certifications, Guarantees and Warranties**.)

If the client refuses to allow you to do construction observation or other appropriate construction phase services, make certain that you get adequate contractual protection. (Refer to **Design Without Construction Phase Services** for a sample paragraph.)

See also:

Certifications, Guarantees and Warranties
Claims Arbiter Service
Definitions
Delays
Design Without Construction Phase Services
Information Provided by Others
Inspection
Jobsite Safety
Shop Drawing Review
Stop Work Authority
Subconsultants
Supplanting Another Design Professional

Exhibit 4

Loss Prevention Points for Construction Observation

- Carefully describe your construction phase duties in your workscope — and then adhere to that workscope.

- Add a precise definition of "construction observation" to the Definitions section of your contract.

- Avoid words such as *inspect* and *supervise* in all your contracts, correspondence and documentation.

- Use your best people for construction observation, and make certain they are properly trained.

- Establish a field manual with proper procedures and require that your field personnel follow these procedures. (The PLAN Project Representative's Manual is a good model to build upon. See the *Bibliography*.)

- If you are the prime consultant, require all your subconsultants to observe their portion of the project.

- Keep proper documentation of each project visit by using logs, videotapes, reports and photographs.

- Caution field representatives not to give direction to contractor personnel on construction means, methods, sequences or any safety procedures. That's the contractor's responsibility.

- Make sure your client is well informed on the progress of the project. Provide copies of your project visit reports to your client and all appropriate parties.

- Work to promote good communications with the contractor — he or she may be more likely to tell you if there is a problem.

CONTINGENCY FUND

No one is perfect. While it's true that people strive for perfection in their work, it's also true that perfection is impossible to attain. Every architect and engineer knows that the perfect set of plans and specifications has yet to be prepared. Even the most well-prepared documents probably contain discrepancies or deficiencies that may result in change orders and increased costs.

Clients should understand that they will encounter unexpected costs caused by contractor problems during construction. Astute clients will anticipate these costs by having contingency reserves set aside in their project budgets. Design professionals must educate their clients about the realities and uncertainties of the design process, too. If clients expect and plan for some changes due to design errors and omissions, there will be less likelihood of claims later.

THE PROBLEM

Architecture and engineering are considered such exacting professions that the public has difficulty understanding the potential for human error. Even your clients often have unrealistic expectations and presume your services will be error-free. These expectations can subject you to liability claims when errors or omissions — no matter how minor — result in change orders and extra costs. (Refer to *Standard of Care* for a related discussion.) Unless you plan for and anticipate by contract the reasonable level of defects, errors, omissions and ambiguities that are a normal part of every design project, your client may expect you to pay for the resulting change orders.

THE SOLUTION

Your client must understand that there will be errors and omissions in your documents. Once you establish this premise, show your client that these errors and omissions can be managed effectively — that your goal is to find problems and fix them quickly. You can do this by establishing a procedure by which you handle problems as they arise.

First, implement an early warning system to identify any difficulty as soon as possible. The sooner a discrepancy can be identified, the sooner it can be remedied — and at far less cost. This is accomplished by obligating the contractor, subcontractors and vendors to advise you and your client immediately of any deficiencies they discover. Insist on a provision in your contract with your client (and a parallel clause in the client's agreement with the contractor) that requires all contractors and vendors to report such defects at once. (Refer to *Defects in Service* for suggested contract language and *Appendix II* for a sample General Conditions provision.)

Second, make the document corrections and negotiate costs of extras at the earliest possible moment. The sooner these are done, the less likely that memories will fade and costs will escalate.

Third, incorporate an alternative dispute resolution clause into each of your client agreements. Such a provision would provide for mandatory mediation as the first step in resolving any dispute, including a disagreement over change orders and extras. If you make certain the owner has a similar provision in his or her contract with the general contractor, you might frustrate those contractors who make their profits on extras for "design deficiencies." (See *Claims Arbiter Service* and *Dispute Resolution* for more information and the *Bibliography* for additional resources.)

Fourth, encourage the owner to plan for extra costs by setting up a contingency fund. Such a fund establishes a percentage of the project budget to cover the costs of changes resulting from design errors and omissions. The recommended contract language includes an agreement that your client will not sue you for extra costs resulting from design errors that are under the contingency amount. Although the percentage set aside depends on the complexity and duration of the project, it must always be realistic.

Successfully negotiating a contingency provision may be easier if you and your client follow a plan such as the one suggested above. Here is a sample provision:

CONTINGENCY FUND

The Owner and the Design Professional acknowledge that changes may be required because of possible omissions, ambiguities or inconsistencies in the plans and specifications and, therefore, that the costs of the project may exceed the construction contract sum. The Owner agrees to set aside a reserve in the amount of ____ percent of the actual project construction costs as a contingency reserve to be used, as required, to pay for any such increased project costs. The Owner further agrees to make no claim by way of direct or third-party action against the Design Professional or his or her subconsultants with respect to any payments within the limit of the contingency reserve made to the construction contractors because of such changes or because of any claims made by the construction contractors relating to such changes.

This clause and all other clauses herein are intended as examples only and should be reviewed and modified by competent legal counsel to reflect variations in applicable local law and the specific circumstances of your contract.

We recommend that you keep a log of change orders that could be attributed to design errors or omissions and assign dollar amounts to each (determined by a method decided upon in advance). If, when the project is completed, the log total is below the agreed upon amount, you've done your job.

If you are unable to negotiate a separate contingency fund for the design team, there is an alternative strategy. If the General Conditions of the construction contract contain a contingency provision, you might persuade your client to include design errors among the allowable causes for change orders chargeable to the general contractor's contingency. Although the contractor will no doubt object to this, your client may prefer to deal with one lump-sum contingency.

See also:

Contractual Reference to the Design Professional

In contracts prepared by architects and engineers, design professional firms are referred to specifically (Smith, Doe & Associates), by acronym (SDA) or generically (Architect, Engineer, Design Professional or Consultant). In some client-prepared agreements, the design professional is referred to as Contractor. Frequently, such contracts have been developed for contractors or suppliers and not specifically for professional service firms.

The Problem

Some people who review a contract may not understand the difference between a construction contractor and a design professional under contract to a client. The importance of the words used can be significant, especially when a judge or jury does not understand that although you are being called a "contractor," as a design professional you are not (or should not be) responsible for jobsite safety, construction means and methods, warranties or a myriad of other things for which construction contractors are responsible. Lawyers thrive on confusion and misuse of terminology.

The Solution

The best solution is to refer to parties specifically by name or acronym in a clause at the beginning of the contract that identifies each. For example:

Parties

This Agreement for professional services has been entered into by Jones Widget Company (hereinafter referred to as JWC), and Smith Architecture & Planning, Inc. (hereinafter referred to as Smith).

This clause and all other clauses herein are intended as examples only and should be reviewed and modified by competent legal counsel to reflect variations in applicable local law and the specific circumstances of your contract.

Some design professional practices use their own pre-printed contracts that refer to their clients generically (Client, Owner) and to themselves specifically. However, it is a better idea to customize your contracts. Given the capabilities and widespread reliance on word processors, it should be a simple matter to produce a contract using the specific names of the parties wherever they appear in the agreement.

If your clients, in their pre-printed contracts, insist on calling you "Contractor" and refuse to refer to you either specifically by your firm name or acronym, or to use a professional designation such as Architect, Engineer, Consultant or Design Professional, insist on having included in the Preamble or Definitions section of the contract some language to mitigate the negative implications. (See *Definitions* for further discussion of that clause.) Consider the following example:

> **Wherever used herein, the term Contractor shall mean Smith Architecture and Planning Inc., AIA, (Smith), a professional corporation rendering professional architectural and engineering services. The term Contractor does not imply that Smith is engaged in any aspect of the physical work of construction contracting, nor is Smith responsible in any way for the construction means, methods, techniques or sequences nor for any aspect of jobsite safety. These duties are and shall remain the sole responsibility of the construction General Contractor.**

SEE ALSO:

Definitions
Jobsite Safety

COPYRIGHTS

Copyright law defines "architectural work" as the design of a building as expressed in plans or drawings, but not individual standard features. The owner of a copyright to an architectural work has the exclusive right to reproduce it, to make derivative works from it, to grant licenses to use the work, to sell the work and to otherwise deal with the copyright. In general, these rights last throughout the life of the owner and extend fifty years beyond that.

Prior to 1990, design professionals had only limited protection under copyright laws. While the drawings for a building design could be protected, the building design itself could not. Anyone with a camera, a tape measure and a calculator could copy a structure without infringing upon the copyrights of the building's designer. However, the 1990 Architectural Works Copyright Protection Act amended the U.S. copyright laws to provide more extensive safeguards for the designs of architects and engineers. The Act prohibits unauthorized construction of buildings depicted in copyrighted drawings created on or after December 1, 1990. Simply put, prior to the Act, an architect's or engineer's drawings were protected by law — now, for the most part, the actual buildings are, too. (Note, however, that building owners can still alter or destroy a structure without the designer's consent.)

THE PROBLEM

Although your rights as a designer have been strengthened by the legislation, it is up to you to safeguard these rights. It is a simple matter to sign away all these hard-earned protections with the stroke of a pen. How? By agreeing, in a client-written contract, to give up your ownership and rights — including copyrights — to your client or even your client's lender. For the most part, such a requirement is inappropriate for traditional design projects. Be aware, too, that if you do contract away your copyrights, it is possible you might not be able to use derivatives of your own design for another client. In addition, assignment provisions that your client or your client's lender might try to impose upon you in a contract may contain language that could transfer your ownership and copyrights to your design. (Refer to *Ownership of Instruments of Service* and *Assignment* for more information.)

Administration of copyright safeguards requires your vigilance for another reason. If you supplant another design professional on a project, depending upon the terms and conditions of that design professional's contract, you may need his or her permission to complete unfinished designs, or you may be liable for copyright infringement. This may be true even if you changed the original design. Usually, your professional liability insurance will not cover claims for copyright infringement.

THE SOLUTION

Although your copyrights exist as soon as you create your drawing or design, it is such a simple matter to mark your designs with an accepted copyright notice that we recommend you do so on every copy of every document you create. You should also register your documents with the United States Copyright Office, a simple and inexpensive procedure that will assist you in the enforcement of your rights. (See the *Bibliography* for details on obtaining registration information.) If you file a registration within three months of publication, you should be eligible for certain rights granted under federal law that are not otherwise available, such as the right to file for an injunction, to claim statutory damages, and perhaps to recoup reasonable attorneys' fees should you prevail against someone who infringes upon your copyright.

If you neglect to register your copyright, you still have some protection. Although by delaying registration you forfeit certain rights, you still have up to five years after publication to add or correct a copyright notice. It is far better, however, to elect one person in your firm to see that all your designs are promptly copyrighted as a matter of office routine. In addition, consider requiring your employees to agree in writing that they are employed on a "work for hire" basis, so that only your firm — and not your employees — can register the copyrights.

To avoid any misunderstandings, your client contract should always address copyrights. It should clearly state that you will retain the copyrights to your drawings and design, as well as the ownership of those documents. (Refer to *Ownership of Instruments of Service* for a related discussion.) We repeat the following suggested contract language:

OWNERSHIP OF INSTRUMENTS OF SERVICE

All reports, plans, specifications, computer files, field data, notes and other documents and instruments prepared by the Design Professional as instruments of service shall remain the property of the Design Professional. The Design Professional shall retain all common law, statutory and other reserved rights, including the copyright thereto.

Since any copying of your plans without your express consent by the contractor might be deemed a technical copyright infringement, it is probably a good idea to grant a limited license to contractors to use and copy applicable portions of your documents so they can go about their work. The AIA A201 General Conditions has such a provision, which also requires that each copy made bear the design professional's copyright notice. If the A201 is not used, you can provide for a limited license for the contractors in whatever document is used.

Before you agree to sign away any right, seek qualified legal counsel. Copyright law is a highly specialized field, and you need a knowledgeable attorney to advise you on your ownership rights. If you do transfer all or any portion of a copyright, either from a consultant to you or from you to another party, you should record that transfer in an appropriate filing with the United States Copyright Office by sending it a copy of the instrument evidencing the transfer (or an abbreviated form to be used for this purpose) along with the required fee.

Should you decide to contract away your copyrights, you will need some additional protection. Your contract should have provisions that guard you against unauthorized reuse and unauthorized changes to your designs. (Refer to *Unauthorized Changes to Plans* and *Prototype Designs* for more information and suggested clauses.)

Normally, ownership of documents created by subconsultants is transferred to the prime consultant. This is a matter of negotiation, however, and a point you and your attorney should carefully consider when drafting your subconsultant or prime consultant agreements. (Refer to *Subconsultants*.)

SEE ALSO:

Assignment
Bibliography
CADD
Lenders' Requirements
Ownership of Instruments of Service
Prototype Designs
Subconsultants
Supplanting Another Design Professional
Unauthorized Changes to Plans

CORPORATE PROTECTION

Of all the parties to a construction project, the architect and engineer are most at risk. That's because, in virtually every state, licensed design professionals can be held personally liable for their professional acts. While the owner and contractors can shield themselves from personal liability for their business activities by forming corporations, such protection is unavailable to the designer. Even if the design firm closed its doors and went out of business, the licensed professional who signed and sealed the plans would remain personally accountable for damages. That liability can extend for years — perhaps even after the architect's or engineer's death to his or her estate. And that liability, in most jurisdictions, stretches to virtually anyone to whom the design professional owes a duty of care, anyone who could foreseeably be injured or damaged. (See *Standard of Care* for a discussion.)

THE PROBLEM

Clients frequently bring added legal pressure to bear by naming not only the architectural or engineering firm in lawsuits, but individual design professionals too. In other words, if you are incorporated, the client might name not only the corporation, but also you personally — if you signed the plans — and any other licensed professionals who provided services on the project. The client might even name your corporation's officers and directors, claiming that they managed or directed the firm's allegedly negligent activities.

Being named in a lawsuit, whether negligence is eventually proven or not, can be devastating. Not only must you spend a great deal of money and time defending yourself, but your personal assets — your home, your savings, your children's future education — might be placed in jeopardy.

Some states have laws that require a corporation to indemnify its employees from claims arising from the normal scope of their employment. However, this is not true in every state and only applies to firms that are incorporated. If you operate as a partnership or proprietorship, individuals may not be protected by such laws. (Check with your lawyer to see if your state has this kind of statutory corporate protection.)

THE SOLUTION

If your firm carries professional liability insurance, such policies generally insure not only the firm but also its employees, partners and principals, and its officers and directors (for claims arising from the normal scope and course of their employment). If an ex-employee is sued for professional acts he or she performed while in your employment, most policies also would provide protection. Check with your professional liability insurance specialist to determine the specific terms of your professional liability policy that apply to both present and former employees. In particular, there is real concern if you drop your coverage or if a new carrier does not provide as broad a coverage for all these potential defendant parties.

Is there any other protection available to you? Perhaps. It may be possible, depending on applicable state laws, to limit your exposure to first-party suits — claims by those with whom you have a contract. In your agreement with your client, you could include a clause providing that, in the event of a claim, your client would sue only your firm and would not name any individual employee, officer or director. Some design professionals have been successful in obtaining such a provision. Discuss the use and wording of this clause with your attorney to see if it is enforceable in your jurisdiction and if it can be adapted to partnerships or proprietorships.

CORPORATE PROTECTION

It is intended by the parties to this Agreement that the Design Professional's services in connection with the project shall not subject the Design Professional's individual employees, officers or directors to any personal legal exposure for the risks associated with this project. Therefore, and notwithstanding anything to the contrary contained herein, the Client agrees that as the Client's sole and exclusive remedy, any claim, demand or suit shall be directed and/or asserted only against the Design Professional, a {state} corporation, and not against any of the Design Professional's employees, officers or directors.

This clause and all other clauses herein are intended as examples only and should be reviewed and modified by competent legal counsel to reflect variations in applicable local law and the specific circumstances of your contract.

If you are successful in negotiating such a provision, bear in mind that while it might protect you from claims by your client, you still may be vulnerable to third party suits. (See *Third Party Claims*.) In some special situations, nevertheless, you might be able to combine the above clause with an indemnity in which your client holds you harmless for third party suits. This is an innovative measure, however, and may be attainable only in high-risk situations where you are in a strong bargaining position. Work closely with your attorney in drafting and negotiating this provision to make it as enforceable as possible.

In the end, if your client doesn't agree to a Corporate Protection clause, it may still serve as a good springboard for discussing risk allocation and help you in negotiating Limitation of Liability and indemnification provisions for your contract. (Refer to *Limitation of Liability* and *Indemnities* for discussions and sample clauses.)

SEE ALSO:

Indemnities
Limitation of Liability
Standard of Care
Third Party Claims

DEFECTS IN SERVICE

The perfect set of plans has yet to be produced. Despite the best efforts of the design professional, minor errors, omissions, inconsistencies, gaps and overlaps do occur in plans and specifications. An enlightened client understands the likelihood of minor defects in the documents. He or she will assist the architect or engineer by requiring the contractor and subcontractors to identify and report these deficiencies as soon as possible so that they can be remedied.

THE PROBLEM

The price tag on a minor defect can rise dramatically if it is not promptly called to your attention so you can make immediate corrections. The cost of removing and reinstalling work after the fact is often a good deal more expensive than doing the work correctly in the proper construction sequence. Sometimes, however, aggressive contractors may remain silent about defects they discover so they can jack up the cost and volume of change orders. Your client may then make claim against you because of these defects, even though they were not reported to you.

THE SOLUTION

The best solution is to work with clients who will select their contractors carefully and require those contractors and their subcontractors to "play straight" by alerting you as soon as they are aware of any problems. Ideally, the client, designers, contractor and subcontractors work together in a partnership to identify and solve problems as they appear. You can encourage this kind of relationship by means of contract language that obligates the owner and his or her constructors to advise you promptly of any deficiency they discover.

There is another important reason for such a clause. Claims of defects often are made after you are forced to press your client for payment. Frequently, a client will attempt to use a lawsuit or threat of one as a lever to delay payment further or to reduce the amount he or she must pay you. By means of a Defects in Service clause, however, the client would be partly responsible for any defects of which he or she was aware but did nothing to mitigate. It is well worth adding such a requirement to your contract. Consider the following:

DEFECTS IN SERVICE

The Client shall promptly report to the Design Professional any defects or suspected defects in the Design Professional's work or services of which the Client becomes aware, so that the Design Professional may take measures to minimize the consequences of such a defect. The Client warrants that he or she will impose a similar notification requirement on all contractors in his or her Client/Contractor contract and shall require all subcontracts at any level to contain a like requirement. Failure by the Client, and the Client's contractors or subcontractors to notify the Design Professional, shall relieve the Design Professional of the costs of remedying the defects above the sum such remedy would have cost had prompt notification been given.

This clause and all other clauses herein are intended as examples only and should be reviewed and modified by competent legal counsel to reflect variations in applicable local law and the specific circumstances of your contract.

If you cannot negotiate this or similar wording into your contract, you might send an occasional notice to clients (perhaps with requests for progress payments) that asks for a report of any defects, or calls on them to relate their satisfaction to date. By having clients on record as satisfied with your services, or at least not expressing dissatisfaction when they had cause and opportunity to do so, spurious claims of defects can be countered. Another way to accomplish this is to write a letter to your client that incorporates such language when your plans and specifications are completed and delivered.

As recommended in the section on Billing and Payment, you also can add language to that clause that suggests payment of any invoice by the client shall be taken to mean that the client is satisfied with your services and is not aware of any deficiencies in those services. (See *Billing and Payment* for specific language and discussion.) Another alternative is to prohibit by contract the withholding of any sum of money from payments due you unless you have been found legally liable for some alleged discrepancy or costs of changes in the work. Consider the following:

> Payments to the Design Professional shall not be withheld, postponed or made contingent on the construction, completion or success of the project or upon receipt by the Client of offsetting reimbursement or credit from other parties causing Additional Services or expenses. No withholdings, deductions or offsets shall be made from the Design Professional's compensation for any reason unless the Design Professional has been found to be legally liable for such amounts.

See Appendix II for a sample owner-general contractor clause that obligates the contractor to report any defects of which he or she has knowledge. You'll note that the sample language intends to establish realistic expectations regarding the standard of care by the designer. (See also *Standard of Care*.)

SEE ALSO:

Appendix II
Billing and Payment
Construction Observation
Non-Negligent Services
Pay When Paid
Standard of Care

100

DEFINITIONS

Very often, words used in a design professional's contract have different meanings than those commonly understood by the public. If conflicts arise, such a difference in interpretation can cause confusion over the original intent of the parties to an agreement — and may even increase the design professional's liability if certain terms are left to laypersons (a jury, for instance) to interpret.

THE PROBLEM

Occasionally a client may insist on using a word or term that you feel is misleading, such as referring to you as a *contractor* (instead of as a *consultant, architect* or *engineer*). (See **Contractual Reference to the Design Professional** for further discussion.) Such usage idiosyncrasies can be baffling to a layperson, but there are other more dangerous words that, when improperly used, may lead to confusion about your duties under the contract — thereby increasing your exposure to risk. These may include *cost estimate* as opposed to *opinion of probable cost* or *inspect* versus *observe*. (See **Opinion of Probable Construction Cost, Construction Observation** and **Inspection** for more information.) Other confusing terminology might include abbreviations, contractions or design and construction industry jargon.

THE SOLUTION

The best way to avoid misunderstandings — and lower your risk — is to draft a contract that uses well-defined and/or universally-understood terms and phrases. If your client is adamant about using a particular word you feel could be misunderstood or might increase your liability, an appendix or contract clause that clearly defines such words may be useful. This way, you can clear up misconceptions surrounding certain industry terms that may not be generally understood and further clarify "bad" words that your client (perhaps through his or her use of a pre-printed contract form) insists on retaining. Consider these examples:

DEFINITIONS

As used herein, the following words and their derivative words or phrases have the meanings indicated, unless otherwise specified in the various sections of this Agreement.

CERTIFY, CERTIFICATION: A Design Professional's opinion based on his or her observation of conditions, knowledge, information and beliefs. It is expressly understood that the Design Professional's certification of a condition's existence relieves no other party of any responsibility or obligation he or she has accepted by contract or custom.

ESTIMATE: An opinion of probable construction cost made by the Design Professional. The accuracy of a probable construction cost opinion cannot be guaranteed.

INSPECT, INSPECTION: The visual observation of construction to permit the Design Professional to render his or her professional opinion as to whether the contractor is performing the Work in a manner indicating that, when completed, the Work will be in accordance with the Contract Documents. Such observations shall not be relied upon by any party as acceptance of the Work, nor shall they relieve any party from fulfillment of customary and contractual responsibilities and obligations.

This clause and all other clauses herein are intended as examples only and should be reviewed and modified by competent legal counsel to reflect variations in applicable local law and the specific circumstances of your contract.

These are merely examples. Your contract should be carefully reviewed and any questionable words or phrases included in a Definitions section.

If your client won't agree to a Definitions clause, another — but much less protective — method is to send the client a cover letter with the final form of the contract, restating the definitions of words and terms you have previously reviewed with him or her. Finally, there is another technique you can employ: if a word is used only once or twice in the contract, you can define it right in the contract clause where it appears.

SEE ALSO:

Certifications, Guarantees and Warranties
Construction Observation
Contractual Reference to the Design Professional
Inspection
Opinion of Probable Construction Cost
Titles

Delays

Delay claims from contractors are a fact of life for design professionals. Fierce competition for contracts, fast tracking or highly complex projects, and a litigious society all contribute to the problem. Sometimes, delays are caused by forces that are beyond anyone's control, such as the weather, labor strikes or acts of God. Other delays may be caused by the belated processing of approvals by the owner or regulatory officials, or slowness by the design professional. But most often, delay claims are instigated by other parties to the construction project who underprice their bids and set unrealistic schedules.

Contractors who submit low-ball bids to win contracts are especially prevalent in public works projects. These contractors intend to make their profit through change orders and delay claims against the design professionals and owner. They will contend that the architect or engineer was tardy in responding to their requests for information (RFIs). They will allege that uncoordinated construction documents required numerous change orders and RFIs, resulting in a loss of efficiency, out-of-sequence work and an accelerated construction schedule that caused interference between the trades. As proof, the contractors and their attorneys will point to the mountain of change orders and RFIs (that they themselves have generated) as well as detailed records of delayed responses.

The Problem

Even the best-staffed design firm can be overwhelmed if suddenly faced with dozens or even hundreds of RFIs. Although each request must be treated seriously, you and your staff could find yourselves scurrying to respond, only to discover many answers are self-evident or are already in the contract documents. The RFIs often arrive at a critical stage in the project and, if your reply is not prompt, the contractor will allege that you delayed the project and caused damages.

An owner's failure to approve the contractor's change orders promptly can also result in delay claims. It could be claimed that you, as the owner's agent during construction, failed to advise the owner to process the change orders quickly and therefore are responsible for some delay damages.

THE SOLUTION

There are several steps you can take to help avoid delay claims. First, you may want to recommend that your client review the contractor's dispute history — before signing the construction contract — and look for a track record of delay-related claims. Explain to your client the importance of his or her own timely decisions too. Sometimes your client is not aware how much his or her failure to act quickly can impact a schedule. On complex projects, consider advising your client to have an independent constructibility review performed before bidding. Some design firms recommend that the owner include in his or her instructions to bidders an estimate of the number of clarifications and percentage of cost changes and require the contractors to factor this into their bids. (See *Exhibit 5* for other suggestions.)

Your contract should have a no-responsibility-for-delays provision, such as the one below. Advise your client to consult with his or her attorney about the inclusion of a No Damage for Delay clause in the Owner-General Contractor agreement, too. Such a clause should allow ample time for both the contractor and the design professional to review and respond to any submittals.

DELAYS

The Design Professional is not responsible for delays caused by factors beyond the Design Professional's reasonable control, including but not limited to delays because of strikes, lockouts, work slowdowns or stoppages, accidents, acts of God, failure of any governmental or other regulatory authority to act in a timely manner, failure of the Client to furnish timely information or approve or disapprove of the Design Professional's services or work product promptly, or delays caused by faulty performance by the Client or by contractors of any level. When such delays beyond the Design Professional's reasonable control occur, the Client agrees the Design Professional is not responsible for damages, nor shall the Design Professional be deemed to be in default of this Agreement.

This clause and all other clauses herein are intended as examples only and should be reviewed and modified by competent legal counsel to reflect variations in applicable local law and the specific circumstances of your contract.

You should be aware, though, that the foregoing provision will protect you only from claims from your client. In many jurisdictions, contractors can pursue delay/ extra claims directly against you based on alleged negligence. They will claim that you owed a duty of care to the contractor in preparing your plans and specifications and in performing your construction phase services — and that the duty was breached. They will further claim that the breach caused delays and extra costs to the contractor. In truth, there is little protection available from such suits.

You may also want to address in your contract the potential costs caused by excessive and inappropriate requests for information and failure by the contractor to properly monitor RFIs:

> **The Client warrants he or she will cause the Contractor to review any requests for information (RFIs) submitted by subcontractors prior to submission to the Design Professional to ensure such RFIs are not already clearly and unambiguously answered in the Contract Documents. The Design Professional shall be paid by the Contractor for his or her time in reviewing RFIs which are already clearly answered or inferable from the Contract Documents in accordance with the Design Professional's standard rates. In the event of a disagreement over such compensation, the judgment of the Client's representative shall prevail.**

Because any delay might result in a large claim against you, and because no airtight contractual protection against such claims exists, your best defense is a good offense. Negotiate with your client to obtain as much protection as you can in your contract. And, perhaps more importantly, institute and follow rigorous loss prevention practices.

SEE ALSO:

Consequential Damages
Construction Observation
Contingency Fund
Fast Track Projects
Liquidated Damages
Shop Drawing Review
Timeliness of Performance

EXHIBIT 5

AVOIDING DELAY CLAIMS

- Develop a project schedule with the owner that allows time for you to coordinate the construction documents with your consultants.

- Develop a contractor's submittal schedule and insist the contractor follow it.

- Appoint a member of your staff to keep an accurate change order and RFI log.

- Process all RFIs promptly. If the information can be found in the contract documents, so indicate on the RFI and return it.

- Explain to your client that a delayed decision on his or her part could impact a project schedule.

- Maintain detailed records of all correspondence and conversations about the project.

- Increase project observation visits and job progress meetings to establish a record of the contractor's actual performance.

DESIGN WITHOUT CONSTRUCTION PHASE SERVICES

Design professionals might find themselves unable to provide full construction phase services for a number of reasons. An architect, for instance, may design a "spec" warehouse. Although his contract provides for construction phase services as an on-call Additional Service, that call from the client never comes. Or an engineer might provide for construction administration and observation in her contract, only to have her services terminated as soon as the client has the building permits in hand. In a military housing project, the government agency may refuse construction phase services from the designer because it has in-house engineers who will perform them. In still another fairly common scenario, the architect for a large residential project may be contracted to provide construction observation of only five model homes, but the finished development will comprise three hundred units.

Clients who eliminate construction phase services do so simply to cut costs. Perhaps they do not understand that the role of the architect or engineer during construction is to minimize expensive problems. Maybe they do not appreciate the importance of project observation, field interpretation of plans and specifications, and submittal review. Or maybe they are simply unconcerned about quality and want only minimal services at minimum cost. Whatever the client's reason, if a designer cannot provide construction phase services, he or she is denied perhaps the single most important loss prevention technique available.

THE PROBLEM

Your involvement during construction is in everyone's best interest: the owner, the builder and you. In any project, issues arise during construction that require a designer's input. No set of plans is perfect; every set requires some interpretation. There are always inconsistencies, discrepancies and questions that are best addressed by the designer. The impact of errors can be mitigated substantially if you are on the scene (or at least available) to resolve problems or to create a field change to minimize the consequences of a mistake.

If your contract does not require construction observation and submittal review, you have no way of assuring that a contractor's interpretation of your design is correct. You cannot determine if construction is proceeding according to your plans and specifications. You cannot call for critical shop drawings. You cannot determine if unauthorized changes have been made to your plans. But your name is on the design, construction phase services or not. If damages can in any way be attributed to your services, it is quite likely you will be named in a suit, either by the owner or a third party.

THE SOLUTION

Your best course by far is to provide for full services in your contract. (Please refer to *Construction Observation* for discussion and a sample provision.) We strongly recommend that you do everything in your power to provide construction phase services on each and every project you undertake. Certainly, in any complex or especially risky project such as renovation work or condominium design, we believe a contractual provision that provides for full construction phase services should be considered a **Deal Maker**. In other words, if construction phase services are not provided for in your contract, strongly consider turning down the project.

In the real world, however, providing for construction phase services is not always possible. If that is the case, tread very carefully. If you cannot provide full services, negotiate for the best contractual protection possible. Show in your workscope's Excluded Services section that the owner has declined your construction phase services, and then get contractual protection for not being allowed to provide those services. Don't let your client promise to decide later or on an if-called-for basis. Chances are he or she will decide against it (or had no intention of asking for it in the first place). Make certain, up-front, that your client either agrees to full construction phase services or gives you protection for the additional risk you assume.

Although a fool-proof hold harmless agreement for design professionals who do not provide construction phase services does not exist, you will want to obtain as strongly worded a waiver and indemnity as you and your attorney can negotiate. Consider the following example:

DESIGN WITHOUT CONSTRUCTION PHASE SERVICES

It is understood and agreed that the Design Professional's Basic Services under this Agreement do not include project observation or review of the Contractor's performance or any other construction phase services, and that such services will be provided by the Client. The Client assumes all responsibility for interpretation of the Contract Documents and for construction observation and supervision and waives any claims against the Design Professional that may be in any way connected thereto.

In addition, the Client agrees, to the fullest extent permitted by law, to indemnify and hold the Design Professional harmless from any loss, claim or cost, including reasonable attorneys' fees and costs of defense, arising or resulting from the performance of such services by other persons or entities and from any and all claims arising from modifications, clarifications, interpretations, adjustments or changes made to the Contract Documents to reflect changed field or other conditions, except for claims arising from the sole negligence or willful misconduct of the Design Professional.

If the Client requests in writing that the Design Professional provide any specific construction phase services and if the Design Professional agrees in writing to provide such services, then they shall be compensated for as Additional Services as provided in Section___.

This clause and all other clauses herein are intended as examples only and should be reviewed and modified by competent legal counsel to reflect variations in applicable local law and the specific circumstances of your contract.

If you are going to do the design work without the protection of performing construction phase services, you will want to include some other very important provisions in your contract. Your attorney may suggest you add clauses such as Unauthorized Changes to Plans, Supplanting Another Design Professional and Ownership of Instruments of Service. (See those titles for additional information and suggested contract clauses.) Because of the high degree of risk involved if you are not providing full services, you should also consider it a **Deal Maker** to negotiate a reasonable Limitation of Liability provision as well as an acceptable means for dispute resolution. (See *Limitation of Liability* and *Dispute Resolution*.)

If your client later wants you to provide limited construction phase services — for instance, to observe only a small or very specific portion of the work — get the request in writing. Then document and get your client's acknowledgement of the exact purpose of the visit and the restrictions on your construction phase services.

It is crucial to look at the General Conditions of the construction contract to make sure they also reflect your duties and responsibilities accurately. If you don't have responsibility for construction phase services, make certain the General Conditions clearly state that fact in order to avoid confusion and inadvertent assumption of liability.

Many seasoned design professionals believe that construction phase services are so important to their overall risk management that they choose to perform those services whether or not their contract provides for them. Anyone who has been involved in a protracted lawsuit probably agrees that the cost of providing construction phase services is modest when compared to the expense of a legal dispute. Just bear in mind that if you decide to perform a service, even if unpaid, you have the duty to do it properly and in accordance with the standard of care. Secondly, if you intend to provide the service regardless, you may want to factor in the cost to the overall project cost equation.

SEE ALSO:

Construction Observation
Dispute Resolution
Excluded Services
Indemnities
Limitation of Liability
Ownership of Instruments of Service
Prototype Designs
Scope of Services
Standard of Care
Supplanting Another Design Professional
Termination
Unauthorized Changes to Plans

DISPUTE RESOLUTION

If an architect or engineer is a party to litigation, chances are his or her case will never get as far as a courtroom. The great majority of all lawsuits are settled before they go to trial — but often only after years of interrogatories, depositions, countersuits, legal maneuvering and mounting legal fees. No wonder parties to disputes often see the litigation process as a frustrating waste of productive time and massive sums of money. It makes one ask: if the chances are that a dispute will eventually end at the negotiating table, why not start there instead?

In fact, there is already a process in place that allows disputing parties to do just that; a comparatively inexpensive and quick process, with established structure and rules. It's called *mediation*. It is a voluntary method of helping disputing parties reach agreement among themselves, thus reopening communications between client and design professional. Unlike arbitration, mediation is usually not binding on the parties. The approach involves a mediator, an impartial third party who helps resolve conflicts. By direct and informed negotiation, consultation with each side and "shuttle diplomacy," the mediator works with the parties until they are able to reach their own settlement.

If total resolution of all issues cannot be reached, the parties can try advisory arbitration, a mini-trial or another consensual method of dispute resolution in which the parties continue, in a voluntary and nonbinding way, to work out their solutions to the remaining issues. Advisory arbitration allows the mediator to slip temporarily into the role of an arbitrator and give opinions as to the merits of a case. For firms whose senior officers need a "preview" of their legal position, a mini-trial is an abbreviated, confidential and nonbinding way to gauge their vulnerability. If methods such as these are not successful, then the parties could proceed to an adjudicative form of formal dispute resolution, in which someone else renders a binding decision — arbitration, or, as a last resort, litigation. (See *Arbitration* for more information.)

THE PROBLEM

To date, few contracts call for mediation as a formalized dispute resolution method. But unless you and your client have agreed beforehand to handle conflicts through mediation, you may miss the chance to resolve your differences this way. It is difficult to explain the benefits of mediation to an angry client and persuade him or her to try it after a claim has been made, a lawsuit filed and relationships increasingly strained. Sadly, once a dispute becomes hostile, as it does in litigation or arbitration, it is unlikely that you will be able to preserve your relationship with your client for work on future projects together.

THE SOLUTION

Provide for mediation in your contract. Mediation has a remarkable track record when it is employed at the appropriate stage of the dispute. (In one study, fully three-fourths of over two thousand claims against design professionals were resolved to the disputants' satisfaction through mediation.) Discuss the problems and expense of senseless litigation or arbitration with your client during contract formation, and explain your wish to have in place a mechanism to resolve conflicts and possibly avoid litigation altogether.

By including such a provision in your agreement, you and your client will have on tap a proven means by which you can inexpensively settle most disputes and very likely emerge from the process with your business relationship intact. Such a clause might read:

MEDIATION

In an effort to resolve any conflicts that arise during the design or construction of the project or following the completion of the project, the Client and the Design Professional agree that all disputes between them arising out of or relating to this Agreement shall be submitted to nonbinding mediation unless the parties mutually agree otherwise.

The Client and the Design Professional further agree to include a similar mediation provision in all agreements with independent contractors and consultants retained for the project and to require all independent contractors and consultants also to include a similar mediation provision in all agreements with subcontractors, subconsultants, suppliers or fabricators so retained, thereby providing for mediation as the primary method for dispute resolution between the parties to those agreements.

This clause and all other clauses herein are intended as examples only and should be reviewed and modified by competent legal counsel to reflect variations in applicable local law and the specific circumstances of your contract.

We recommend you and your client together select the mediator when a dispute arises rather than have a mediator predetermined by contract provision. Check with your attorney, professional liability insurance specialist or insurance carrier for the names of recommended mediation services in your area; they should be able to commend a service to you. There are several local and national organizations that provide mediation services for design and/or construction industry disputes. Generally, they have a detailed set of rules and procedures. When you and your client agree on the mediation service, you have agreed to be guided by their rules.

There are many other alternatives for dispute resolution available to you, such as arbitration, rent-a-judge, project review panels or mini-trials. Start with mediation, however, and provide for it in your contracts. Because the cost in time and dollars required for mediation is so low and the success ratio so high, mediation is an effective problem-solving device you should include in every contract. Although you need legal representation in most mediation and alternative dispute processes, your legal fees should be substantially less than those involved in a full-blown court or arbitration proceeding. You have everything to gain and nothing to lose by trying the process. In fact, DPIC Companies believes so strongly in mediation that we consider this clause a **Deal Maker** — a must have — in your contracts.

Interestingly, many professional societies are recognizing the power of mediation and have created contract language to incorporate into their standard agreements. [Refer to: AIA Document B 511 (1990), Article 7.5; CASE Contract Document 2 (1991), Exhibit B, Section 6.5; ASFE Standard Forms of Agreement; EJCDC Document 1910-1 (1992), Exhibit G 8.6.]

SEE ALSO:

Arbitration
Bibliography
Partnering Supplement

ENVIRONMENTAL AND HEALTH HAZARDS

PART ONE:
IF YOU DON'T EXPECT TO ENCOUNTER POLLUTANTS

Over the last century, literally hundreds of differing toxic substances have been buried, dumped, burned or otherwise discharged into the earth, its waters or atmosphere. Now, more and more often, design professionals are encountering these pollutants unexpectedly on the jobsite. Of course, not all hazardous materials are man-made. Naturally occurring substances such as radon and methane gases are very real dangers too, not only to public health but also to the architect or engineer who discovers them.

There is another, equally troubling problem: as technology evolves, so does the realization that certain materials we once believed to be safe are in truth hazardous. Who can say with certainty that some process or product we are confidently speci-fying today might not become the lead paint or asbestos of tomorrow? (Refer to Part Four of this section for more information on the special considerations of asbestos-containing products.)

THE PROBLEM

No one is immune to risk from environmental hazard claims. Almost any discipline in which you practice can expose you to some environmental liability. Consider the mechanical engineer who designs an adequate ventilation system according to code, but after occupancy there are allegations of Sick Building Syndrome. Or the archi-tect who faces claims that furniture and finishes specified for an interiors job had given off toxic gas in a fire. Or a civil engineer whose design of a water treatment plant did not anticipate that heavy metals would be illegally dumped in an indus-trial sewer system.

THE SOLUTION

No matter how unlikely it seems that you will encounter toxic substances on a project, you must plan for that eventuality. This may be the most important provision in your agreement with your client. In every contract you negotiate, insist on a clause that provides for the possibility of discovering hazardous materials on the jobsite. We consider this type of clause to be a **Deal Maker** — a must have —and recommend that it become a standard part of all your contracts — whether or not you anticipate encountering environmental hazards:

HAZARDOUS MATERIALS

It is acknowledged by both parties that the Design Professional's scope of services does not include any services related to asbestos or hazardous or toxic materials. In the event the Design Professional or any other party encounters asbestos or hazardous or toxic materials at the jobsite, or should it become known in any way that such materials may be present at the jobsite or any adjacent areas that may affect the performance of the Design Professional's services, the Design Professional may, at his or her option and without liability for consequential or any other damages, suspend performance of services on the project until the Client retains appropriate specialist consultant(s) or contractor(s) to identify, abate and/or remove the asbestos or hazardous or toxic materials, and warrant that the jobsite is in full compliance with applicable laws and regulations.

This clause and all other clauses herein are intended as examples only and should be reviewed and modified by competent legal counsel to reflect variations in applicable local law and the specific circumstances of your contract.

The right to suspend your services and to have an opportunity to negotiate an indemnity from your client is important. You could try to include an indemnity provision along with the above clause in your original contract — as we suggest on the next page — but indemnities are often difficult to obtain.

If you encounter hazardous substances when none were anticipated, all bets are off. It should be obvious to your client that under these new circumstances it is now appropriate to give you stronger protection. Your client should see that the risks are different. The workscope and fee may need to be changed, and indemnity protection is now imperative if you are to continue your services.

If your contract does not contain a general indemnity from your client (see *Indemnities* for discussion and suggested language), try to obtain a special indemnity against the possibility of encountering unexpected environmental hazards. But be careful: some states have anti-indemnification laws or are very reluctant to enforce contract indemnities. It is crucial that you obtain competent legal counsel familiar with local laws to help you write and negotiate any indemnities and to ensure that the language you use is, to the maximum extent possible, enforceable in your jurisdiction. Consider the following suggested language:

> **The Client agrees, notwithstanding any other provision of this Agreement, to the fullest extent permitted by law, to indemnify and hold harmless the Design Professional, his or her officers, partners, employees, agents and consultants from and against any and all claims, suits, demands, liabilities, losses, or costs, including reasonable attorneys' fees and defense costs, resulting or accruing to any and all persons, firms, and any other legal entity, caused by, arising out of or in any way connected with the detection, presence, handling, removal, abatement, or disposal of any asbestos or hazardous or toxic substances, products or materials that exist on, about or adjacent to the jobsite, whether liability arises under breach of contract or warranty, tort, including negligence, strict liability or statutory liability or any other cause of action.**

Make certain your contract has a very strong Changed Conditions provision that allows you to renegotiate your workscope and terms — or terminate the project — in light of these developments. It is important to include Interpretation, Public Responsibility, Severability and Survival, Specification of Materials and Confidentiality clauses too. (Refer to those sections for suggested language and discussion.)

Part Two:

If you know or suspect you will encounter pollutants

Since the late 1970s, the environmental clean-up business has grown into a multi-billion dollar industry. In the United States alone, thousands of toxic sites have been identified that will require massive clean-up efforts, and more are being uncovered every day. Such enormous expenditure represents an appealing business opportunity for design professionals. Sadly, many design firms are finding that the dangers of such work far outweigh potential profits.

The Problem

The price tag for cleaning up the environment is almost incalculable – some estimates reach into the trillions of dollars in the United States alone. Clearly, somebody has to foot the bill. The result: huge liability claims and a hunt for an agglomeration of deep pockets, in which everybody who has had any connection with a given site — or had anything even remotely to do with the generation, storage, transportation or handling of toxic material — is being named in suits.

Environmental hazards represent a massive liability problem for design professionals too. Many companies who may want to get into remediation work fear that they might be grouped in court with the people who put the pollutants there in the first place. While there are laws that separate the clean-up companies from the polluters, they are not airtight. Because polluters and property owners are subject to strict liability or liability imposed by statute, they can be made to pay even if they are not proven negligent. By the time a claim is filed, the polluters may be long gone. If your company is the only one still in business, or the only worthwhile target the lawyers can find, you may have to defend the claim or pay damages, even if your role was to remediate the problem.

Nor is insurance the answer. Design firms may remember when pollution coverage was summarily taken away in 1984-85 and realize that they cannot depend on insurance coverage being available in the future. Many professional liability insurance policies still exclude most pollution claims. When coverage is available, it usually comes at a steep price.

THE SOLUTION

All environmental work involves significant hazards. Even if you engage in the lower-risk aspects — such as remedial investigation, feasibility studies or EIRs — you still subject yourself to a high likelihood of claims. If, on the other hand, your firm is directly involved in high-risk projects — such as designing facilities for clean-up, mitigation or handling of hazardous materials — do everything in your power to insulate yourself from the serious risk you face.

The solution lies in two areas: professional practice and contractual protection. You must develop and follow sound business and technical practices (See *Exhibit 6*) and then wrap yourself in the broadest contract safeguards you can devise. This is not the time to practice do-it-yourself lawyering. Retain the best legal counsel you can find who is familiar with environmental and construction law.

If you are not involved in the clean-up, but are providing professional services on a site that probably contains hazardous materials, your contract must include an indemnity from your client. We offer such a provision in Part One of this section. Even though your work does not involve clean-up, if it is known there are hazardous materials on the site, your contract should go much further. You need to obtain extremely strong contractual language to limit your liability to a level you are willing to accept for the work you perform in this high-risk situation. We strongly recommend that you insist on a Limitation of Liability provision in every contract you sign that involves environmental hazards, in addition to an indemnity. (See *Limitation of Liability* for more information and suggested contract language.) The remaining risk should rest where it belongs — squarely on the shoulders of the property owner. It is, after all, the owner who either polluted the property or who acquired the property with the pollutants already there. In either event, you didn't cause the problem and should not be held responsible.

In addition, your contract must have several other provisions if you are to provide these services. We consider these clauses to be **Deal Makers** — must-haves. (See *Exhibit 7* for a list, and refer to those specific clauses for further discussion.)

It is essential to get an indemnification from your client for any environmental hazards work. If your contract does not have a general indemnity (see *Indemnities*) and you have not included the indemnity for Environmental Hazards suggested in Part One of this section, talk to your lawyer about adding strong indemnity language such as the following:

KNOWN AND SUSPECTED
ENVIRONMENTAL HAZARDS

In consideration of the substantial risks to the Design Professional posed by the presence or suspected presence of asbestos or hazardous or toxic materials on or about the project site, the Client agrees, to the fullest extent permitted by law, to indemnify and hold harmless the Design Professional, his or her officers, directors, employees, agents and independent consultants and any of them from all claims and losses, including reasonable attorneys' fees and defense costs, arising out of, or in any way connected with, the performance or nonperformance of the obligations under this Agreement unless and until there has been an adjudication by a court or forum of competent jurisdiction that the claims at issue are a direct result of the sole negligence of the Design Professional.

This clause and all other clauses herein are intended as examples only and should be reviewed and modified by competent legal counsel to reflect variations in applicable local law and the specific circumstances of your contract.

Be especially careful to develop a clear and precise scope of services, stating exactly what services you will provide, what services you will not provide and what consequences may result from excluding those services. (Refer to *Scope of Services* and *Excluded Services* for discussion.)

No amount of compensation could begin to cover your legal costs and lost billable time if you face a claim arising from hazardous materials. Such claims are likely to be class action. They are very difficult to get out of or to settle. Before you enter contract negotiations, know precisely the terms you must have — and be prepared to walk away if your client is unwilling to cooperate.

A point to keep in mind when considering a clean-up project: You did not generate the pollutants in the first place, nor did you store them, handle them or dispose of them. Why, therefore, should you accept liability in any way for claims that probably will arise from the clean-up effort? Remember, you're the good guys — the cavalry on the white horses — doing your best to eliminate a dangerous condition. Your only responsibility is to perform your job reasonably and competently.

EXHIBIT 6

PROFESSIONAL PRACTICE CHECKLIST FOR ENVIRONMENTAL HAZARDS PROJECTS

- Is your firm technically qualified for work with hazardous materials?

- Do you have enough trained staff for the project?

- Have appropriate staff members completed legally mandated health and safety training that complies with OSHA and state requirements?

- Do key staff members receive relevant continuing education?

- Have you established a press and public affairs policy?

- Has your firm developed a written quality control, procedural and technical manual for in-house and field personnel?

- Do you have a written health and safety plan to establish the baseline condition of your field employees? Do you monitor their health periodically?

- Do you undergo a comprehensive risk assessment of each potential project?

- Are the owners sophisticated, stable and adequately financed?

- Have you worked with the owners on previous projects? Are they litigation-prone? Do they pay their bills on time?

- How complex is the project? Is there a good fit between your personnel and the design requirements?

- Who are the adjacent landowners? Do you have a potential for conflict of interest?

- Can you obtain insurance? Is project insurance available?

- Do you have a properly worded professional contract that has been reviewed by competent legal counsel?

EXHIBIT 7

DEAL MAKERS — MUST-HAVE CLAUSES FOR ENVIRONMENTAL HAZARDS PROJECTS

Changed Conditions

Confidentiality

Dispute Resolution

Excluded Services

Information Provided by Others

Interpretation

Limitation of Liability

Public Responsibility

Scope of Services

Standard of Care

Termination

PART THREE: PRELIMINARY SITE ASSESSMENTS

A Preliminary Site Assessment (PSA) is a study performed — usually as part of a
real estate transaction — to discover and evaluate the existence of contamination by
hazardous materials on, under, above and around a parcel of land. While many
states now require PSAs, buyers and lenders also often demand an environmental
clean bill of health before the sale or development of property, regardless of state
regulations.

A PSA (which goes under a variety of other names, such as pre-acquisition site
assessment, environmental site assessment, site reconnaissance and site audit) is
most often conducted in three separate phases. Phase One typically consists of a
historical and public document search and a site reconnaissance with a preliminary
report to the client. If hazardous materials are indicated or suspected, a Phase Two
PSA would most likely be recommended. This phase includes intrusive exploration
and sampling, soil, groundwater and surface water analyses, and a report of these
findings. Phase Three comprises the remedial recommendations and specifications
for the removal or containment of the environmental hazards.

THE PROBLEM

The increasing number of PSA-related claims underscores the high risk involved in
providing these services. Design professionals are discovering that, although their
fee for a Phase One PSA may be only a few thousand dollars, they could face a
potential pollution claim for many times that amount.

Although the market for PSA services has increased dramatically, the field is still
largely unregulated, and with few established protocols. Consequently, there are
engineers and architects offering PSAs who may not fully realize the risks involved.
Clients and their lenders may believe that PSAs guarantee detection of all existing
substances. Clients sometimes want you to certify a site as pollution-free. Even
worse, some clients will try to shift their environmental liability to you by various
clauses in their contract.

Looking ahead, there is no certainty that insurance coverage will always be available for the pollution risk. Although you may be able to obtain coverage now, you cannot count on it in the future. You may remember when pollution coverage for design professionals disappeared in 1984-85; some insurance carriers still do not offer such coverage. If too many PSA-related claims arise, that coverage could indeed disappear as well.

THE SOLUTION

Talk openly with your clients about the risks and problems you both face and the need to address these in your contract. Explain that even the most thorough (and costly) PSA may fail to identify all existing pollutants, simply because it is impossible to test every square inch of a site. Underscore that it is not the purpose of a PSA to guarantee or certify a clean site, but rather to reduce the uncertainty as much as practicable. (See *Certifications, Guarantees and Warranties*.) Make sure your clients also understand that you need enough time in order to do an adequate job. By contract, have them agree to provide all the necessary site data and give you the right to rely on that data. (See *Information Provided by Others*.) Explain your legal obligation to notify regulatory agencies if you discover pollutants. (See *Public Responsibility*.) For various reasons, you or your client might want your final report to remain confidential; if so, you'll need to address that issue too. (See *Confidentiality*.)

Before undertaking any PSA, analyze the project and client with care: How large is the site? (Larger sites can mean a greater likelihood that a hazardous substance might go undetected.) What are the time constraints or other limitations that would affect your services? Are those limitations realistic? What reliable information is available concerning the existing site conditions and historic use of the site? Has public or media attention been focused on the project? Is the client willing and able to invest enough time and money for an adequate PSA? (Review the loss prevention checklist on *Exhibit 6* in Part Two of this section for special recommendations to consider when dealing with environmental hazards.)

It is important to work with your client to develop a detailed and specific work-scope. Explain exactly what services you will and will not provide. Outline additional services that may be necessary if Phase One indicates possible pollutants. Furthermore, if you don't intend to be responsible for the detection of asbestos, PCBs or radon, or for historical, archeological or endangered species identification, clearly state in your contract that these services are excluded. You might consider using a special PSA workscope checklist and have the client initial any services declined. If necessary, have your client confirm in writing that the workscope is suitable to the lender's needs, too. Last, append a copy of the workscope to your final report with a notation that these were the services agreed to by your client in your contract. (See *Scope of Services* and *Excluded Services*.)

The ASFE: Professional Firms Practicing in the Geosciences has developed a contract for PSAs you might consider. (See the *Bibliography* for details on contacting ASFE.) If you develop your own, remember it must give you adequate protection. Above all, your client should understand that you cannot assume any risk that rightfully belongs to him or her. Insist on limitation of your liability and a full indemnification. Consider the following:

PHASE ONE PSA SERVICES

In consideration of the substantial risks to the Design Professional in performing Phase One PSA services on this project, the Client agrees, to the maximum extent permitted by law, to indemnify and hold the Design Professional harmless from any damage, liability or cost, including reasonable attorneys' fees and costs of defense, arising out of or resulting from the performance of the services under this Agreement or related in any manner whatsoever to the existence, release or disposal of toxic or hazardous substances, excepting only those damages, liabilities or costs arising directly from the sole negligence or willful misconduct of the Design Professional.

In addition, the Client agrees, to the maximum extent permitted by law, to waive any claims against the Design Professional arising out of the performance of the services under this agreement.

This clause and all other clauses herein are intended as examples only and should be reviewed and modified by competent legal counsel to reflect variations in applicable local law and the specific circumstances of your contract.

A contract for a Phase Two PSA should contain similar terms but go further to require the client to provide information on the whereabouts of any subsurface structures (pipes, tanks, utilities and so on) and to retain responsibility for any damage to those structures not correctly identified or located by the client. (See *Buried Utilities* and *Information Provided by Others*.) In addition, the client should agree to accept responsibility for disposal of all contaminated samples and decontamination of or compensation for your contaminated equipment. (See Part Two of *Environmental and Health Hazards* and *Testing Laboratories*.)

Sometimes insurance companies hire design professionals to perform PSAs before issuing an environmental impairment policy. If you are retained for such work, make sure your contract with the insurance company contains a waiver and indemnity from first and third party claims. You should also ask for a Waiver of Subrogation from the insurer. (See *Indemnities*, *Insurance* and *Third Party Claims*.)

There are several other provisions you should have in your contract. (See *Exhibit 8* for a list of desirable clauses.) We consider these to be **Deal Makers** — must-have clauses. As always, carefully review any contract terms with your attorney.

We strongly recommend that any firm performing PSAs contract directly with the owner. If that is impossible, and if your client requires you to hire an environmental specialist as your subconsultant, make certain that subconsultant is technically qualified, indemnifies you and has adequate insurance. (Refer to *Subconsultants* and *Indemnities* for more information.)

When conducting a PSA, it is important to follow the contract scope of services duties precisely and document your services well. Put in writing all research, sources, and interviews for your files and describe in your client report all work done both on and off the site. Any verbal amendments to your scope of services should be followed up with a letter to your client that confirms the additional or excluded service agreed upon. Also document any risk options or warnings you have given to your client. Make certain you check and recheck all your data and, finally, have another senior person in your firm review your final report.

Remember, PSAs are risky undertakings. In addition to the contractual protections you obtain from your client, you must do your job competently, using qualified environmental professionals who possess adequate technical experience and knowledge of regulatory requirements.

EXHIBIT 8

DEAL MAKER CLAUSES FOR PRELIMINARY SITE ASSESSMENT CONTRACTS

Buried Utilities
Certifications, Guarantees and Warranties
Changed Conditions
Corporate Protection
Dispute Resolution
Environmental and Health Hazards
Excluded Services
Indemnities
Information Provided by Others
Integration
Lenders' Requirements
Limitation of Liability
Public Responsibility
Right of Entry
Scope of Services
Standard of Care
Termination
Testing Laboratories

PART FOUR: ASBESTOS

More than twenty years have passed since health officials began to acknowledge that exposure to asbestos causes very real health problems. Resulting mainly from the inhalation of airborne fibers, diseases such as asbestosis (a debilitating lung disease) and cancers of the lung, stomach and other organs were found in significant numbers of workers exposed to asbestos in various industries. Clearly, there was reason for concern. The federal government reacted with strict regulations that would, over time, limit or ban the use of asbestos altogether.

Nevertheless, over three-quarters of a million public and commercial buildings still contain materials made with asbestos. The scope of the problem is enormous. Asbestos may be found in some cement pipe products, acoustical plaster, floor and ceiling tiles, wallboard, insulation, textiles and other materials. Friable materials — materials that are brittle or can be readily crumbled or reduced to powder by handling — are the most immediate problem. Such materials are considered dangerous because dust resulting from damage or disturbance to the asbestos-containing material (ACM) can be inhaled. But any ACM can be considered hazardous if asbestos fibers are released when the substance is cut, drilled or sanded during installation or broken during building repairs or renovation.

The magnitude of the problem and the resulting costs of remediation and potential injury have led to strict legislation on both the federal and state levels. Stiff civil and criminal penalties have been levied on building owners and asbestos removers alike. Literally hundreds of thousands of asbestos-related claims have been filed; the resulting litigation and damages have driven some of the largest industrial corporations into bankruptcy. Still, claims continue to be filed every day.

THE PROBLEM

The likelihood that claims will arise from asbestos abatement design services is so great that insurance coverage for this risk is very difficult to obtain. What insurance there is costs a great deal and, worse, may not be obtainable in the future.

In renovation and rehabilitation projects, you face the very real probability of encountering asbestos, especially in pre-1972 buildings. If your firm is not prepared for and does not react appropriately in such situations, you may face substantial civil or criminal repercussions. Even in jobs where you do not anticipate asbestos, its discovery could result in significant delays and increased costs. Conversely, you also could be held responsible for failure to discover asbestos on a site. (Refer to *Renovation/Remodeling, Consequential Damages* and Parts One, Two and Three of *Environmental and Health Hazards.*)

There is yet another concern. While the EPA is trying to effect a ban on all asbestos products by the end of this decade, there are still several ACMs on the market that can be specified under most building codes. If you specify such a material, and it is later banned or deemed unsafe, you probably will face claims.

THE SOLUTION

Providing asbestos abatement design services is so risky that many firms avoid such work altogether. That lessens but does not eliminate the problem, however. Even if you refuse abatement design projects, you still should protect yourself on every project in the event that you unexpectedly encounter asbestos on the jobsite. Always address the issue in your contracts.

There are three differing situations to consider:

IF YOU DON'T EXPECT TO ENCOUNTER ASBESTOS

Even if you believe there is no chance of encountering asbestos during the project, address the possibility in your contract anyway by adding a general protective clause. In Part One of Environmental and Health Hazards, we suggest you always insert a contract clause that provides for the possibility of discovering unanticipated hazardous materials. Your client should have no objections to the clause since neither of you anticipates the discovery of asbestos or hazardous materials. Both the AIA and the EJCDC standard contracts have such clauses. If you choose not to use a standard contract, however, we repeat the suggested Hazardous Materials clause:

HAZARDOUS MATERIALS

It is acknowledged by both parties that the Design Professional's scope of services does not include any services related to asbestos or hazardous or toxic materials. In the event the Design Professional or any other party encounters asbestos or hazardous or toxic materials at the jobsite, or should it become known in any way that such materials may be present at the jobsite or any adjacent areas that may affect the performance of the Design Professional's services, the Design Professional may, at his or her option and without liability for consequential or any other damages, suspend performance of services on the project until the Client retains appropriate specialist consultants or contractors to identify, abate and/or remove the asbestos, hazardous or toxic materials and warrant that the jobsite is in full compliance with applicable laws and regulations.

This clause and all other clauses herein are intended as examples only and should be reviewed and modified by competent legal counsel to reflect variations in applicable local law and the specific circumstances of your contract.

If you do encounter asbestos where none is expected, you need the right to suspend your services and renegotiate your fees, workscope and indemnification. Therefore, it is important that your contract also include a Changed Conditions provision that will allow you to do that. (See *Changed Conditions* for a discussion and suggested contract language.)

IF YOU KNOW OR SUSPECT YOU WILL ENCOUNTER ASBESTOS

If there is any chance asbestos is present on the site, we recommend you insist on a Limitation of Liability provision and the strongest indemnity possible. (See *Limitation of Liability* and *Indemnities* for further information.) If your contract does not contain a good general indemnity in your favor, we suggest you negotiate, with the help of your attorney, a specific indemnity for asbestos, such as the one following:

KNOWN OR SUSPECTED
PRESENCE OF ASBESTOS

It is understood that the existing building may contain asbestos or products containing asbestos, a substance known to present health hazards. The Client acknowledges that the Design Professional's scope of services for this project does not include any services related in any way to asbestos. Should the Design Professional or any other party encounter such materials on the jobsite, or should it in any other way become known that such materials are present or may be present on the jobsite, or any adjacent areas, which may affect the Design Professional's services, the Design Professional may, at his or her option, and without liability for consequential or any other damages, suspend performance of services on the project until the Client retains a qualified specialist contractor to abate, encapsulate and/or remove the asbestos or asbestos-containing materials and warrant that the jobsite is in full compliance with all applicable laws and regulations. The Client agrees to waive all claims against the Design Professional and his or her officers, directors, employees and subconsultants arising from or in any way connected with the existence of asbestos or asbestos-containing materials on or about the site.

The Client further agrees, to the fullest extent permitted by law, to indemnify and hold harmless the Design Professional for any and all damages, liabilities or costs, including reasonable attorneys' fees and defense costs, arising in any way from the existence of asbestos or asbestos-containing materials on or about the site, except for those damages, liabilities or costs attributable to the sole negligence or willful misconduct of the Design Professional. The Design Professional shall not be responsible in any way for any safety precautions, including measures for the protection of the contractor or any subcontractor, nor for the protection of the public. Such responsibility for safety precautions is and shall remain that of the Client and the Contractor.

This clause and all other clauses herein are intended as examples only and should be reviewed and modified by competent legal counsel to reflect variations in applicable local law and the specific circumstances of your contract.

We consider this a **Deal Maker** — a must-have clause. If your client won't agree to both a Limitation of Liability provision and indemnity when there is a possibility of encountering asbestos, we suggest you decline the project.

Specifying Materials Containing Asbestos

Last, we recommend that you avoid specifying any asbestos-containing material, although it still may be legal to do so under many building codes. Such material might be banned in the future, and you could be sued or even held liable for remediation costs, the costs of replacement, or even claims of injury to installers or the public.

What if your client insists on such products, perhaps because of lower costs? We suggest some contract language that may be helpful in Specification of Materials. (Refer to that section for further discussion.)

SEE ALSO:

Bibliography
Buried Utilities
Certifications, Guarantees and Warranties
Changed Conditions
Confidentiality
Consequential Damages
Corporate Protection
Dispute Resolution
Excluded Services
Indemnities
Information Provided by Others
Insurance
Interpretation
Jobsite Safety
Limitation of Liability
Public Responsibility
Renovation/Remodeling
Right of Entry
Scope of Services
Severability and Survival
Specification of Materials
Standard of Care
Subconsultants
Termination
Testing Laboratories
Third Party Claims

EXCLUDED SERVICES

To help assure client awareness and reduce their own exposure to risk, design professionals should include in their agreements a list of services they have offered to the client which may be necessary but which the client has refused or decided to obtain from another source.

THE PROBLEM

Since the client relies on your professional expertise, it could be alleged you were negligent by not informing your client that certain services might have been needed for the project and were either available from you or should have been obtained from another source, such as a specialist consultant.

THE SOLUTION

Work with your client to develop your scope of services. It is important that you review together a comprehensive workscope matrix or checklist, go over all needed and recommended services, and discuss those rejected by your client that you believe will be needed, are advisable and/or should be obtained from another source. By so doing, you not only alert the client to potentially needed and recommended services, you also protect yourself should your client later claim that he or she was unaware of such services. (Refer to *Scope of Services*.)

In addition, you will want to add an Excluded Services clause to your contract. Consider the following:

EXCLUDED SERVICES

Other services available from the Design Professional and applicable to the project have been made known and explained to the Client. Where the Design Professional has deemed a service needed or advisable, the Design Professional has made this opinion known to the Client and the Client has confirmed his or her opinion that such services are not requested of the Design Professional and/or that the Client has made or shall make arrangements to obtain those services from a source other than the Design Professional. These excluded services included:

{Listing or annotated listing of excluded services.}

The Client hereby agrees, to the fullest extent permitted by law, to indemnify and hold the Design Professional harmless from any claim, liability or cost (including reasonable attorneys' fees and costs of defense) for injury or loss arising or allegedly arising from the Design Professional's failure to perform a service listed above and excluded at the Client's direction.

This clause and all other clauses herein are intended as examples only and should be reviewed and modified by competent legal counsel to reflect variations in applicable local law and the specific circumstances of your contract.

You might want to consider highlighting any service you believe is essential.

It may be difficult, but try to obtain the suggested indemnity. However, if the client objects strenuously, you may be able to eliminate it. Check with your attorney. Depending on the law in your jurisdiction, and with the list of excluded services in place, an indemnity might not be needed.

If, as discussed in the Scope of Services section of this book, you choose to append a checklist of services, you can reference this fact by modifying the above paragraph to read:

**. . . These excluded services are listed in the appended Scope of
Services, Exhibit ____ , and are shown in the column headed
"Not Included." The Client hereby agrees to indemnify. . .**

Caution: if such a checklist is used to delineate both included and excluded services, be thorough in marking each and every item on the checklist as "in" or "out," in order to avoid confusion. A better practice is to retype the list, grouping the included services together in one place and those excluded in another.

SEE ALSO:

Construction Observation
Indemnities
Inspection
Opinion of Probable Construction Cost
Scope of Services

EXTENSION OF PROTECTION

Unless design professionals specifically provide for it in their contracts, protection they have obtained from their clients — such as an indemnification or limitation of liability — may not be applicable to the design professionals' subcontractors and subconsultants.

THE PROBLEM

If your subconsultants are not protected, they may file a claim against you in response to any claim filed against them. Or they may develop contracts that require you to indemnify them, which could confuse the issue should a claim arise.

THE SOLUTION

If you obtain some form of contractual protection (such as the client indemnifying you or limiting your liability) in your client contract, we recommend that you pass this protection on to your subconsultants. The best solution may be a clause such as the following:

EXTENSION OF PROTECTION

The Client agrees to extend any and all liability limitations and indemnifications provided by the Client to the Design Professional to those individuals and entities the Design Professional retains for performance of the services under this Agreement, including but not limited to the Design Professional's officers and employees and their heirs and assigns, as well as the Design Professional's subconsultants and their officers, employees, heirs and assigns.

This clause and all other clauses herein are intended as examples only and should be reviewed and modified by competent legal counsel to reflect variations in applicable local law and the specific circumstances of your contract.

If you are unable to negotiate this provision, you might be able to accomplish much the same thing by including your subconsultants among those to be indemnified by your client. (See *Indemnities*.)

SEE ALSO:

Delays
Indemnities
Limitation of Liability
Subconsultants

FAST TRACK PROJECTS

Fast track projects — those in which construction begins before all of the design professional's drawings and specifications are complete — have a single purpose: to augment the owner's pocketbook. Also known as phased construction, the method is intended to save time by bypassing the traditional sequence of completing plans, bidding or negotiation, and then starting construction.

If everything goes just right, fast tracking can expedite certain projects and result in savings to the owner. Materials can be purchased early, for instance, thus locking in lower prices. Rising labor costs can be anticipated, too, and averted. Buildings can be completed quicker and the owner's use or rental income begun sooner. Contractor selection may be improved. If all parties to the construction are motivated and well-meaning, cooperation between owner, contractor and designer may be enhanced. As with any shortcut, however, there are risks — especially to architects and engineers.

THE PROBLEM

It is almost never in your best interests to provide your design services in a fast track mode. Unless all conditions are ideal, you may incur tremendous risk by interrupting the normal sequence and flow of a project.

In the early stages of a fast track project, you have to make many assumptions that could prove to be untrue later as the project takes shape. Because of this, your early plans probably will need revision as design and construction proceed. Changes that are needed might not be design errors at all, or would not have been necessary had there been the normal amount of time to check and coordinate. If your client does not understand the facts of fast track life, he or she might also not understand that those modifications to your plans are probably not due to errors or negligence on your part and may balk at additional fees such changes require.

Design changes may mean some of the construction work itself will also need to be modified. Unless you are prescient, it is unlikely you could precisely anticipate an HVAC system that has yet to be specified by a subconsultant who has yet to be hired. What's more, the traditional delivery system gives you time to work closely with municipal building officials to anticipate and design around code problems. In fast tracking you may not have that luxury. A contrary code interpretation could mean costly modifications.

Unless your client clearly understands the process and pitfalls of fast tracking and unless the likelihood of design changes and change orders — with their resulting delays and costs — are acknowledged, your client's expectations of savings may be much too high. And unrealistic expectations often are the harbingers of claims.

THE SOLUTION

Because it is your client who will profit from the fast track process, it is your client who must bear the resulting risk. To avoid later disputes and hard feelings, your client needs to understand the process and acknowledge the risks involved. Explain that there will be changes, delays and resulting extra costs. Recommend that these costs be anticipated in the project budget and that a larger than usual contingency fund be established to include both design and construction changes. (Refer to *Contingency Fund* for more information.) To encourage full cooperation, consider suggesting a *partnering* agreement between the owner, contractors and all design professionals. (See the *Bibliography* and *Partnering Supplement*.) Finally, your contract should reflect the risks the client must retain. Consider the following sample clause:

FAST TRACK DESIGN AND CONSTRUCTION

In consideration of the benefits to the Client of employing the fast track process (in which some of the Design Professional's design services overlap the construction work and are out of sequence with the traditional project delivery method), and in recognition of the inherent risks of fast tracking to the Design Professional, the Client agrees to waive all claims against the Design Professional for design changes and modifications of portions of the Work already constructed due to the Client's decision to employ the fast track process.

In addition, the Client agrees, to the maximum extent permitted by law, to indemnify and hold the Design Professional harmless from any and all damage, liability and cost, including reasonable attorneys' fees and defense costs, except for those damages, liabilities and costs resulting from the sole negligence or willful misconduct of the Design Professional.

The Client further agrees to compensate the Design Professional for all Additional Services required to modify, correct or adjust the Construction Documents and coordinate them in order to meet the Client's program requirements because of the Client's decision to construct the project in a fast track manner.

This clause and all other clauses herein are intended as examples only and should be reviewed and modified by competent legal counsel to reflect variations in applicable local law and the specific circumstances of your contract.

No matter how strongly your contract is worded, you should go to extraordinary lengths to document every step of your involvement in the project. Keep detailed notes on why certain decisions were made, why some things were done out of sequence, who made the decisions and under what set of assumptions. On risky work of this nature, you must make every reasonable effort to protect yourself. The decision to participate in a fast track project should start with careful client selection and proceed only if all signals are go: a quality project, a strong contract, an adequate fee, experienced contractors and good working relationships.

SEE ALSO:

Bibliography
Codes and Standards Compliance
Contingency Fund
Delays
Limitation of Liability
Standard of Care
Timeliness of Performance

FOREIGN PROJECTS

With the opening of Eastern Europe, the rising economic power of the European
Community and the development of the Pacific Rim countries, design professionals
are finding expanding foreign markets available to them. In addition to normal
business concerns, however, an architect or engineer who provides services in a
foreign country must surmount a host of cultural differences. Language barriers,
disparity in construction industry practices, variances in social and business cus-
toms, unfamiliar legal standards and requirements, even novel contracting and
pricing procedures — all present as great a challenge to a designer as the project
itself.

THE PROBLEM

Laws and industry custom vary so widely from country to country that it is difficult
to know your professional obligations. In many countries, for example, the U.S.-
style standard of care is unheard of. Instead, under some laws, you are presumed
liable as soon as a defect in a structure becomes evident; the burden of proof that
you are not responsible lies with you. (This is sometimes known as the "Duty of
Result," which differs significantly from our own standard or "Duty of Care." For
more information, refer to *Standard of Care*.) Some countries even embrace the
doctrine of strict liability for design professionals — that is, you are held responsible for a defect even if you are not negligent. Even more confusing, the definition
of "defect" can range from "unfit for intended purpose" in some places to a complete failure in others. Similarly, the guarantee period, during which an owner can
claim compensation from a contractor or designer for that defect, varies from six
months in one country to thirty years in another — with every possible permutation
in between. The manner in which such a guarantee is applied also can vary from
nation, to region, to building function, to type of client.

There are two areas of particular concern: First, you should do everything you can to ensure a fair trial should you have to defend yourself against a claim of professional negligence. This means not only to determine where a suit would be tried, but what body of law would be applied to the suit. It is important that both these issues be addressed. Second, you need to understand how your professional liability insurance applies to foreign projects.

THE SOLUTION

Before you market your services abroad, consult with a good lawyer who is knowledgeable in both international law and the design professions. Once you have begun preliminary negotiations with a potential foreign client, you should retain local counsel in that country as well. These lawyers will help you address special business issues such as how and in what currency you will be paid, repatriation of funds, tax considerations and possible protection in politically unstable situations.

If your client or the project is in a country where the legal system is substantially different from that of the United States, specify in your contract the venue and governing law that will be applied to any claim. It is important to understand that a civil judgment of a foreign court usually can be enforced against your assets in the United States. After consulting with your lawyers, you may decide that the local laws of the country where the project or client is located would be preferable. Some countries, for instance, have laws regarding jobsite safety that completely protect the design professional. And in many places, limitation of a design professional's liability is an accepted standard contract provision. (See *Governing Law*, *Jobsite Safety* and *Limitation of Liability* for related discussions.) Most often, however, you should strive to negotiate a provision requiring that all disputes be heard and resolved under the applicable laws of the principal place of your business. Here is a sample clause:

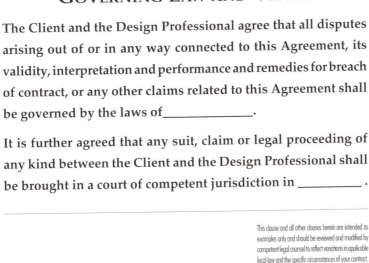

GOVERNING LAW AND VENUE

The Client and the Design Professional agree that all disputes arising out of or in any way connected to this Agreement, its validity, interpretation and performance and remedies for breach of contract, or any other claims related to this Agreement shall be governed by the laws of_____.

It is further agreed that any suit, claim or legal proceeding of any kind between the Client and the Design Professional shall be brought in a court of competent jurisdiction in _____ .

This clause and all other clauses herein are intended as examples only and should be reviewed and modified by competent legal counsel to reflect variations in applicable local law and the specific circumstances of your contract.

Another possibility is to specify the laws of a country that is neutral to both you and your client, but preferably one whose laws are based on the English Common Law. Recognize, however, that despite the venue and law you and your client decide upon for your disputes, that decision will not be binding upon third party claims.

Professional liability insurers differ on how coverage applies for suits brought outside the United States and Canada. Some provide coverage for claims brought anywhere in the world. Some exclude coverage in certain countries. Some require you to defend yourself and will reimburse you after the claim is resolved. You must check with your professional liability insurance specialist. Find out what coverage is available under your various insurance policies for any services you perform in foreign countries and what, if any, "gaps" need to be filled.

To help overcome difficulties with cultural and business differences abroad, some American firms choose to work with a local design professional firm. (In fact, some countries require this.) Such a liaison may be especially useful in unraveling unfamiliar building codes and construction practices. Other U.S. architects or engineers keep local designers on staff to help them with the intricacies of shop drawing and submittal review. And some U.S. firms choose to limit their work to "front end" design services on foreign projects. They will work up through the design development phase and require the owner to hire a local design firm to do construction documents and construction phase services. If you do affiliate with a local firm, you should (as always) ascertain the amount and type of professional liability insurance it carries and remember to address dispute resolution in your contract.

Finally, consider this: many foreign clients are appalled by the high rate of liability claims U.S. design professionals incur. This reputation may put American design firms at a disadvantage when competing in the foreign market. Perhaps one way to counter this is to demonstrate to your client that reliance on alternative methods of dispute resolution — rather than litigation — is your firm's policy. And to prove it, ask that your contract provide for mandatory nonbinding mediation should problems between the two of you arise. (See *Dispute Resolution*.)

SEE ALSO:

Dispute Resolution
Governing Law
Insurance
Jobsite Safety
Limitation of Liability
Standard of Care

GOVERNING LAW

Statutory laws and their judicial interpretations vary from state to state. It is possible that the laws in some states will be more favorable toward design professionals than the laws in others, especially on such issues as statutes of limitation, indemnification, limitation of liability, liens, responsibility for jobsite safety and certificates of merit.

THE PROBLEM

Difficulties can arise when you and your client are headquartered in different states or when the project is located in another state or country. Should litigation become necessary, under which state's laws will the contract be interpreted or claims adjudicated?

THE SOLUTION

Talk to your attorney. Your contract should clearly specify which state's laws will govern. Generally speaking, you may receive more favorable consideration in your "home" jurisdiction — where you and your employees live, pay taxes and vote. If your firm has branch offices, and thus more flexibility, you may wish to choose a state where, in your lawyer's opinion, you would stand the best chance of winning a claim, given existing law or prior court decisions. If clients want to rely on the laws in the state where they are headquartered or where the project is located, that may or may not be acceptable to you.

GOVERNING LAW

The laws of the State of _____ will govern the validity of this Agreement, its interpretation and performance. Any litigation arising in any way from this Agreement shall be brought in the courts of that State.

This clause and all other clauses herein are intended as examples only and should be reviewed and modified by competent legal counsel to reflect variations in applicable local law and the specific circumstances of your contract.

You should keep in mind, too, that if your client (or project) is located outside the United States, its possessions or territories, it is especially important that the jurisdiction of the governing law be one in which your firm will be treated fairly and your insurance carrier will defend any claims against you. Check with your professional liability insurance specialist concerning coverage under all your insurance policies for work in foreign countries. (See *Foreign Projects* for more information.)

SEE ALSO:

Attorneys' Fees
Foreign Projects
Indemnities
Jobsite Safety
Limitation of Liability
Statutes of Repose or Limitations

INCORPORATION BY REFERENCE

Incorporation by reference is a contract term that says that a party to a contract agrees to be bound by the terms and conditions contained in another document that is not quoted in its entirety in or appended to the contract. It may refer to a body of regulations or laws, a section of code, the General Conditions or the prime contract between the design professional's client and another party.

THE PROBLEM

Agreeing to incorporate and abide by the contents of another contract or document without reviewing it is foolhardy, especially since the incorporated terms and conditions may increase your liability and/or may be uninsurable. In effect, agreeing to terms that you have not seen is like signing a blank check.

THE SOLUTION

Before agreeing to be bound by the terms of any other document, insist that your client provide a copy of the referenced item or contract, read it thoroughly (and, if appropriate, have your attorney do the same), append a copy to your agreement with your client and modify any contract language to reflect the appended document:

INCORPORATION

The Client has a contract with _____ , a copy of which is appended to this Agreement. Regarding his or her services, the Design Professional agrees to be bound by the terms and conditions contained therein to the same extent as the Client is bound.

This clause and all other clauses herein are intended as examples only and should be reviewed and modified by competent legal counsel to reflect variations in applicable local law and the specific circumstances of your contract.

If you find certain provisions of the appended document unacceptable to you, the clause could be modified to read:

> **. . . contained therein to the same extent as the Client, except as indicated through deletions or other modifications made therein, and initialed by both the Client and the Design Professional.**

You also can reference only those sections of the contract in question that pertain to you or to which you agree. If your client doesn't wish to show you the entire contract, ask to see only those portions that would affect you, and list them in your agreement.

> **. . . contained therein in only the following clauses:**
>
> _____
>
> _____
>
> _____
>
> **The Design Professional shall not be bound by any other provision of said contract unless specifically listed in this paragraph.**

Ask to review the actual General Conditions (or the owner's draft) of the contract between the owner and the general contractor. You'll want to see that any references to you are consistent with the terms and conditions of your own agreement with the client.

SEE ALSO:

Assignment
Lenders' Requirements
Right to Retain Subconsultants
Subconsultants

INDEMNITIES

Of all the provisions in a contract for design professional services, indemnities have the most far-reaching liability implications. They are also the most difficult clauses to negotiate — especially if a client (or a client's attorney) is not inclined to be reasonable. Furthermore, enforceability, restrictions and interpretations vary widely from state to state. Some states prohibit most forms of indemnities while others allow broadly written, mutually agreed upon provisions. For these reasons, it is critical that design professionals understand the issues and work closely with their attorneys and professional liability insurance specialists to review and negotiate any contract indemnification language.

Pared down, the concept of indemnification (or *hold harmless*) is simple: It is an agreement to assume someone else's liability in the event of a loss. It's a means of shifting risk from one party to another, a kind of insurance. When a design professional indemnifies a client, he or she is agreeing to assume some of the client's potential or actual legal liabilities and thereby to act as an insurer, of sorts, for that client.

When a contractor takes over control of someone else's property to build something on it to make a profit, it's reasonable to ask the contractor to hold the owner of the property harmless from liability caused by the contractor's negligence. The same logic does not apply to architects and engineers. Design professionals do not take over nor exercise constructive control over the jobsite. They are not building something tangible on a site. Instead, they're rendering their professional and rather intangible services (planning, designing, observing and collecting data) for the benefit of their clients. It makes no sense, therefore, for designers to agree to the same kinds of indemnity clauses imposed on contractors. What's more, clients are not simply passive parties to the construction process. They are in the inherently risky business of construction. In this situation, it's only logical that all parties (owner, contractor and design professional) be responsible only for their own risks or those they can control. If no one can control a risk, then it must remain with the owner. In fact, a project may be so hazardous or the design services so risk-prone that it would make more sense for the owner to indemnify the designer for those risks in return for the benefit the owner derives from the professional services provided under such circumstances.

A design professional may encounter at least four different types of indemnity situations. Ways to handle each will be suggested here. Two points must be kept in mind, however: First, there is no guarantee that a particular jurisdiction will necessarily enforce an indemnity in a designer's favor, given the great disparity in the enforceability and interpretation of indemnity clauses resulting from various state statutes and court decisions. When it comes to indemnities, design professionals should expect the worst of both worlds — that a client's indemnity will be enforced and the designer's will not. This is why good legal advice is especially important on any indemnity language. (See *Interpretation*.)

Second, many of the sample clauses offered throughout this book include specific indemnifications simply because each contract topic is considered separately. Many attorneys believe that a contract should have as few indemnities as possible, although everything for which a designer seeks indemnification should be included. This often can be accomplished by combining several related issues into one general indemnity clause.

When Your Client Wants an Indemnity From You

In that cleverly crafted agreement sent to you by your client's attorney probably lurks a clause requiring you to indemnify the client. The language may be short and innocuous-sounding, or it may be pages long, convoluted and confusing. In either case, proceed with caution. With the help of your attorney, your professional liability insurance specialist and the suggestions below, you can unravel the most offensive legal verbiage and, if you can't dispose of the provision altogether, perhaps you can make it more equitable.

The Problem

Your most significant dilemma is the existence of the clause itself. By including this indemnity, your client is attempting to transfer some or perhaps all of his or her risk to you — and likely demanding that you take on more liability exposure than law or custom requires. If you doubt this, ask yourself: without this indemnity, whose risk would it be? Almost invariably, it would be the client's.

Several other critical factors must be examined:

- Client-drafted indemnities often ask you to pay for the client's own negligence. Your client has control over the budget and workscope. During design and construction, he or she frequently participates in discussions and may make decisions that save money but also increase your risk — by specifying cheaper grades of materials, for instance, or a less expensive construction method. This is especially dangerous if your contract has you bearing all the risk — including the risk for your client's negligent decisions. Typically, a client requests indemnity for claims caused in *whole or in part* by the design professional, except for the *sole* negligence of the client. The inference is clear: the client intends that you pay all of the loss jointly caused by you and the client, even if he or she is ninety nine percent at fault and you are a mere one percent negligent. Keep in mind that even the most inept lawyer can convince a jury that the design professional is one percent at fault for just about anything.

- Client-drafted indemnities often are uninsurable. Under the law, you already have an obligation to perform your services in a non-negligent manner. Accordingly, your professional liability insurance covers you against damages resulting from your *negligent* professional acts, errors or omissions. To prove negligence, a claimant must establish the standard of care, establish a duty to adhere to that standard of care and establish your failure to do so — and then prove that this failure proximately resulted in injury or damage to the claimant. If you sign a client's indemnity that is not limited to your negligence, you are accepting liability beyond that required by law and beyond that for which you are insured. Your professional liability policy may include such language as, "This insurance does not apply to liability assumed by you under any 'contract'; but this exclusion does not apply if you would have been liable in the absence of such 'contract,' due to your own error, omission or negligent act." However it is worded, check with your professional liability insurance specialist or knowledgeable legal counsel to determine if a proposed indemnity clause would be covered or if your policy would exclude certain aspects of it.

- Client-drafted indemnities frequently contain onerous, overreaching language. For instance, a client may ask for indemnity for your "intentional acts, errors." The truth is, virtually everything you do could be interpreted by an enterprising attorney as intentional. (It is possible your client means *willful* or *malicious* instead. Keep in mind, however, that malicious acts are not insurable.) Sometimes clients want you to indemnify against *allegations* or *claims* of your negligence. That, too, is excessive language, because anyone can allege or claim anything, and you could conceivably find yourself indemnifying someone simply on the strength of those allegations. Beware, also, of any extreme phrasing, such as *at any time, from any cause whatsoever* or *any or all* claims. These only serve to broaden your liability and may render the clause uninsurable.

- Client-drafted indemnities frequently ask you to defend the client. If an indemnity is not tied directly to your negligence (see following sample clause), this provision could be interpreted as an obligation on your part to retain an attorney for your client and pay for his or her defense — even before your legal liability for actual negligence (if any) has been established. You might find yourself having to pay for your client's defense attorney from your own pocket even if you're proven to be non-negligent because your professional liability carrier is not responsible for paying such expenses. (In most instances, your insurer will reimburse for defense costs after the fact if they are part of your client's damages and your negligence has been proven.) Again, discuss the terms of your coverage with your insurance specialist.

- Client-drafted indemnities sometimes attempt to include inappropriate parties as *indemnitees* (parties to be indemnified). Such clauses often list a long series of indemnitees, some of whom can be indemnified and others who cannot. For example, it is not unusual to indemnify a client's partners, principals, officers, directors and employees. However, you should not agree to indemnify a client's agents, contractors, attorneys, contract employees, lenders, volunteers or anyone else who is not directly part of the client entity. You do not owe these parties the same obligations, and they can always seek their own legal remedies should your negligence somehow damage them.

THE SOLUTION

Refuse to accept unlimited liability. Your goal is to keep the risk in the hands of the party who is most able to control it or who has the most to gain from it. This is almost never the design professional. Many design firms are guided by a strict policy: "If we can't insure a risk, we won't assume it."

Your best solution? Delete any provision that requires you to indemnify the client. Explain you are already obligated by law to perform in a non-negligent manner and, if you fail to do so, the client has recourse in tort. (Assuming you make the changes we suggest to the client's indemnity language, he or she will gain very little, if any, protection anyhow.) Your client also may be more agreeable if you can show that the clause as presented is uninsurable and, therefore, too great a liability for you to accept.

Failing that, if your client insists on some indemnification, counter with a *mutual indemnity*, in which each of you indemnifies the other for your own negligent acts. This should seem equitable to a fair-minded client. Consider:

INDEMNIFICATION

The Design Professional agrees, to the fullest extent permitted by law, to indemnify and hold the Client harmless from any damage, liability or cost (including reasonable attorneys' fees and costs of defense) to the extent caused by the Design Professional's negligent acts, errors or omissions in the performance of professional services under this Agreement and those of his or her subconsultants or anyone for whom the Design Professional is legally liable.

The Client agrees, to the fullest extent permitted by law, to indemnify and hold the Design Professional harmless from any damage, liability or cost (including reasonable attorneys' fees and costs of defense) to the extent caused by the Client's negligent acts, errors or omissions and those of his or her contractors, subcontractors or consultants or anyone for whom the Client is legally liable, and arising from the project that is the subject of this Agreement.

The Design Professional is not obligated to indemnify the Client in any manner whatsoever for the Client's own negligence.

This clause and all other clauses herein are intended as examples only and should be reviewed and modified by competent legal counsel to reflect variations in applicable local law and the specific circumstances of your contract.

As a final — and, by far, least desirable — alternative, you may be forced to give your client some kind of unilateral indemnity. However, you must limit the indemnity to that which is insurable. Make certain the indemnity is tied to your negligence and purge the clause of any client-generated onerous language. Include the concept of *comparative negligence*, which holds you liable for only that portion of the damages for which you are responsible; and, finally, see that the indemnity is limited to the services called for under the agreement. These concepts are reflected in the following suggested language:

> **The Design Professional agrees, to the fullest extent permitted by law, to indemnify and hold the Client harmless from damages and losses arising from the negligent acts, errors or omissions of the Design Professional in the performance of professional services under this Agreement, to the extent that the Design Professional is responsible for such damages and losses on a comparative basis of fault and responsibility between the Design Professional and the Client. The Design Professional is not obligated to indemnify the Client for the Client's own negligence.**

If you feel your client is forcing you to sign an unfair indemnity, you may want to suggest that he or she is using *disparate bargaining power*; that is, adopting a "sign this or forget the job" stance occasionally used by those in a superior bargaining position, which constitutes a refusal to bargain in good faith and results in what courts may call a *contract of adhesion*. Under certain circumstances, this may allow you to claim that the clause is unenforceable. Public officials are becoming more sensitive to this issue, so it may be worthwhile to raise it if you feel the client is refusing to negotiate on an indemnity. If you do nothing else, at least document your concerns with a letter to the client and keep complete records of your negotiation efforts for your files.

We regard harmful or inappropriate indemnities as **Deal Breakers.** A client who insists on keeping unfair and one-sided indemnity provisions has an obvious agenda: to lay all or most of the project risk at your feet. If you cannot either delete the provision or negotiate an equitable indemnity, walk away from the project.

When You Want Protection From Your Client

Never assume liability out of proportion to the potential profit you will make on a high-risk project. Unless you use protective contract language, such extraordinary risks could be yours.

The Problem

Certain situations are so risk-prone or hazardous to the health of your business that it is imperative your client keep all the risk. Such instances may involve hazardous waste, asbestos, condominiums, renovations or the possibility of unauthorized reuse of your documents. (See *Environmental and Health Hazards*, *Condominiums*, *Renovation/Remodeling* and *Ownership of Instruments of Service* for further discussion on these topics.)

The Solution

There are times when indemnity by your client from third-party claims is the only approach that seems to make sense. In high-risk projects, you should consider such a clause a **Deal Maker** provision; if your client won't give you indemnity, consider declining the project. But remember that an indemnity is only as good as your client's net worth. If your client doesn't have the financial resources or appropriate insurance to back up the indemnity or if he or she refuses to indemnify you, strongly consider declining the project.

On very risky projects or projects you cannot properly insure, you also should ask your client to agree not to sue you. This is called a *waiver*. Although an important protection, it is one of the most difficult provisions to obtain and to enforce. You and your attorney must be extremely cautious in its wording and presentation, since there are wide variations in state statutes pertaining to waivers. When drafting your contract, keep the waiver and indemnity in separate paragraphs. If a court declares the waiver invalid, you don't want an attached indemnity thrown out as well. (This is a good reason to insist on a severability provision in your contracts. Refer to *Severability and Survival* for sample language.) Finally, to avoid any conflict, your attorney must be certain to coordinate the waiver with any Limitation of Liability provision. Consider the following sample waiver and indemnity provisions:

WAIVER

In consideration of the substantial risks to the Design Professional in rendering professional services in connection with this project, the Client agrees to make no claim and hereby waives, to the fullest extent permitted by law, any claim or cause of action of any nature against the Design Professional, his or her officers, directors, employees, agents or subconsultants which may arise out of or in connection with this project or the performance, by any of the parties above named, of the services under this Agreement.

INDEMNIFICATION

In addition, and notwithstanding any other provisions of this Agreement, the Client agrees, to the fullest extent permitted by law, to indemnify and hold harmless the Design Professional, his or her officers, directors, employees, agents and subconsultants from and against all damage, liability or cost, including reasonable attorneys' fees and defense costs, arising out of or in any way connected with this project or the performance by any of the parties above named of the services under this Agreement, excepting only those damages, liabilities or costs attributable to the sole negligence or willful misconduct of the Design Professional.

Remember, in projects where the potential risk is great, you and your attorney must make every effort to obtain indemnity language that gives you the maximum protection possible under the laws of your jurisdiction.

When You and Your Client Want Indemnity From the Contractor

More and more often, design professionals are being sued for jobsite accidents where injured construction workers claim that the architect or engineer had an obligation to monitor safety precautions or provide a safe jobsite.

The Problem

When a contractor's employee is injured, the search for "deep pockets" takes a predictable course. Whether triggered by the contractor's insolvency or inadequate workers' compensation, the search usually turns to the architect or engineer — even if the design professional's share of the blame is minimal or nonexistent.

The Solution

To protect yourself against injured workers' claims, add language to your contract with the owner that requires the owner to include provisions in the owner-general contractor agreement requiring that the contractor(s) indemnify you, your subconsultants and the owner for claims by the contractor's employees. You also will want to have the contractor name you and the owner as additional insureds on the contractor's general liability policy. (See *Jobsite Safety*.) In addition, you should require the contractor to procure contractual liability coverage sufficient to cover the indemnity obligations being assumed and provide evidence of this coverage to all indemnified parties.

When You Want an Indemnity From Your Subconsultants

Prime consultants often require indemnities from their subconsultants to protect them from damages and costs caused by the subs.

THE PROBLEM

If your subconsultant is sued for negligence, you, as the prime consultant, will almost certainly be named in the suit. Even if you are blameless, the very act of defending yourself may well cost you your deductible (if you are insured) besides your time and staff costs expended in your own defense — a considerable sum.

THE SOLUTION

We recommend that in your subconsultant agreements, you use a reasonable indemnity clause that is both mutual and insurable and that allows you to recover your costs in the event of a claim. Consider the following:

> **The Design Professional and the Subconsultant mutually agree, to the fullest extent permitted by law, to indemnify and hold each other harmless from any and all damage, liability or cost, including reasonable attorneys' fees and costs of defense, arising from their own negligent acts, errors or omissions in the performance of their services under this Agreement, to the extent that each party is responsible for such damages, liabilities and costs on a comparative basis of fault.**

Remember, indemnities are extremely complex and have enormous liability implications. Have your lawyer examine any indemnity language with respect to the laws of the governing jurisdiction to determine exactly what your rights and exposures may be. Work, too, with your professional liability insurance specialist to determine if any indemnities you intend to sign are insurable under your various policies.

SEE ALSO:

Condominiums
Environmental and Health Hazards
Extension of Protection
Governing Law
Insurance
Interpretation
Jobsite Safety

Non-Negligent Services
Ownership of Instruments of Service
Renovation/Remodeling
Severability and Survival
Standard of Care
Subconsultants

INFORMATION
PROVIDED BY OTHERS

Design professionals are often required to rely on data and documents prepared or collected by other parties. Such information might range from the location of underground utilities to the original plans and specifications for an older building undergoing renovation. If one design professional is replacing another in a project, the second designer may need to rely on the partially completed plans of the first. Whatever the original source, if the client or someone on the client's behalf provides information to a design professional, the client should be responsible for the accuracy and completeness of that material.

THE PROBLEM

The information you need others to provide can be extensive and critically important to the design or economic feasibility of the project, especially when renovation, remodeling and similar work is involved. It may be impossible to indicate beforehand all the documents you may need and, indeed, some sources may be long gone. (See *Renovation/Remodeling*.) It is also expensive, time consuming or impossible for scheduling or other reasons to conduct the research and investigation necessary to verify someone else's data; your client may not be willing to pay for such an effort.

THE SOLUTION

One solution is an expressed understanding that, for purposes of expediency and economy, you are entitled to rely on information supplied or produced by others — including the client — and that the client will underwrite the resulting risk. A clause that accomplishes this could read:

INFORMATION PROVIDED BY OTHERS

The Design Professional shall indicate to the Client the information needed for rendering of services hereunder. The Client shall provide to the Design Professional such information as is available to the Client and the Client's consultants and contractors, and the Design Professional shall be entitled to rely upon the accuracy and completeness thereof. The Client recognizes that it is impossible for the Design Professional to assure the accuracy, completeness and sufficiency of such information, either because it is impossible to verify, or because of errors or omissions which may have occurred in assembling the information the Client is providing. Accordingly, the Client agrees, to the fullest extent permitted by law, to indemnify and hold the Design Professional and the Design Professional's sub-consultants harmless from any claim, liability or cost (including reasonable attorneys' fees and costs of defense) for injury or loss arising or allegedly arising from errors, omissions or inaccuracies in documents or other information provided by the Client to the Design Professional.

This clause and all other clauses herein are intended as examples only and should be reviewed and modified by competent legal counsel to reflect variations in applicable local law and the specific circumstances of your contract.

Sometimes you are asked by the client to coordinate the work of consultants hired by the owner. Since these are not your consultants, you need to be able to rely on the accuracy and completeness of the work they perform for the owner and not assume responsibility for their inaccuracies, errors or omissions. In these instances, you may want to change the wording as follows:

> . . . for rendering of services hereunder. The Client and such consultants whose work the Client has required the Design Professional to coordinate, shall provide to the Design Professional such information as is available to the Client and the Client's consultants and contractors, and the Design Professional shall be entitled. . . provided by the Client or the Client's consultants to the Design Professional.

Some clients may object to the above language because it forces them to accept a liability without having the benefit of your evaluation of the extent of risk involved. They may say, "You're the expert. You tell me whether we should rely on this or not." You might offer to help evaluate the risk associated with information or work provided by others as an additional service, without subjecting the client to expensive research and testing. And, of course, clients may not be the only sources of other information. In such instances you could modify the wording as follows:

> . . . for rendering of services hereunder, as well as likely sources of this information, with such sources to include but not be limited to the Client. The Design Professional shall review information provided by others and shall give the Client an opinion of the risk associated with reliance on such information. The Client understands that it is impossible to eliminate all risk, because of the inherent limitation of the techniques available to develop the information, and/or because of errors, omissions or inaccuracies which may exist in the information. Accordingly, the Client agrees to the fullest extent permitted by law. . .

In accepting or offering such a provision, you should recognize that your evaluation must be provided (i.e., you must now review and render an opinion of the risks to the client) — and provided in accordance with the standard of care. The extra work needed would be provided and paid for as an additional service.

SEE ALSO:

Buried Utilities
CADD
Environmental and Health Hazards
Indemnities
Multiple Prime Contracts
Record Documents
Renovation/Remodeling
Standard of Care
Subconsultants
Supplanting Another Design Professional

INSPECTION

The dictionary tells us that to "inspect" something is to examine it carefully and critically for flaws. In the construction industry, inspection is a comprehensive examination of the work in progress. However, it is a common misconception that the purpose of a design professional's project visit is to "inspect" the contractor's work to uncover any code violations or construction defects. Because the words *inspect* and *construction observation* have been widely and inaccurately used to describe the same function, they are often confused. Many clients — and more than a few juries — don't understand that, unlike inspection, construction observation is generally quite limited in scope and purpose.

There are times when a client truly needs the services of an inspector — and some of these services can be provided by architects or engineers. A client may want a full-time resident inspector on a complex construction project, or may need a building inspected before purchase to fulfill a lender's requirements or to determine whether it is safe for occupancy following an earthquake or other disaster. Sometimes a design professional contracts with a municipality as a city building inspector. Sometimes special inspection services are mandated by municipal or state code to assure the integrity of certain structural elements of a building. Whatever the nature of the inspection, however, these are high-risk services and require special contractual protection.

THE PROBLEM

The word *inspect* and its derivatives imply a much more detailed examination than mere *observation* of a project. Inappropriate use of these words in contracts, correspondence or even in conversation can establish obligations you never intended. A layperson may believe that an "inspector" should uncover each and every error, unsafe condition and violation of law. It could be alleged you are responsible for any errors or omissions that are not discovered. In fact, agreeing to provide inspection services raises the standard of care to which you must perform. The liability implications are immense. What's more, if you are "inspecting" a project, it also could be claimed you failed to detect unsafe conditions on the site — and be blamed, at least in part, for workers' injuries. (Refer to *Jobsite Safety*.)

A simple "walk-through inspection" of a building for lenders or potential buyers or for owners requiring a survey under ADA legislation may seem straightforward enough. The time spent and the corresponding fee received hardly seem to merit the trouble of getting a written contract. But if a financial decision or safety determination is based — even partially — on your inspection report and troubles surface later, your losses could amount to hundreds of times your fee.

THE SOLUTION

Unless you intend to provide actual inspection services, you should avoid the use of the word *inspect* to describe your basic observation or role. If a client-written contract contains the offending word, delete it and replace it with *observation*. If that is not possible, carefully define *inspect* in the Definitions or Scope of Services sections of your contract to mean exactly the service you will provide. (You may want to refer to the AIA contract document B352 for a well defined scope of services for full-time resident inspectors or project representatives. Also refer to *Construction Observation*, *Definitions* and *Scope of Services*.)

If your client asks you to provide inspection services, first determine if he or she truly wants an inspector or is misinterpreting the term and really intends a normal level of contract administration and project visits instead. If a full-time, on-site inspector is what is required, your client should contract with a qualified inspector directly. The vicarious liability you could assume for subcontracting with an inspector is significant and should be avoided. If you must retain an inspector, however, get an indemnification from your client and make certain the inspector is adequately insured. You should also consider the greater risk you must bear when negotiating your fee. (See *Indemnities*, *Insurance* and *Subconsultants* for related discussions.)

As we recommend for every project you undertake, insist on some form of written contract — no matter how small the inspection job. Even if it's a quick "walk-through" survey, at least obtain a signed letter of agreement or a "short-form" contract. (The Coalition of American Structural Engineers (CASE) has developed a limited services agreement. Refer to the *Bibliography* for information on contacting CASE.)

When providing visual, on-site inspection services of an existing building — whether to verify compliance with codes, to look for damage following an earthquake, fire or other disaster, or to check the integrity of a building for potential buyers — you will be making certain assumptions about the building and its condition. Without extensive invasive testing, you cannot know certain facts about the building. Therefore, you should protect yourself with a strong contractual provision. Here is one example:

VISUAL ON-SITE OBSERVATION SERVICES

Because evaluation of the existing structure requires that certain assumptions be made regarding existing conditions, and because some of these assumptions cannot be verified without expending additional sums of money or destroying otherwise adequate or serviceable portions of the building, the Client agrees, to the fullest extent permitted by law, to indemnify and hold the Design Professional harmless from and against any and all damage, liability and cost, including reasonable attorneys' fees and defense costs, arising or allegedly arising out of the professional services under this Agreement, except for the sole negligence or willful misconduct of the Design Professional.

This clause and all other clauses herein are intended as examples only and should be reviewed and modified by competent legal counsel to reflect variations in applicable local law and the specific circumstances of your contract.

In the event of a natural disaster, only a few states have "Good Samaritan" laws to provide some protection to design professionals who, at the request of a public agency, inspect buildings to determine if they are safe for occupancy. Check with your attorney and your professional society. If your state does not yet have such a law, you and your professional society should urge your state legislators to pass one. In the meantime, protect yourself by contract.

When inspecting existing buildings, always make sure that you have a provision that protects you from the discovery of unexpected hazardous materials (See Part One of *Environmental and Health Hazards* for recommended language). We also recommend that you include a clause that addresses your right to rely upon information given to you concerning the condition of the building. (See *Information Provided by Others* for a sample clause.)

If your firm provides contract municipal services as a building inspector or other type of building official, you can attempt to wrap yourself in whatever municipal immunity might be available. You also might want to use such phrases as "appointed by the City" and "authorized representative of the City" in your contracts and reference appropriate sections of the Uniform Building Code pertaining to the duties and powers of a building official. The following example could be inserted in the agreement between you and a city for whom you provide contract services:

MUNICIPAL INSPECTION SERVICES

The Design Professional, acting as the City Building Inspector {or other applicable title}, **when acting in good faith in the discharge of his or her duties, shall not thereby render himself or herself liable personally and is, to the maximum extent permitted by law, relieved from all liability for any damage that may accrue to persons or property by reason of any act or omission in the discharge of his or her duties. Any suit brought against the Design Professional because of the acts or omissions performed by him or her in the enforcement of any provisions of the City Building Code shall be defended by the legal department of the City until final termination of the proceedings. The Design Professional shall be entitled to all defenses and municipal immunities that are, or would be, available to the City if the same services were provided by City employees.**

This clause and all other clauses herein are intended as examples only and should be reviewed and modified by competent legal counsel to reflect variations in applicable local law and the specific circumstances of your contract.

Finally, if you are to provide services as a Special Inspector to review certain structural components of a building (such as special welding, concrete or bolting details), there are specific contracts available for such services. (CASE publishes one such contract for Special Inspection Services. See *Bibliography*.) No matter what contract you use, be very sure you are qualified to provide such services.

SEE ALSO:

176

INSURANCE

Almost every professional service contract written contains detailed and often confusing insurance requirements, usually phrased in mind-numbing "insurance-speak." To make sense out of these requirements and know how to deal with them, design professionals must master some insurance basics. They need to understand the various types of policies, what these policies cover, and what extra endorsements they can and cannot get. Most importantly, designers must be able to spot impossible or ambiguous insurance requirements in client-written contracts and negotiate reasonable alternatives.

THE PROBLEM

Perhaps because some clients are used to specifying insurance requirements for contractors, they think design professionals should carry the same types of coverage. But quite often, agreements drawn up by clients or their attorneys will specify insurance requirements that are impractical or impossible for you to meet.

THE SOLUTION

Take the initiative. Offer a paragraph that in simple, straightforward language says you will attempt to maintain appropriate policies with reasonable limits of coverage and list them on an addendum attached to your contract. (See *Exhibit 9* for a sample format.) If you offer such a paragraph up front, you may forestall drawn out negotiations with your client over insurance requirements:

INSURANCE

During the term of this Agreement, the Design Professional agrees to provide evidence of insurance coverage as shown on Addendum ___, attached hereto. In addition, the Design Professional agrees to attempt to maintain continuous professional liability coverage for the period of design and construction of this project, and for a period of ___ years following substantial completion, if such coverage is reasonably available at commercially affordable premiums. For the purposes of this Agreement, "reasonably available" and "commercially affordable" shall mean that more than half the design professionals practicing in this state in this discipline are able to obtain such coverage.

This clause and all other clauses herein are intended as examples only and should be reviewed and modified by competent legal counsel to reflect variations in applicable local law and the specific circumstances of your contract.

Your best source for insurance assistance and information is a specialized professional liability insurance agent or broker who is knowledgeable about the design professions and construction industry. (Refer to the *Bibliography* for information on how to obtain a listing of specialized agents and brokers.) This individual can help you analyze contract requirements for the types of insurance discussed below.

PROFESSIONAL LIABILITY INSURANCE

Professional liability is insurance that protects you from claims arising from your negligent acts, errors or omissions in the performance of your professional services. Because this coverage is peculiar to licensed professionals, few clients fully understand its function and limitations.

Professional liability policies have several unique features that narrowly define coverage:

First, policies are written on either a *claims-made* or a *claims-made and reported* policy form. Both policies cover claims made against you during the policy period and require that the claims be reported to your carrier in accordance with policy terms. To be covered, such claims must have arisen from acts, errors or omissions occurring after the retroactive date stated in your policy.

Second, in order to keep your *retroactive date* and to have your *prior acts* covered, you normally must continue to renew your policy every year. In other words, if you don't renew your policy, you won't have coverage for projects you designed while you were previously insured.

Third, professional liability policies are *aggregate limit* policies. The policy limit you purchase is the total amount your insurer would pay for both defense costs and indemnity, regardless of the number of claims made during the policy period.

Fourth, they are *expense within the limits* policies. This means that after you meet your deductible, additional defense costs paid on that claim by your insurer will decrease the policy limits available for payment of that claim or other claims.

Because of these limitations and because the insurance market for this coverage is somewhat volatile — in both price and availability — it would be chancy for you to agree to a contract requirement to maintain specific levels of professional liability coverage for any extended time. You might not be able to comply in the future.

Clients often confuse professional liability with general liability insurance (discussed later in this section) and try to specify the same coverage they require of contractors. Because of this, it is important to review and negotiate client-drawn contracts and to delete unattainable or unreasonable requirements — such as the inclusion of "additional insureds" on your professional liability policy. Despite the clients' demands, there often are provisions to which you simply cannot or should not agree. (We've listed some of those provisions in *Exhibit 10*.)

Professional liability insurance is written by relatively few insurance carriers. While there are some similarities among them, there are also significant differences in underwriting, policy language and its interpretation, and claims services. Once again, the advice of a professional liability insurance specialist can be invaluable in designing insurance coverage suited to your firm's needs and when selecting or changing carriers.

PROJECT INSURANCE

One solution to the limitations of professional liability practice policies (such as the length of coverage and the aggregate limits) is to obtain a professional liability project policy. Project policies provide *extended coverage* for the design and construction period of a single project, plus a preselected *discovery period* after substantial completion of the project. These policies provide a separate project limit so that claims on other projects will not erode the limits available for this project. And, because they are written on a multi-year basis and guaranteed noncancelable under most circumstances, there is less administrative burden on you and your client to ensure continuous coverage.

Another advantage to project coverage is that the entire design team — including all the subconsultants — can be covered under a single policy by a single insurance carrier. This cuts down on intramural conflict or finger-pointing among project team members if a claim arises and reduces lawsuits, counterclaims and blame shifting within the project team, which in turn reduces overall liability costs.

Because of the significant advantages of project insurance, owners often will pay the cost — or some part of it. Sophisticated owners recognize project insurance as a solution to many of their liability concerns and will treat it as a normal project cost in much the same way they treat insurance required of contractors. Project insurance also is an excellent solution in those instances where your client wants a higher limit than your practice policy offers.

Check with your professional liability insurance specialist to see if coverage is available for your projects. If you feel that project insurance is appropriate, you may be able to negotiate with your client to include the cost as a direct reimbursable item. Here is a sample provision that incorporates these ideas:

PROJECT INSURANCE

The Design Professional agrees to obtain professional liability project insurance specifically to cover this project. This project policy will cover the design and construction period and will include a discovery period of ___ years after substantial completion. The policy will provide a project aggregate limit of $_____ and a deductible of $_____. The cost of this coverage shall be paid by the Client as a Direct Reimbursable Cost in accordance with paragraph ___ hereof.

This clause and all other clauses herein are intended as examples only and should be reviewed and modified by competent legal counsel to reflect variations in applicable local law and the specific circumstances of your contract.

COMMERCIAL GENERAL LIABILITY

Another frequently required insurance is commercial general liability (also called comprehensive general liability, CGL, or public liability). It insures your firm for liability claims for bodily injury and property damage arising from your nonprofessional activities and your business operations. Claims arising from your professional acts, errors or omissions are excluded. For instance, this policy would provide coverage should a visitor slip and fall while in your offices. Because, as a design professional, almost everything you do — attending a planning commission meeting, drawing plans, or observing work at the jobsite — is considered a professional act, there is little risk of a general liability claim. Sometimes, however, you might find it difficult to obtain general liability if you do not also maintain professional liability insurance.

Many coverage endorsements (amendments to your policy) that cannot be added to your professional liability can be provided under your general liability policy. Your clients might ask for endorsements they believe will give them additional protection under your policies, such as being named an additional insured or provisions called *Waiver of Subrogation*, *Severability of Interest* or *Cross Liability*. Depending on the insurer, all of these endorsements may indeed be possible under your general liability policy.

General liability also differs from professional liability in that it is written on an *occurrence* basis instead of a claims-made form. This means that if an insured event takes place while the policy is in force and results in a claim — perhaps years later and even after the policy had been dropped — coverage would still be provided under that policy.

WORKERS COMPENSATION

Workers compensation is a no-fault insurance that protects employers and employees when workers are injured, become ill or are killed on the job as a direct result of their employment. It is paid for by the employer and provides benefits set by law for medical costs and lost wages. Although required by statute in every state, your clients' contracts usually require proof that you carry workers compensation coverage.

Once again, clients may confuse you with contractors and specify endorsements to be added to your workers compensation policy that may or may not be attainable. Before agreeing to provide more than basic coverage, check with your professional liability insurance specialist to be sure you can meet your clients' requirements. Availability of endorsements like Waiver of Subrogation and Additional Insureds varies from state to state and insurance carrier to carrier. You should negotiate your contract language to agree to provide only that coverage which is available from your insurers.

AUTOMOBILE LIABILITY

Clients often require that you provide evidence of automobile liability insurance, whether or not you are likely to use vehicles on the project. If you have a business automobile policy, this is usually not a problem; you can provide a certificate of insurance to your client. Smaller firms, however, in which employees drive and insure their own personal automobiles sometimes face a dilemma because private passenger auto insurance companies often are reluctant to issue certificates or to name your clients as additional insureds. Some firms have solved the problem by having one vehicle — the company delivery truck or the president's car — owned (or leased) and insured by the firm so that there is a business automobile policy for which they can provide evidence of coverage.

NON-OWNED AUTOMOBILE LIABILITY

There is a common companion contract requirement to provide evidence of *non-owned auto coverage*. This is insurance carried by the firm for automobiles it does not own — such as your employees' cars — but are used on company business. It provides liability coverage for your firm in addition to the primary limits carried by the car owner. This coverage often is attached to your firm's owned automobile policy (discussed earlier), but in some states it may be possible to obtain a free-standing Non-Owned Auto Policy. Check your policy or ask your professional liability insurance specialist how to meet this contract requirement.

FOREIGN PROJECTS INSURANCE

Special problems may arise if a project is in a foreign country. Many insurance policies are limited to providing coverage only in the United States (and perhaps U.S. territories and Canada). If the job is in a country where coverage is not provided under your existing policies, separate foreign coverage insurance may be needed for workers compensation, general liability or automobile liability. Professional liability policies often provide or can be endorsed to provide international or worldwide coverage. Check with your professional liability insurance specialist before undertaking any foreign project to determine the foreign projects coverage available under each of your insurance policies. (See *Foreign Projects* for more information.)

Remember, it is crucial that you review and negotiate the insurance terms of any contract before you sign it. You must be sure you can obtain the required coverage, and you need to know the costs of having special endorsements added to your policies. Often, by contract or practice, clients will withhold your fees until you provide the required insurance certificates. If you can't get an insurance certificate that reads exactly as your contract requires, your fees may be held up.

It's just not good business to promise to provide insurance coverages you can't obtain, either knowingly or unwittingly. Lawyers earn high fees extricating people from contract promises they later realize are impossible to keep.

Neither should you give advice to your clients about insurance or surety (bonding) matters, since claims arising out of such advice are typically excluded under most professional liability policies. Instead, refer your clients to their insurance agents or brokers.

If you are interested in learning more about insurance, the *Bibliography* includes information on available resources.

EXHIBIT 9

If you use a contract provision which references an Insurance Addendum listing coverages you intend to provide, you might start with this as a model. In consultation with your professional liability insurance specialist, you should develop specific wording to correspond to the coverages you intend to carry and that are available in your locale.

Addendum ___

To Contract Between __{Design Professional}__ and ____{Client}____ , dated _____ .

SCHEDULE OF INSURANCE

In accordance with the terms of this Agreement, the Design Professional shall attempt to obtain and maintain the insurance policies with coverages and limits as indicated hereon:

☐ **Professional Liability Practice Policy** with limits of $_____ per claim and $_____ aggregate.

or

☐ **Professional Liability Project Policy** with limits of $_____ per claim and $_____ project aggregate. This policy shall remain in force for the period of design and construction (estimated to be ____ years, ____months) but not beyond __{date}__ and shall include a discovery period of ____ years, ____ months, to commence upon substantial completion of the project.

☐ **Commercial General Liability Insurance** with limits of $_____ per occurrence and $_____ aggregate. This policy shall be written or endorsed to include the following provisions:

    ☐ ____{Client}____ shall be named as an additional insured.
    ☐ Waiver of Subrogation.
    ☐ Severability of Interest (Separation of Insureds).
    ☐ Cross Liability Endorsement.
    ☐ Other: _____

☐ **Workers Compensation Insurance** as required by statute, including **Employers Liability**, with limits of:

    $_____ each accident.
    $_____ disease - policy limit.
    $_____ disease - each employee.

☐ **Automobile Liability Insurance** with limits of $_____ per occurrence, combined single limits.

☐ **Non-Owned Automobile Liability Insurance**, including coverage for hired and leased vehicles, with limits of $_____ per occurrence.

The above indicated coverages shall be subject to all of the terms, exclusions and conditions of the policies. Certificates of Insurance shall be provided to _{Client}_ upon execution of the Agreement and prior to the commencement of services by _____{Design Professional}_____ .

EXHIBIT 10

Your professional liability insurance policy cannot:

. . . be written on an **Occurrence** basis.

. . . name the client as an **Additional Insured**.

. . . contain a **Waiver of Subrogation**.

. . . contain a **Severability of Interest** clause.

. . . be written to cover claims beyond the terms of the policy.

. . . cover "any act" of the design professional.

. . . cover the client for his or her own negligence.

Furthermore, you should not agree by contract to:

. . . maintain coverage for any extended period of years (unless it's a project policy).

. . . maintain a deductible not to exceed a specific amount.

. . . provide insurance coverages, endorsements or certificates you are unsure of without checking with your qualified professional liability insurance specialist.

SEE ALSO:

Bibliography
Foreign Projects
Limitation of Liability

INTEGRATION

It is a principle of contract law that a written agreement supersedes all prior contemporaneous understandings and oral agreements.

THE PROBLEM

Unless your agreement specifically states otherwise, your client may claim the agreement was supposed to say something it did not say, or that a last minute change was made with wording that sounded similar to what had been agreed to, but in fact changed the intent substantially.

THE SOLUTION

You and your client should review the final written agreement in detail to assure that it contains all your intentions regarding services to be performed and the terms and conditions of performance. In addition, we recommend you add an Integration clause to your contract. Such a clause generally appears just before the signature lines in the agreement:

INTEGRATION

This Agreement comprises the final and complete agreement between the Client and the Design Professional. It supersedes all prior or contemporaneous communications, representations, or agreements, whether oral or written, relating to the subject matter of this Agreement. Execution of this Agreement signifies that each party has read the document thoroughly, has had any questions explained by independent counsel and is satisfied. Amendments to this Agreement shall not be binding unless made in writing and signed by both the Client and Design Professional.

This clause and all other clauses herein are intended as examples only and should be reviewed and modified by competent legal counsel to reflect variations in applicable local law and the specific circumstances of your contract.

SEE ALSO:

Authorized Representatives
Notices

INTERPRETATION

Most lawsuits against design professionals allege multiple causes of action, or theories under which an architect or engineer is being sued. For example, if a client claims the architect omitted something from the plans or specifications, the architect will be sued for negligence. But the client could also plead breach of contract if the architect had agreed in his or her contract to perform services according to the standard of care — and failed to do so. Furthermore, the client could charge breach of warranty, that there was an implied warranty that the architect would perform to the standard of care. Of course, if the architect had neglected to remove such onerous words as *warrant* or *guarantee* from the contract, the client could claim breach of express warranty too. If the client doesn't prevail on one cause of action, perhaps another will work.

THE PROBLEM

Although the number of causes of action under which you can be sued doesn't affect the total amount of damages, it gives the plaintiff more leeway and creates more discovery and legal expense. It could be likened to scattershot. The lawyers fire off a round or two, hoping that at least one pellet will find its mark — which, in this case, is your pocketbook.

Courts vary widely in their acceptance and interpretation of indemnities and other limitations of a design professional's liability. Some courts may narrowly interpret these protective clauses and apply them under very limited circumstances. If, for instance, your client agrees by contract to limit your liability to $50,000, a court may nevertheless decide this limitation applies only to your negligence. Such a ruling would leave the way open for a plaintiff to sue for a higher amount under a variety of other actions, such as breach of contract, warranty or strict liability — despite the intent of your agreement with your client.

THE SOLUTION

Add a provision to your contract that makes it clear that any protective clauses (limitations of liability, indemnities, limits on consequential damages) apply not only to claims in tort (negligence) but also to any other cause of action except willful misconduct or sole or gross negligence. Such a provision may serve to avoid narrow interpretations by the courts and may help to strengthen your protective clauses too. Consult with your attorney about including contract language such as the following:

INTERPRETATION

Limitations on liability and indemnities in this Agreement are business understandings between the parties and shall apply to all the different theories of recovery, including breach of contract or warranty, tort (including negligence), strict or statutory liability, or any other cause of action. These limitations on liability and indemnities will not apply to any losses or damages that have been found by a trier of fact to have been caused by the Design Professional's sole or gross negligence or the Design Professional's willful misconduct. "Parties" means the Client and the Design Professional, and their officers, partners, employees, agents and subconsultants. The parties also agree that the Client will not seek damages in excess of the contractually agreed limitations indirectly through suits with other parties who may join the Design Professional as a third-party defendant.

This clause and all other clauses herein are intended as examples only and should be reviewed and modified by competent legal counsel to reflect variations in applicable local law and the specific circumstances of your contract.

The above clause encompasses not only you but also your officers, partners, employees, agents and subconsultants, and further strengthens your indemnities and limitations of liability. However, if your client won't agree to include those other parties and you need a fallback position, you could agree to omit reference to your agents and subconsultants. It also might be worthwhile to insert a similar provision in any agreements with your subconsultants if those contracts contain indemnities in your favor.

The provision also contains language that attempts to prevent your client from coming "around through the back door" and suing other parties who, in turn, might sue you for amounts over your limitation of liability. This provision, too, might be difficult to obtain from your client — but it's certainly worth the effort.

As a caution, if your contract doesn't have a limitation of liability or an indemnification in your favor, then you will want to eliminate reference to that provision. Some attorneys suggest you place this Interpretation clause at the very end of a contract so it could be construed to apply to all foregoing clauses in the agreement.

SEE ALSO:

Certifications, Guarantees and Warranties
Consequential Damages
Indemnities
Limitation of Liability
Subconsultants
Third Party Claims

JOBSITE SAFETY

Among the most dangerous of all industrial workplaces, construction sites are treacherous for design professionals, too. Roughly one in every ten liability claims against architects and engineers is related to safety on the site. Moreover, the federal government increasingly seeks to impose substantial and uninsurable fines on architects and engineers for construction worker injuries. Jobsite safety has become such a vital concern that it is imperative that designers understand the issue thoroughly. They must be able to explain it to their clients and, more importantly, conduct their practices prudently by training their employees and avoiding any contract language that could make them liable for safety on the site.

THE PROBLEM

When a contractor's employee is injured, he or she generally cannot sue the contractor and must accept as sole remedy from that employer the state-mandated workers compensation benefits. Of course, these benefits are lower than awards possible through successful litigation against a third party. This inequity can set into motion a search for "deep pockets" and an attempt to impose responsibility on a source other than the employer — in other words, you.

Jobsite safety usually — and rightly — is the primary responsibility of the general contractor because he or she has control of his or her own employees and of the site, and is the overall coordinator of the work. You must do your utmost to ensure that nothing in your contract or your actions can be taken to imply that you will in any way assume these responsibilities. Under no circumstances should you accept a contract clause that makes you responsible for any losses or injuries that occur at the jobsite.

THE SOLUTION

Carefully negotiate agreements so that they accurately reflect the responsibilities you intend to assume. Make it clear to the owner and the contractor that you are not responsible in any way for the means, methods, sequence, procedures, techniques or scheduling of construction — or for jobsite safety. These duties belong with the general contractor. Delete any language in an owner-drafted agreement that calls for your "supervision" on a jobsite. (See *Construction Observation* for more information.) Likewise, do not accept any extreme contract language that calls for you to "assure strict compliance" with plans and specifications. Your observation of the work is meant only to determine general conformance with the design concept and information contained in the contract documents. (See *Stop Work Authority* for a related discussion.) Consider the following clause:

JOBSITE SAFETY

Neither the professional activities of the Design Professional, nor the presence of the Design Professional or his or her employees and subconsultants at a construction site, shall relieve the General Contractor and any other entity of their obligations, duties and responsibilities including, but not limited to, construction means, methods, sequence, techniques or procedures necessary for performing, superintending or coordinating all portions of the Work of construction in accordance with the contract documents and any health or safety precautions required by any regulatory agencies. The Design Professional and his or her personnel have no authority to exercise any control over any construction contractor or other entity or their employees in connection with their work or any health or safety precautions. The Client agrees that the General Contractor is solely responsible for jobsite safety, and warrants that this intent shall be made evident in the Client's agreement with the General Contractor. The Client also agrees that the Client, the Design Professional and the Design Professional's consultants shall be indemnified and shall be made additional insureds under the General Contractor's general liability insurance policy.

This clause and all other clauses herein are intended as examples only and should be reviewed and modified by competent legal counsel to reflect variations in applicable local law and the specific circumstances of your contract.

As noted in the provision, have the client make sure you are named (along with your client and your subconsultants) under the general contractor's general liability policy. This allows you to tender back to the general contractor any claims from an injured worker in the event you are named in a jobsite injury suit. In addition, you should ensure the client has a provision in the General Conditions to the construction contract requiring the contractor to indemnify your client, your subconsultants and you for all claims arising from the performance of the contractor and his or her subcontractors. (AIA A201-1987 General Conditions of the Contract for Construction contains such an indemnity. Refer to Section 3.18.) It is important that you consult with knowledgeable legal counsel and your professional liability insurance specialist to develop such language and to make certain it is insurable.

When you and your client develop your scope of work, carefully define your construction phase services to avoid inadvertently assuming responsibility for site safety, especially if you are offering expanded field services. (See *Scope of Services*.)

Finally, you and your employees must work cautiously and safely. Develop a field manual for your project representatives that establishes standard procedures to be followed if they observe an unsafe condition on a construction site. (Refer to the *PLAN Project Representative's Manual* for an example of these procedures. See the *Bibliography* for details on how to order a copy.) Reinforce these procedures by requiring that field personnel receive periodic training, and be certain to insist on adequate documentation of your project representative's visits to the construction site.

SEE ALSO:

Bibliography
Certifications, Guarantees and Warranties
Construction Observation
Indemnities
Information Provided by Others
Inspection
Insurance
Scope of Services
Shop Drawing Review
Stop Work Authority

LENDERS' REQUIREMENTS

Client-drawn agreements sometimes call for the design professional to cooperate fully with the client's lender and to execute whatever documents that lender might demand. Such vague language can mean tremendous liability problems for the unwary architect or engineer.

THE PROBLEM

A provision that requires you to "cooperate in every respect" with the lender is overreaching and far too open-ended. Imagine what you might have to do to comply with such a requirement!

Even worse is the demand that you sign any document required by a lender. Your clients' lenders may ask you to guarantee the absence of hazardous materials or asbestos. They might require you to guarantee that your design will achieve a specified level of production or result. (See *Certifications, Guarantees and Warranties* and *Environmental and Health Hazards* for more information.) They might require you to certify that your design is in strict compliance with all codes and standards. (See *Codes and Standards Compliance*.) They might demand that you turn over ownership or other rights to your plans and specifications to them. (See *Copyrights* and *Ownership of Instruments of Service*.) They might insist that you consent to an assignment clause that would allow transfer of your client's rights to the lender. (See *Assignment*.) Or they might impose additional insurance requirements on you without allowing sufficient time to consult with your professional liability insurance specialist or attorney as to cost and availability.

Absent any contractual protection to the contrary, your clients' lenders could exert undue pressure on you to hurriedly sign documents you have never seen before and deny you sufficient time to review or negotiate for insurability and liability implications. It isn't unusual to be told that if you don't sign immediately, you could delay the funding of the projects or even cause the loans to be denied, resulting in irreparable damage to your clients. No one should have to submit to this kind of business blackmail.

The Solution

Delete from contracts any language that would require you to cooperate with the lender in every respect or to execute any and all documents the lender requests. If you refuse such a contractual requirement, you are under no obligation to the lender. If you can't delete the provision entirely, however, at least modify it to state you will comply with only those lender requirements that are, in your judgment, reasonable and consistent with the common law and with your agreement with your client. (The common law doesn't require guarantees from you, only that you perform your services in a non-negligent way. See *Standard of Care* for further discussion.)

Perhaps the best solution is an aggressive approach. Insert a clause that would exempt you from signing anything that might affect your insurance or increase your contractual or liability risk. Consider the following suggested clause:

Lenders' Requirements

The Design Professional shall not be required to execute any documents subsequent to the signing of this Agreement that in any way might, in the sole judgment of the Design Professional, increase the Design Professional's contractual or legal obligations or risks, or the availability or cost of his or her professional or general liability insurance.

This clause and all other clauses herein are intended as examples only and should be reviewed and modified by competent legal counsel to reflect variations in applicable local law and the specific circumstances of your contract.

Another solution is to include a provision that would require your client "to append to the Agreement any document the Design Professional will be required to sign during the course of the project." This clause may not be appropriate, though, since your client may not have selected a lender before your contract negotiations and would not have the necessary documents available.

An alternative might be to require in your contract that you be given sufficient time to review and approve documents presented to you for execution by lenders. You should still reserve the right to change or negotiate any language that would alter your risks or insurance cost or availability, as we suggest in the preceding clause.

Discuss these alternatives with your attorney to be sure your contract protects you from having to sign any onerous documents your clients' lenders may put in front of you. And when such documents are presented, review them carefully with legal counsel and your professional liability insurance specialist. You must make certain you are not increasing your risk and that your future insurance coverage is not jeopardized.

SEE ALSO:

Assignment
Certifications, Warranties and Guarantees
Codes and Standards Compliance
Copyrights
Environmental and Health Hazards
Insurance
Ownership of Instruments of Service
Standard of Care

LIMITATION OF LIABILITY

A Limitation of Liability (LoL) clause is an agreement between the design professional and client to limit the amount of liability the architect or engineer will
assume if there is a problem on the construction project. The purpose is simple: to
allocate risk in reasonable proportion to the profits to be derived. In other words, if
the providers of a service obtain a small benefit (their profit) while helping their
clients achieve a much larger one, the risk these service providers must bear should
rightfully be in proportion to their benefit.

To place the theory in a construction industry context, it may be helpful to consider
a simple hypothetical project. An owner who plans to build a $20 million office
building expects a minimum of five percent profit a year over perhaps twenty to
forty years — and to have a saleable building at the end of that time. The general
contractor expects to earn at least five percent of that $20 million — or a $1 million
profit. The architect or engineer who designs the same building expects perhaps a
five percent fee — or $1 million. With luck, and assuming he or she doesn't have to
chase down the client to collect the fee, the designer may realize a five percent
profit from that fee — or $50,000. And yet, should problems develop with the
building, this same designer might have to pay damages far in excess of the fee,
despite his or her modest profit. It is the inequity of this situation that limitation of
liability seeks to address.

THE PROBLEM

The standard of care that governs design professionals asks only that you provide your services with the ordinary degree of skill and care that would be used by other reasonably competent practitioners of the same discipline under similar circumstances. Yet clients often expect and demand perfection from you. If perfection is not attained (and, truthfully, it can never be), litigation frequently follows.

Today's construction projects have a degree of complexity and sophistication of design that involves numerous parties in the design and construction process. Simply put, more things can go wrong, and even though you may not be primarily at fault, you will probably be brought into the dispute.

In our sue-first-ask-questions-later society, litigation — and even the threat of litigation — is so costly that without some sort of limit to the damages, a single protracted lawsuit can put a small design practice out of business. Any firm that continually accepts unlimited risks can expect eventual huge losses and, perhaps, bankruptcy. Even worse, a firm's principals also could face personal bankruptcy in some circumstances.

THE SOLUTION

Your survival in the marketplace may depend as much on effective risk management as anything else. This means a resolute refusal to accept unlimited liability. You need to balance your risk in proportion to your return, and insist that the lion's share of the risk remains with the party who stands to profit the most — the owner.

You can learn to manage those risks by first critically evaluating each potential project and by placing Limitation of Liability provisions in all your contracts. While LoL always is an important provision, we consider it a **Deal Maker** — a must-have — when the risk of a project increases. Jobs involving hazardous materials, asbestos, condominiums, design without construction phase services, renovation or any other work that increases risk and the cost of insurance demand strong limitation of liability language. Keep in mind, however, that since LoL clauses do not protect you from third party claims, they are only effective in claims between you and your client. Although attorneys representing design professionals often recommend clauses to protect them from third party claims, such clauses are not yet tested. Discuss with your attorney whether or not you should try to implement such a clause. (See *Third Party Claims*.)

Obtaining LoL in all or most of your agreements is not an unrealistic goal. True, in the past, clients and even some design professionals have resisted the idea. But the climate is changing. There are now many firms who routinely ask for and get Limitation of Liability clauses in all their contracts. These firms have come to realize — and are convincing their clients — that LoL is a reasonable way to decide the level of responsibility to which an architect or engineer will be held in the event something should go wrong. They recognize, too, that there are many instances in which fault may not originate with the design professional (or may to a very minor degree), but that the designer will most likely be brought into a costly suit, regardless.

Your success in negotiating LoL with your client depends on several factors. Your first step must be a frank discussion of risk allocation concepts — and specifically LoL — to help the owner understand and accept that having something built is a speculative business and that a major portion of risk rightly belongs with him or her. To help your client see the issue in a different light, ask, "How can you ask me to assume risk that is rightfully yours?" Demonstrate that your liability is always limited anyhow: you don't have unlimited resources or unlimited insurance. Nor is insurance the answer. Clients must understand that professional liability insurance carries an aggregate policy limit, is not always available for a particular risk, is expensive, and does not assure future coverage.

You may have more success in obtaining LoL if you use a preprinted contract that contains an LoL provision. Several professional societies have come to recognize this — and the importance of LoL — by including the clause in the body of their standard agreements. Other societies also recognize LoL as an important risk management tool and provide Limitation of Liability clauses as addenda. Whether or not you use a professional society contract, you should develop your own "standard" contract language — one that includes an LoL clause.

An important factor in enforcing a Limitation of Liability provision is to be able to show that the provision was negotiated or at least was negotiable.[1] You and your client should discuss and decide on an equitable limit to your liability. We suggest clauses that provide a blank in which you can insert an agreed-upon liability dollar cap. Some firms believe, however, they have greater success in obtaining LoL provisions if they offer contracts with a dollar figure preprinted in the body of the contract. If you decide to use a preprinted liability cap, however, bear in mind that you may weaken the premise that the clause was negotiated. Many firms choose $50,000 or $100,000 as a preselected liability limit. If your client objects to limiting your liability to this figure or the amount of your fee and demands a higher dollar cap, at least you are negotiating for some limit — rather than leaving your liability unlimited. Any limitation is better than none. Talk with your attorney. He or she can help you decide which is the better course in your jurisdiction.

There are some clients who insist on equating the dollar cap to the amount of professional liability insurance you carry. If you agree to this, make certain the wording reflects "insurance coverage available at the time of settlement or judgment" in the event your policy limit has been eroded by another claim. This provides an excellent opportunity to raise the issue of project insurance with your client. (See *Insurance* for more information.)

Depending on your attorney's advice, and considering your jurisdiction, you may want to highlight the clause in some manner. Some design professionals (or their attorneys) prefer that the clause be printed in bold, large type, capital letters, or with space provided for both parties to initial. Still others include a paragraph just before the signature line of the agreement that states the contract contains a Limitation of Liability clause and that the client has read and consents to all terms. You could also place the LoL clause at the very end of the contract, immediately above the client's signature line.

Some standard form contracts — such as those published by the AIA or EJCDC — have developed Limitation of Liability clauses that are coordinated with the rest of

---

[1] A 1991 California appellate court decision (Markborough v. Superior Court (1991) 227 Cal.App.3d 705) held that a Limitation of Liability clause in a preprinted contract was valid, even though it was not specifically negotiated or initialed. An important consideration for the court was the existence of an **opportunity to negotiate**, which was present in the form of a cover letter from the design professional, giving the client the option to accept, reject or modify any element of the contract. Another consideration was the relative bargaining power of the parties.

their contracts. If you don't use these forms, are using your client's contract, or would like another option, there are several alternatives, beginning with the following:

LIMITATION OF LIABILITY

In recognition of the relative risks and benefits of the project to both the Client and the Design Professional, the risks have been allocated such that the Client agrees, to the fullest extent permitted by law, to limit the liability of the Design Professional and his or her subconsultants to the Client and to all construction contractors and subcontractors on the project for any and all claims, losses, costs, damages of any nature whatsoever or claims expenses from any cause or causes, so that the total aggregate liability of the Design Professional and his or her subconsultants to all those named shall not exceed $___ , or the Design Professional's total fee for services rendered on this project, whichever is greater. Such claims and causes include, but are not limited to negligence, professional errors or omissions, strict liability, breach of contract or warranty.

This clause and all other clauses herein are intended as examples only and should be reviewed and modified by competent legal counsel to reflect variations in applicable local law and the specific circumstances of your contract.

The above clause is a reasonable provision that incorporates most of the features necessary to give you sufficient protection but should be relatively acceptable to your clients.

Some design firms believe that a simplified version of LoL is preferable. Although not as broad or protective as the above clause, it may be easier to obtain. These firms argue that the client who agrees to a basic form of LoL clause has agreed to the principal of reasonable risk allocation and will be more willing to work out problems as they occur on the project. Such a clause might read:

> To the maximum extent permitted by law, the Client agrees to limit the Design Professional's liability for the Client's damages to the sum of $_____ or the Design Professional's fee, whichever is greater. This limitation shall apply regardless of the cause of action or legal theory pled or asserted.

In high-risk projects — condominium design, renovation, PSAs and other jobs that may involve hazardous materials — where obtaining an LoL provision is a **Deal Maker** (a must-have) or in other instances where you are less than comfortable with the client, contractor or other design team members, you may prefer a clause that gives you more protection:

> To the fullest extent permitted by law, and not withstanding any other provision of this Agreement, the total liability, in the aggregate, of the Design Professional and the Design Professional's officers, directors, partners, employees, agents and subconsultants, and any of them, to the Client and anyone claiming by, through or under the Client, for any and all claims, losses, costs or damages of any nature whatsoever arising out of, resulting from or in any way related to the Project or the Agreement from any cause or causes, including but not limited to the negligence, professional errors or omissions, strict liability, breach of contract or warranty, express or implied, of the Design Professional or the Design Professional's officers, directors, employees, agents or subconsultants, or any of them, shall not exceed the total compensation received by the Design Professional under this Agreement, or the total amount of $_____, whichever is greater.

Note that the above clause limits your liability — and that of your subconsultants — to the owner to a certain sum for not only your negligence but also any joint negligence with others. By including your subconsultants, you preclude the possibility of paying for joint liability claims — and may even prevent the subconsultant from later seeking damages against you.

DPIC Companies, as well as ASFE: Professional Firms Practicing in the Geosciences, has been advocating and recommending limitation of liability for more than twenty years. In fact, DPIC feels so strongly about LoL that it offers substantial premium credits to its insureds who implement LoL in their contracts. (If you want more information about LoL, see the *Bibliography* for suggested resources. In addition, your professional liability insurance specialist and professional society also can offer assistance.)

Limitation of liability may not be attainable in every one of your contracts, but it is a worthy goal. The important thing is to start the education process for both yourself and your clients. Remember, no firm ever got limitation of liability without asking for it.

SEE ALSO:

Asbestos
Bibliography
Condominiums
Design Without Construction Phase Services
Environmental and Health Hazards
Information Provided by Others
Insurance
Interpretation
Renovation/Remodeling
Standard of Care
Subconsultants
Third Party Claims

LIQUIDATED DAMAGES

Liquidated damages are a specified amount agreed upon in advance to represent damages for breach of contract, usually due to delay. Rather than try to quantify the actual damages (which can be imprecise, time-consuming or downright impossible), an owner and contractor simply agree by contract that delay in completion of their project will cost the contractor so much per day. For example, an owner and a contractor might agree that if the contractor failed to complete construction of a toy store by November 1, the owner would stand to lose substantial holiday season profits. They could stipulate that $500 per day would represent those lost profits. If the contractor is ten days late in completing the toy store, therefore, he or she will forfeit $5,000 as liquidated damages.

THE PROBLEM

While the use of liquidated damages is commonplace with contractors and subcontractors, professional services do not customarily lend themselves to strict schedules. As a design professional, you provide an intellectual service; you do not provide a tangible product nor perform a physical task. During the proposal and contract negotiation stages of a project, it is impossible to know precisely how long you will need to complete your services professionally and competently. Nor do you have any control over the responsiveness of the owner, the contractor or public agency personnel. It would be unreasonable, therefore, to expect you to accept liability for delays in the completion of your work. (For more discussion, see *Timeliness of Performance*.)

What's more, if you agree by contract to pay liquidated damages, those damages may not be fully covered by your insurance. All professional liability insurers exclude coverage for penalties and fines and any type of liability assumed by contract that is not the result of your negligence. Some insurance companies do not cover any claims for late delivery of plans and specifications. Some cover the direct, provable damages that result from late delivery of your plans and specifications. For instance, if you are able to substantiate actual damages of only $300 a day but you have agreed to $500 per diem in liquidated damages, the $200 balance may be considered by your insurance company to be a penalty and would not, therefore, be covered.

THE SOLUTION

The solution is simple: review all your contracts carefully and delete any reference to liquidated damages in any agreement with your client. Explain that such a provision is intended for contractors and is inappropriate for professional services. And because it is uninsurable, it represents an unacceptable risk to you anyway.

Instead, substitute a Standard of Care provision in which you agree to do what is expected of you as a professional: to perform your duties in a manner consistent with the ordinary degree of care and skill practiced by your peers. (See *Standard of Care* for discussion and specific clause suggestions.) Or you might agree — if absolutely necessary — to a Timeliness of Performance clause, using language that suggests that your work toward an established schedule must be governed by sound professional practices. We repeat one such sample clause below. (For more information, refer to *Timeliness of Performance*.)

TIMELINESS OF PERFORMANCE

The Design Professional acknowledges the importance to the Client of the Client's project schedule and agrees to put forth reasonable efforts in performing the services with due diligence under this Agreement in a manner consistent with that schedule, as provided in Exhibit ___ hereto. The Client understands, however, that the Design Professional's performance must be governed by sound professional practices.

This clause and all other clauses herein are intended as examples only and should be reviewed and modified by competent legal counsel to reflect variations in applicable local law and the specific circumstances of your contract.

We believe liquidated damages are unreasonable and inappropriate for professional service contracts and, because of their questionable insurability, an unnecessary risk for you to assume. Therefore, we regard the inclusion of a liquidated damages clause as a **Deal Breaker.** If a client-written contract contains a liquidated damages provision and you cannot persuade your client to delete it, give serious consideration to walking away from the project.

SEE ALSO:

Consequential Damages
Delays
Standard of Care
Timeliness of Performance

Multiple Prime Contracts

Multiple prime projects are those in which a client contracts with all or most of the consultants directly, rather than using the more traditional hierarchal method of contracting — owner to prime consultant to subconsultants. Although owners sometimes contract directly with multiple construction contractors as well, the focus here is on multiple prime design services contracts.

As projects become more complex and engineering systems increasingly critical, more responsibility rests with the consultants who design them. Owners may wish to retain the best specialists in a given field or ones with whom they have worked before. One way to accomplish this is for clients to contract with them directly, bypassing the traditional prime consultant.

Some consulting engineers, whose role is typically that of a subconsultant, believe that the "multi prime" system makes sense. They may feel a more prominent role in the design process will improve communication among all consultants. If they are brought into the project earlier and get input directly from the owner — rather than having information filtered down through the prime — they reason they can better understand the owner's needs. Some also feel that, because they do not have to transmit their invoices through the prime designer, they may be paid more promptly and might even enhance their profitability by negotiating their fees directly with the owner. (See *Pay When Paid*.)

In some ways, the multiple prime — also termed *separate contracts* — system offers advantages for the architect or engineer who usually acts as the prime. By sidestepping the traditional contracting arrangement, the prime's liability is reduced somewhat, and his or her professional liability insurance premium may also be reduced. There is the further inducement of avoiding the added administrative duties that are part and parcel of acting as the prime consultant. (Refer to *Subconsultants*.)

Unfortunately, some owners choose multiple prime contracting not because of better communications or enhanced quality, but to save money by squeezing down the fees for subconsultants or by eliminating the administrative fees paid to the prime for coordinating the work. These owners are deceiving themselves, however, and may be setting the stage for a problem-plagued project.

THE PROBLEM

If your clients elect to use separate contracts believing the move will save money, they will be disappointed. Multiple prime contracting rarely results in lower project costs to the owner. Whether there are separate contracts or not, the work of the various consultants must be coordinated. And proper coordination of all the designers requires time and expertise to integrate the documents and resolve technical issues. The effort and corresponding fees required for such coordination remain fairly constant, whatever contracting approach your client chooses.

If there is no designated project coordinator, the workscope of each multiple contract must be exceptionally detailed and coordinated with that of every other consultant. Even so, your client may find that the resulting confusion over who is legally responsible for what and the inevitable inconsistencies can be very costly indeed. It could prove to be expensive for you too. If something goes wrong, chances are all the consultants will be named in a lawsuit, and you might spend a great deal of time and money extricating yourself from a situation in which you had no culpability.

If it is not provided for by contract, no one will be required to take the lead in coordinating the design. Nor will other consultants be required to cooperate with the appointed coordinator. With many disciplines working on the same design without a single focal point, details are bound to "fall through the cracks."

THE SOLUTION

There are several alternative approaches. The AIA contracts offer a paragraph for use with the B141 series that addresses a multiple prime contract situation. Paragraph 4.12 of the B511 would put responsibility on each consultant to coordinate his or her designs with the architect. Another school of thought, however, holds that it might be better to designate someone — probably whoever would traditionally be the prime consultant — as project coordinator. If you are to be coordinator, that designation should be spelled out in your workscope and included in your fee calculations. You and your attorney might want to discuss this with your client. If you follow this approach, your client should also agree that all the owner-consultant contracts he or she enters into should likewise identify the coordinator.

If you are the design firm who would otherwise be prime but you are not responsible for coordination, you should obtain an indemnity from your client against claims arising from lack of coordination by others. Consider the following suggested contract clause:

Owner's Consultants

It is understood and agreed that the Client shall contract directly with other design professionals for the following services:

Design Professional Firm   Professional Services

_____   _____

_____   _____

_____   _____

The Client agrees that the Design Professional shall have no responsibility for any portion of the project designed by the Client's other consultants. The Design Professional shall not be required to check or verify other consultants' construction documents and shall be entitled to rely on the accuracy and completeness thereof, as well as the compliance of such documents with applicable laws, codes, statutes, ordinances and regulations.

The Client agrees, to the fullest extent permitted by law, to indemnify and hold the Design Professional harmless from any damage, liability or cost, including reasonable attorneys' fees and defense costs, arising in any way from the services performed by any other consultants to the Client.

This clause and all other clauses herein are intended as examples only and should be reviewed and modified by competent legal counsel to reflect variations in applicable local law and the specific circumstances of your contract.

If your client requires the other consultants to coordinate their designs with yours, you may want to add the following:

> The Client further agrees to require all other consultants under separate contract to coordinate their construction documents with those of the Design Professional, to promptly report any conflicts or inconsistencies to the Design Professional and to cooperate fully in the resolution of those conflicts or inconsistencies.

On the other hand, if your client wants you to take responsibility for coordinating the work of the other consultants, consider this addition:

> It is further agreed that the Design Professional shall coordinate the construction documents of the professional consultants listed above but only for conformance with the aesthetic aspects, space constraints and design concepts as expressed in the construction documents prepared by the Design Professional. The Client agrees to require all other consultants under separate contract to cooperate fully with the Design Professional in the resolution of any conflicts or inconsistencies discovered.

If you or your client decide against naming a project coordinator, it is important that both your work and your contract reflect that fact. Do not assume responsibility for coordinating anyone's work but your own. Make sure your contract also has provisions that protect you from delays by others and faulty information provided to you. (Refer to *Delays* and *Information Provided by Others* for discussions and possible contract language.) Ask your client to review with you the other agreements with his or her consultants; it is critical that all these contracts reflect the same understandings and responsibilities.

SEE ALSO:

Delays

Indemnities

Information Provided by Others

Pay When Paid

Subconsultants

Non-Negligent Services

Sometimes clients will include a phrase in their contracts that states the design professional will perform in a non-negligent manner.

The Problem

The clause may seem harmless, but it is not. We are all obligated to perform non-negligently in whatever we do, or we are subject to damages under tort law. However, by agreeing specifically by contract to perform your services in a non-negligent manner you could aggravate your liability exposure. A negligent act could also be considered a breach of contract — perhaps even a breach of a warranty. In many jurisdictions, the statute of limitations to bring suit for negligence is several years shorter than that governing breach of contract suits. And, lawsuits for breach of warranty are excluded from coverage under all professional liability policies. Why agree to such a clause and expose yourself unnecessarily to greater liability?

The Solution

You should delete the clause and be frank with your client about the liability issue. If architects and engineers could guarantee non-negligent performance, the professional liability insurance industry would be far smaller.

You could go one step further in distancing yourself from this sort of problem by inserting a No Warranty clause. (See *Certifications, Guarantees and Warranties* for more information.) Consider the following:

NO WARRANTY

The Design Professional makes no warranty, either expressed or implied, as to his or her findings, recommendations, plans, specifications, or professional advice. The Design Professional has endeavored to perform the services pursuant to generally accepted standards of practice in effect at the time of performance.

This clause and all other clauses herein are intended as examples only and should be reviewed and modified by competent legal counsel to reflect variations in applicable local law and the specific circumstances of your contract.

SEE ALSO:

Certifications, Guarantees and Warranties
Defects in Service
Insurance
Standard of Care
Statutes of Repose or Limitation

NOTICES

Many contracts stipulate that any notices given to the client are only considered served if sent by registered or certified mail to the address listed in the contract.

THE PROBLEM

While this provision may seem innocuous, it precludes other forms of communication that you may find more convenient or effective. Furthermore, it may fail to stipulate just when notice is considered to have been served: when sent or when received. The difference of a few days can be a major issue in some critical contractual matters.

THE SOLUTION

The best solution is a provision that does not limit delivery of notices to the mails and is clear as to when a notice is effective. You and your client will want to discuss what forms of submittal you prefer. Consider:

NOTICES

Any notice given hereunder shall be deemed served immediately if hand-delivered in writing to an officer or other duly appointed representative of the party to whom the notice is directed, or if transmitted by facsimile to the facsimile number contained in this Agreement or listed below. Notices shall also be deemed served _____ business days after transmittal by registered, certified, express, or regular mail or by {name} courier service(s) to the business address identified in this Agreement.

This clause and all other clauses herein are intended as examples only and should be reviewed and modified by competent legal counsel to reflect variations in applicable local law and the specific circumstances of your contract.

Clients should have no objection to this provision, as it simply helps to clarify notice requirements for both parties under the contract terms.

SEE ALSO:

Authorized Representatives
Timeliness of Performance

Opinion of Probable Construction Costs

Quite often, a client will include in the workscope a provision that requires the architect or engineer to prepare an estimate of project costs. Construction cost estimates are certainly critical planning tools for project owners, but many clients have unrealistic expectations of the accuracy or reliability of cost forecasts provided by the design professional. These clients mistakenly believe the designer can provide them with definitive pricing information.

The Problem

Many clients (and certainly the public) fail to understand that a cost estimate is only an estimate — and not a guaranteed maximum price. The labor market, future costs of equipment and materials, and the actual construction process are all beyond your control. Other than render your professional opinion based on your firm's recent experience, you cannot be expected to provide infallible construction cost figures.

Unfortunately, clients may have other ideas. The result: if your estimates are far off the mark and your clients fail to appreciate the limitations of those estimates, a dispute could ensue, and your clients might claim that critical decisions were made based on your figures.

Without a contract clause that clearly explains the limits to your estimates, your client (and a jury) might not accept the figures you give as mere opinions. If your contract is silent on the issue, a court may even allow the argument that your client had a right to rely on your estimate.

But be forewarned: no matter how airtight your contract language seems, some courts may remain unsympathetic. Depending on the location and size of the project and your firm, some courts seem to feel that if the actual construction cost comes within approximately five to ten percent of your figures, you have made a reasonable estimate. If your estimate varies from the actual construction cost by more than this percentage, you are on much shakier ground, and a trier of fact may decide you had a duty to provide a better figure.

Finally, you should be aware that although DPIC Companies does provide coverage for claims arising from cost estimates based on your designs, many professional liability insurers do not; you may find coverage for such services is excluded under more limited insurance policies.

THE SOLUTION

Your best solution is to not provide construction cost estimates. Discuss the matter candidly with your client and explain that there are many firms who choose not to perform this service simply because of the difficulties and liability issues involved. Instead, suggest that your client hire a professional cost estimator. Failing that, you could hire the cost estimator as your subconsultant, although that would represent taking on some increased risk. At the very least, you would need to make certain the cost estimator has adequate insurance coverage. (See *Subconsultants*.)

A less attractive alternative — if you have no other choice — is to provide the service and attempt to protect yourself as best you can. Don't rely on the courts and even the most tightly constructed contract clause for total protection, however. You must do a good job in giving your estimate. But first, clearly assess the project and your potential client. Are the owner's expectations realistic given the project budget? Will adequate funds be set aside to cover contingencies? If the contractor has been selected (as is prudent) on a negotiated basis rather than low bid, suggest he or she be brought into the planning stages early. In this way, the contractor can provide valuable input while gaining a better understanding of the owner's desires and budgetary confines.

It is also helpful to avoid the word *estimate* in your discussions with your client and in your contract, substituting *opinion of probable cost*, a term that might help clarify the intent. Alternatively, you could define the term *cost estimate* in the Definitions section of your contract. Incorporate language into your contract that states your limitations in providing an estimate. Such a clause might read:

OPINIONS OF PROBABLE COST

In providing opinions of probable construction cost, the Client understands that the Design Professional has no control over costs or the price of labor, equipment or materials, or over the Contractor's method of pricing, and that the opinions of probable construction costs provided herein are to be made on the basis of the Design Professional's qualifications and experience. The Design Professional makes no warranty, expressed or implied, as to the accuracy of such opinions as compared to bid or actual costs.

This clause and all other clauses herein are intended as examples only and should be reviewed and modified by competent legal counsel to reflect variations in applicable local law and the specific circumstances of your contract.

As a further protective measure, attach a cover letter to your cost estimate when you deliver it to your client, reminding him or her that you make no warranty as to the accuracy of your opinion of probable cost.

Finally, you may want to consider offering to your client redesign services as a sole remedy in the event that your figures are less than the construction bid by a certain predetermined percentage (ten or perhaps fifteen percent) — and only on the condition that these services be performed prior to the award of the construction contract. As an example, the following could be added to the clause above:

In the event the construction bids or actual costs exceed the Design Professional's opinion of probable construction cost by more than _____ percent, the Design Professional, upon notice from the Client and prior to the award of the construction contract, agrees to perform a redesign of the project (or those portions of the project where bids exceeded the stipulated percentage). This redesign effort shall constitute the Design Professional's sole responsibility and Client's sole remedy related to the adequacy of his or her opinion of probable construction cost.

By limiting your responsibility to performing this redesign, you may be able to cut off claims of any other responsibility for inadequacy of your opinions of probable construction cost.

SEE ALSO:

Contingency Fund
Definitions
Excluded Services
Scope of Services
Subconsultants

OWNERSHIP OF INSTRUMENTS OF SERVICE

As a design professional, the architect or engineer provides a *service* rather than a product. Construction documents — plans, specifications and reports — are *instruments* of that service; that is, they are the written depiction of the intellectual process that is architecture or engineering. As such, these documents should remain the property of the design professional who prepared them. It is not unusual, however, for clients to insist on ownership. They may want to "own" the designs for one of several reasons: to prevent the design from being repeated on other projects; to facilitate operation and maintenance of the project; or to reuse the design on other projects without involving the designer again.

THE PROBLEM

Unauthorized reuse is the most serious problem that can arise if you transfer ownership of your plans and specifications to others. It could result in a claim filed against you years after the fact by someone who relied on work you did for another project in another location at another time. Worse still, a client who owns your documents could make unauthorized changes which could result in a claim against you. (Refer to *Unauthorized Changes to Plans*.)

Another problem may also arise. When instruments of service are treated as products, defects in them (errors or omissions) may be considered "product defects" subject to strict liability rather than professional liability. (The doctrine of strict liability says that a damage- or injury-causing defect in a product is enough to establish liability, whether or not the producer of that product was negligent in the design or production of the product. Professional liability is based on negligence only.) Thus far, courts have not generally deemed designs to be products, but the current trend is toward liberalizing liability. You are far better off not tempting the courts by appearing to have "sold" your plans.

THE SOLUTION

Do your utmost to retain ownership of your plans and specifications. Work with clients; educate them. If you explain the problems that could arise from reuse under differing site conditions or geographic locations and without your construction phase involvement, your client should understand your concern over your potential liability. If you suspect your client intends to reuse your designs elsewhere without your involvement, you will have to take steps to deal with the corresponding risk. Either refuse the job, get a "gold-plated" indemnity or charge such an exorbitant fee that you can afford failures.

If necessary, you can give your client a reproducible copy of the final documents for use in maintenance and operation of the project. In any case, attempt to obtain a clarifying clause such as the following:

OWNERSHIP OF INSTRUMENTS OF SERVICE

All reports, plans, specifications, field data and notes and other documents, including all documents on electronic media, prepared by the Design Professional as instruments of service shall remain the property of the Design Professional.

This clause and all other clauses herein are intended as examples only and should be reviewed and modified by competent legal counsel to reflect variations in applicable local law and the specific circumstances of your contract.

An acceptable alternative might be to give your client possession of the original documents while you retain ownership; check with your attorney to determine if this would have any legal validity in your jurisdiction.

If your client insists on ownership of documents, it should be possible to strike a compromise whereby you transfer ownership of the final documents to him or her on completion of the project and upon payment in full for your services and if the client indemnifies you against unauthorized reuse and unauthorized changes to your documents. (Refer to *Prototype Designs* for a discussion of designs intended for reuse.) Note that "final documents" means just that and not drafts, notes, sketches and preliminary documents.

A transfer-of-ownership clause may read as follows:

> The Client acknowledges the Design Professional's construction documents as instruments of professional service. Nevertheless, the plans and specifications prepared under this Agreement shall become the property of the Client upon completion of the work and payment in full of all monies due to the Design Professional. The Client shall not reuse or make any modification to the plans and specifications without the prior written authorization of the Design Professional. The Client agrees, to the fullest extent permitted by law, to indemnify and hold the Design Professional harmless from any claim, liability or cost (including reasonable attorneys' fees and defense costs) arising or allegedly arising out of any unauthorized reuse or modification of the construction documents by the Client or any person or entity that acquires or obtains the plans and specifications from or through the Client without the written authorization of the Design Professional.

Another effective measure might be to copyright your materials and grant your client a license to use the design for future projects. (See *Copyrights* for more information.)

SEE ALSO:

CADD
Confidentiality
Copyrights
Indemnities
Prototype Designs
Record Documents
Statutes of Repose or Limitation
Subconsultants
Unauthorized Changes to Plans

PAY WHEN PAID

When one design professional is a subconsultant to another architect or engineer, chances are the subconsultant may be asked to accept a Pay-When-Paid provision. This means that the subconsultant's client, the prime design professional, will invoice the owner (in most cases) for services rendered by the prime and his or her subconsultants, and the subconsultant would then receive payment only after the owner pays the prime.

THE PROBLEM

This type of provision can delay your payments if you're the subconsultant, and give you little recourse. In addition, the owner may become involved in a dispute with the prime, go out of business or, for some other reason, not make payments. Courts generally have held that a Pay-When-Paid provision does not relieve your client (the prime) of responsibility to pay you if his or her client defaults, unless your agreement specifically provides that if your client does not get paid, you do not get paid either.

THE SOLUTION

It seems reasonable to assume that subconsultants hope to be treated by the prime as the prime wants to be treated by the owner. The prime expects to be paid for work done for his or her client; so do you, the subconsultant. Therefore, the best solution is to avoid any type of Pay-When-Paid provision and insist that your standard payment terms be included in the contract.

If, however, your client (the prime) insists on a Pay-When-Paid provision, you should consider seeking whatever late payment penalty you normally require and/or attempt to secure an outer limit by which time you must be paid, whether your client has been paid or not. The clause, which should be incorporated into the language indicated under Billing and Payment, can read:

PAY WHEN PAID

The Subconsultant recognizes that his or her invoices will be presented by the Prime Design Professional to the Owner, and that the Prime Design Professional will pay the Subconsultant the amount due for services rendered and expenses incurred within ____(___) calendar days after the Prime Design Professional is paid by the Owner. The Prime Design Professional recognizes that this procedure differs from standard procedures employed by the Subconsultant. Accordingly, notwithstanding any action or inaction by the Owner, the Prime Design Professional will pay all the Subconsultant's invoices within ___(___) calendar days of the invoice date. The Prime Design Professional shall pay an additional charge of one-and-one-half (1.5) percent (or the maximum percentage allowable by law, whichever is lower) of the invoiced amount per month for any payment received by the Subconsultant more than ___(___) calendar days from the date of the invoice.

This clause and all other clauses herein are intended as examples only and should be reviewed and modified by competent legal counsel to reflect variations in applicable local law and the specific circumstances of your contract.

SEE ALSO:

Billing and Payment
Subconsultants
Suspension of Services
Termination

PERFORMANCE BONDS

Some clients, particularly those in the public sector, occasionally attempt by contract to require a design professional to obtain a performance bond. In most instances, such a bond is intended to guarantee completion of a project by a contractor. Usually it is a simple matter to determine whether or not a contractor has delivered what was required or, if the work is not finished, what additional tasks are necessary. Although such bonds are costly, many owners find them essential because of the financial instability of the construction industry.

THE PROBLEM

Performance bonds are almost never available for design professional services. As an architect or engineer, you do not deliver a product; you provide a service. The nature of this service can be defined only in somewhat general terms, which makes it difficult to determine whether or not the service has been fully completed. For instance, is an error or omission a performance failure?

A surety company is not likely to serve as guarantor of perfection if no such perfection can be guaranteed. Therefore, few sureties, if any, would be willing to issue performance bonds for the professional services you normally provide. Even if available, such bonds would be extremely costly and might not cover what you or your client intend. Furthermore, a dispute may well emerge between a bonding company and your professional liability carrier as to who should provide coverage in the event of a claim — and this possibility only serves to increase your client's risks.

THE SOLUTION

Delete any clause that requires you to obtain a performance bond. Explain to your client why such bonds are virtually impossible to obtain for design professionals. You can remind your client, however, that architects and engineers are registered professionals and remain personally responsible long after the work is completed — in contrast to contractors who can disappear overnight. Such a bond would not only increase your client's risks and expense, but, in reality, would serve no useful purpose.

SEE ALSO:

Insurance
Retainage
Standard of Care

PERMITS AND APPROVALS

Client-provided contracts sometimes call for the architect or engineer to obtain "all approvals and permits necessary to the performance of the services in the contract." Such vague wording could get the design professional into trouble. In some cases, this language is intended to apply only to the design professional's work; in others, it might apply to the overall project.

THE PROBLEM

Keep in mind that it is the owner's ultimate responsibility to obtain permits and approvals. True, architects and engineers normally help their clients obtain permits and approvals for construction by completing appropriate forms and providing necessary data. But, regardless of how helpful you would like to be, you cannot promise to provide something over which you have no control. Approval and permit procedures can be slow, and it is impossible to guarantee the action or inaction of any governmental agency. In addition, agreeing to help obtain all such permits establishes an absolute condition which may be impossible for you to meet. You cannot know at the outset of a project just what will be required, and you don't want to inadvertently agree to an open-ended requirement for any new approvals that might be imposed in the future.

THE SOLUTION

Find out exactly what clients really expect from you by their contract language. Are they referring to permits and licenses you need in order to perform your work? If so, it is your responsibility to maintain your professional and business licenses in any case, so there is no reason to include them in the contract. Or do your clients really want you to assist them in obtaining the necessary approvals for construction to proceed? If so, consider the following:

PERMITS AND APPROVALS

The Design Professional shall assist the Client in applying for those permits and approvals typically required by law for projects similar to the one for which the Design Professional's services are being engaged. This assistance consists of completing and submitting forms as to the results of certain work included in the scope of services.

This clause and all other clauses herein are intended as examples only and should be reviewed and modified by competent legal counsel to reflect variations in applicable local law and the specific circumstances of your contract.

Sometimes additional services are needed — such as special research, documentation and reports, or attendance at more than a specified number of public meetings — for an additional fee. You can address this possibility in your contract clause, saying that you will discuss the scope and expense of these special services with the client before you perform them. Consider adding the following:

. . . This assistance does not include, however, special studies, special research, attendance at meetings with public authorities for more than ___ hours, special testing or special documentation not normally required for this type of project. The Design Professional will provide such special services as Additional Services as authorized by the Client.

Finally, beware of the client who attempts to make your fee contingent upon obtaining the necessary permits and approvals. It is a gamble you needn't take and one that could cost you a great deal of time and money.

SEE ALSO:

Certifications, Guarantees and Warranties
Codes and Standards Compliance
Delays
Excluded Services
Scope of Services

236

PROTOTYPE DESIGNS

Designs that are intended to be built repeatedly have a special set of risks associated with them. For instance, an engineer may design a prototype of a building that will be reiterated many times in different geographic or climatic conditions. Or an architect might design the models for a tract of 500 homes. In a perfect world, the owner would want the design professional involved every time a building is reproduced. The reality, however, is that the design professional may never be involved when his or her design is constructed.

The designer who site-adapts or modifies pre-engineered buildings is also at risk, as is someone who agrees to modify "package plans." In both cases, without specific contract safeguards, he or she may incur substantial liability for defects in someone else's design.

THE PROBLEM

Your liability exposure on prototype designs or the reuse of your plans can be enormous. To put the problem in perspective, let's suppose you are asked to design a prototype restaurant for a new fast-food chain. If the chain is successful, the owner might want to reuse your plans repeatedly all over the country — conceivably hundreds of times on hundreds of sites. Now, imagine your potential liability for a single design error — multiplied dozens or even hundreds of times. If you haven't protected yourself by contract, the possible damages could be staggering. (See *Ownership of Instruments of Service* for more information.)

Unable to provide construction phase services, you are deprived of your most
effective loss prevention tools just when you need them most. Even the best
designed prototype buildings require some code, site and geographic adaption, but
you are not likely to be allowed to provide them. You will not usually be hired to
perform normal project observation nor will you be asked to provide necessary
interpretation of your plans and specifications. (Refer to *Design Without
Construction Phase Services* for a related discussion.) Furthermore, as the owner
and contractors acquire experience with a structure, they could begin to cut corners
or modify your drawings to save money — without consulting you. (See *Unauthorized Changes to Plans*.)

In a related problem, if you design some changes or additions to a pre-engineered
building — such as interior partitions, exterior add-ons or even site adaptation —
you could incur liability for defects in the design of portions of the building not
affected by your work.

Finally, magazines and catalogs advertise numerous package designs, plans for
everything from A-frame vacation cottages to twenty-room mansions. Be aware,
however, that if you put such a design over your title block and sign or add your
seal (perhaps only to help a client obtain a building permit), you might be placing
yourself at risk. The plans could be seriously flawed and the builder incompetent or
worse. You could find yourself assuming liability — or at least having to defend
yourself — for claims of defects in another designer's work. There also may be
problems under your state's licensing laws regarding signing plans prepared by
others.

THE SOLUTION

If you design a structure you know or suspect will be used as a prototype — to be
rebuilt without your involvement — you'll want broad contractual protection. Your
contract should contain a waiver of claims (an agreement that your client will not
sue you) and a strong indemnity for third party claims arising from the reuse of
your documents:

PROTOTYPE DESIGNS

The Client intends to reuse the construction documents produced by the Design Professional under this Agreement on other sites and on other projects. The Client acknowledges that the Design Professional has been requested to provide no construction phase services in connection with any of these reuses. Therefore, the Client agrees to waive all claims against the Design Professional that might be contributed to or caused by the Design Professional's exclusion from the construction phase, and any claims which may, with reasonable certainty, have been avoided or lessened by the Design Professional's participation in the construction phase of any future project involving the reuse of the construction documents.

In addition, the Client agrees, to the fullest extent permitted by law, to indemnify and hold the Design Professional harmless from all damage, liability or cost (including reasonable attorneys' fees and costs of defense) arising from any reuse of the construction documents on any other project or site without the involvement of the Design Professional in the construction phase services normally associated with such a project.

This clause and all other clauses herein are intended as examples only and should be reviewed and modified by competent legal counsel to reflect variations in applicable local law and the specific circumstances of your contract.

Be certain your contract also has provisions that protect you from changes to your plans without your approval. (See *Unauthorized Changes to Plans*.)

PRE-ENGINEERED BUILDINGS

If your client has hired you to specify or modify a pre-engineered building, you need to protect yourself from the inadvertent assumption of someone else's liability. After all, the structure was designed and manufactured by others and you should not be expected to assume responsibility for anything beyond your own negligent acts. Your contract should have a waiver and indemnity against claims arising out of the design, fabrication or installation of any pre-engineered or prefabricated structures.

PRE-ENGINEERED BUILDINGS

The Client acknowledges that he or she has requested the Design Professional to specify a pre-engineered building otherwise identified as a {model number or other specification, if known}. **The Client further acknowledges that the Design Professional will not engineer, design, manufacture, assemble or erect said building and is not responsible in any way for defects or deficiencies in the building. Therefore, the Client waives all claims against the Design Professional arising in any way from the specification of the building or for any defects, deficiencies, errors or omissions in the design, fabrication or erection of the building.**

In addition, the Client agrees, to the fullest extent permitted by law, to indemnify and hold the Design Professional harmless from all damage, liability or cost, (including reasonable attorneys' fees and defense costs) arising in any way from the specification, design, fabrication, erection or use of the buildings.

This clause and all other clauses herein are intended as examples only and should be reviewed and modified by competent legal counsel to reflect variations in applicable local law and the specific circumstances of your contract.

PACKAGE PLANS

To avoid liability associated with "package plans," your best defense is to simply refrain from any such projects. If you do provide such services, however, first make sure that you are operating within the law if you review and sign plans prepared by others not employed by you or not acting under your direct supervision. You should also take drastic steps to protect yourself. Start with a thorough discussion of risk allocation with your client — assuming you have carefully preselected him or her. Include the broadest possible waiver and indemnity clauses in your contract, along with provisions for Limitation of Liability, Attorneys' Fees, Dispute Resolution, Scope of Services and the other **Deal Maker** clauses that pertain to your project. (Refer to these sections for suggested sample clauses.) Insist on sufficient fees and adequate time so that you can check the plans carefully — just as if you had designed them yourself. If all of this is not possible, then pass the job on to someone less mindful of his or her professional responsibilities and survival instincts.

SEE ALSO:

Attorneys' Fees
Copyrights
Design Without Construction Phase Services
Dispute Resolution
Indemnities
Limitation of Liability
Ownership of Instruments of Service
Scope of Services

PUBLIC RESPONSIBILITY

Court decisions have made it clear that design professionals owe a duty of care to
those who could be damaged or injured as a result of their services. This duty is
based on the philosophy that persons or organizations with whom design professionals do not have a contract should nonetheless be able to file claims if they have
been injured or damaged. This is also why a second or successive owner of a project
can sue the design professional, particularly in those circumstances where the
design professional knew or should have known that the structure would be sold to
someone else — as with condominiums or speculative projects specifically built for
resale.

THE PROBLEM

What happens when a client tells you to do — or not do — something you believe
could cause you to violate professional standards, laws, codes or regulations? Your
clients must be made to understand that your duty of care goes beyond that owed
to them as clients. The implications for projects involving public health and safety
are obvious. If your client fails to take action you know is necessary, such as
reporting discovery of hazardous materials, asbestos or PCBs, and you do nothing
about it, you might be found liable or worse, jeopardize your professional
registration. At best, you would have to pay substantial fees for your defense. But if
you do report the situation to building officials, the EPA, OSHA or some other
authority, your client may claim that no violation was involved and your
"precipitous behavior" had caused significant financial loss. If faced with such a
dilemma, you need to be able to take professional action to fulfill your
responsibility under your license and to do so without concern for future liability.
(See *Environmental and Health Hazards*.)

THE SOLUTION

The best solution begins with careful client selection. If you're entering into an agreement worrying about whether or not your prospective client is likely to do the right thing, you may have picked the wrong client.

Know your state and local laws and your professional responsibilities. In virtually all jurisdictions, design professionals are licensed to protect the public health and safety, and that duty overrides any obligation to the client. If you are at all uncertain about your duties, consult with your attorney.

Decide on an appropriate course of action should you discover or suspect hazardous materials or dangerous conditions. First, advise your client of the situation and carefully document your actions. If you make your concerns known in person, follow them up in writing. You may want to suggest to your client that another qualified professional be retained in order to get an independent evaluation. Never knowingly violate building codes, even at the client's request. This could expose you to tremendous legal liability, loss of your professional license and possibly criminal prosecution. Give your client a reasonable amount of time, depending on the situation, to report to the responsible authorities. If your client fails to take the appropriate action, you must do so. Therefore, you need some contractual protection if you must take an action which may be the primary responsibility of your client, but also imposes a duty on you to the general public.

Also, make sure your contract has an adequate Termination clause that allows you to withdraw from the project if you believe your client's actions or inactions are in conflict with your public responsibility. (See *Termination* for specific language.)

The following clause addresses most of these concepts:

PUBLIC RESPONSIBILITY

The Client recognizes that both the Client and the Design Professional owe a duty of care to the public that requires them to conform to applicable codes, standards, regulations and ordinances, principally to protect public health and safety. The Design Professional will do his or her best to alert the Client to any matter that requires the Client's immediate action to protect public health and safety or conform to applicable codes, standards, regulations or ordinances. Should the Client decide to disregard the Design Professional's recommendations in these respects, the Client agrees the Design Professional has the right to employ his or her best judgment in deciding whether or not to notify public officials or take other appropriate action. The Client agrees the Design Professional should not be held liable in any respect for reporting or failing to report said conditions. Accordingly, the Client agrees, to the fullest extent permitted by law, to indemnify and hold the Design Professional harmless from any claim, liability or cost (including reasonable attorneys' fees and costs of defense) for injury or loss arising or allegedly arising from the Design Professional's notifying or failure to notify public officials.

This clause and all other clauses herein are intended as examples only and should be reviewed and modified by competent legal counsel to reflect variations in applicable local law and the specific circumstances of your contract.

Clients may object to being completely in your hands when it comes to reporting or not reporting an incident. They may say that a matter is questionable and a report on your part would be premature, and could result in a costly delay that may be shown as unnecessary. If clients reject your suggestion that an independent expert be brought in to weigh the situation, you could modify the clause above simply by striking "notifying or" from the indemnification, while leaving the "failure to notify" provision intact:

> . . . for injury or loss arising or allegedly arising from the Design Professional's failure to notify public officials.

As a last alternative, you can use a clause that permits you to terminate your work but does not give you indemnity protection for reporting or not reporting certain conditions. Talk to your attorney. You should coordinate any such clause with your Termination provision:

> **The Client understands that the Design Professional owes a duty of care not only to the Client but also to the public and to persons who may later own or use the facilities associated with this project. The Client grants to the Design Professional an absolute right to terminate this Agreement when the Design Professional believes the Client's actions or inactions or the Design Professional's fulfillment of the Client's requests or directives will expose the Design Professional to claims or other charges filed by persons to whom the Design Professional owes a duty of care.**

If your client refuses this provision, consider declining the project.

SEE ALSO:

Changed Conditions
Codes and Standards Compliance
Condominiums
Confidential Communications
Confidentiality
Consequential Damages

Environmental and Health
  Hazards
Indemnities
Jobsite Safety
Permits and Approvals
Termination

QUALITY CONTROL

Some owner-provided contracts require the design professional to have written quality control standards and procedures during the performance of the project. Sometimes a contract will go further and require the architect or engineer to adhere strictly to these quality control procedures and may even dictate that they be submitted for the owner's review and approval. While such conditions probably seem reasonable to the owner, they may put an unreasonable condition on the designer.

THE PROBLEM

If you agree by contract to follow a set of rigid rules and guidelines, you may be changing the standard of care by which you are judged. (See *Standard of Care* for a related discussion.) In fact, you could be agreeing to abide by yet another set of standards and procedures — in addition to the standards of your profession you are legally obliged to follow.

No one objects to the need for well-defined quality assurance procedures. Most good design firms will already have such programs in effect if they want to remain competitive and reduce claims. Your office may have written quality control manuals that you and your staff refer to continually. But such procedures — even if they were developed in-house — are by definition generalized and are written to fit all kinds of situations. They are intended as guidelines, examples of how you might approach a given situation. It makes little sense to try to impose by contract inflexible rules and procedures on what is, in truth, a creative process. Each project you undertake is unique. You cannot know, when you begin a design, what difficulties you will face or what decisions you will need to make. You might follow the guidelines to the letter ninety-nine percent of the time, but ultimately, you must rely on your professional skill and training to make the right decisions. You must retain the prerogative to veer away from "standard operating procedures" and to do what your professional judgment tells you is best for your client or to protect the health and safety of the public.

THE SOLUTION

If a client-written contract requires you to maintain and adhere to written quality control procedures and standards, your best approach is to delete the clause. Find out what your client really means. Perhaps he or she simply wants assurance that you intend to provide quality professional services. Explain that you are already legally obligated to uphold a high standard; the law requires you to perform your services in a manner consistent with the degree of skill and care used by other competent practitioners of your discipline under similar circumstances. (Refer to *Standard of Care* for a sample clause you can offer your client.)

Certainly, it would be helpful if you could demonstrate to your client that your firm is vitally concerned about quality assurance — with a formalized Total Quality Management program, for instance. (See the *Bibliography* for resources on TQM.) Many firms find that having been peer reviewed impresses quality-conscious clients — a side benefit to a peer review's main purpose of improving your in-house procedures. (For information about available peer review programs, contact your professional society or your professional liability insurance specialist. DPIC Companies strongly advocates peer review and offers incentives to its insureds who undergo the process.)

If, however, your client insists that your contract specify that you have quality control procedures, you may agree — with certain limitations. You can agree to have such written procedures. But be sure the provision allows you to use your best judgment as a design professional to apply or not apply those procedures as appropriate. Here is a sample clause:

QUALITY CONTROL

The Design Professional agrees to maintain written quality control procedures. The Design Professional further agrees to follow those procedures to the extent that, in the Design Professional's judgment, the procedures are appropriate under the circumstances.

This clause and all other clauses herein are intended as examples only and should be reviewed and modified by competent legal counsel to reflect variations in applicable local law and the specific circumstances of your contract.

We suggest that you not agree to submit your procedures to your client for review and approval. Quality manuals are "living documents" and are subject to periodic change. If you were required to submit them to your client, you could find yourself locked into a set of procedures that become static instead of growing and changing along with your experience and practice. As a fallback, you might offer to maintain a current set in your offices and make them available to your client in your offices for review at reasonable times.

You are retained by your client to be his or her professional advisor. To fulfill that obligation, you must be able to rely on your best judgment and experience. It is neither appropriate to your profession nor in the best interest of your client or the public to be bound by an uncompromising set of rules.

SEE ALSO:

Codes and Standards Compliance
Non-Negligent Services
Standard of Care

RECORD DOCUMENTS

Design professionals are often required to provide "as-built" drawings and "corrected specifications" at the completion of a project to show what was actually built. Owners may plan to use these documents for facilities maintenance or future remodeling of the structure. Whatever the ultimate purpose, the design professional must make clear that such documents are compiled by the designer based on information supplied by the contractor — information that is unverifiable and, in some cases, unreliable.

THE PROBLEM

Owners often do not understand that Record Documents are created from input over which you have no control. Jurors understand this even less. And while architects and engineers bemoan the confusion, the design community continues to add to the problem by calling such documents "as-builts." To an unsophisticated owner or a jury, the term "as-built" can only mean "as it was built" — or design professionals wouldn't call it that.

THE SOLUTION

Be sure your client understands the limitations of Record Documents and just how they are compiled. Refrain from using the term "as-built" drawings, a phrase that tends to imply "plans without error." Stress instead "Record Documents," a term which is more accurate and can help reduce misunderstandings. Plan to use it in all your contracts, correspondence and drawing stamps.

Suggest it might be more appropriate for the general contractor to prepare (and take responsibility for) Record Documents — especially if you have not provided on-site construction observation services. If this is not possible, make certain the contractor understands his or her duty to provide you with complete and accurate information on the location of all work. (See *Information Provided by Others* for further discussion.)

If your client insists you provide the Record Documents, make sure your contract reflects the source of and responsibility for information provided by others. Consider the following:

RECORD DOCUMENTS

Upon completion of the Work, the Design Professional shall compile for and deliver to the Client a reproducible set of Record Documents conforming to the marked-up prints, drawings and other data furnished to the Design Professional by the Contractor. This set of Record Documents will show the reported location of the Work and significant changes made during the construction process. Because these Record Documents are based on unverified information provided by other parties which will be assumed reliable, the Design Professional cannot and does not warrant their accuracy.

This clause and all other clauses herein are intended as examples only and should be reviewed and modified by competent legal counsel to reflect variations in applicable local law and the specific circumstances of your contract.

Make sure each page of your Record Documents contains a warning stamped onto it. Such a stamp could read:

These Record Documents have been prepared based on information provided by others. The Design Professional has not verified the accuracy and/or completeness of this information and shall not be responsible for any errors or omissions which may be incorporated herein as a result.

There are some alternative solutions. First, you can delete the Record Documents provision from a client-developed agreement but use your warning stamp on record plans and specifications. But if a client insists on deleting the sentence regarding nonwarranty of accuracy, demand to know why and then carefully consider the client's motives. Are you being set up?

If you need to weaken the contract language, include an explanation of Record Documents in the Definitions section of your agreement instead. (See *Definitions.*) You could also strengthen the clause by adding an indemnification that protects you in the event your warnings on Record Documents are ignored. (See *Indemnities*.) Alternatively, you could reword Information Provided by Others to add a reference to Record Documents.

Finally, be certain that your contract addresses the issue of Ownership of Instruments of Service. (Refer to that section for further discussion.)

SEE ALSO:

CADD
Definitions
Indemnities
Information Provided by Others
Ownership of Instruments of Service
Renovation/Remodeling

RENOVATION/REMODELING

In today's market, the restoration or remodeling of older structures makes up a significant portion of total architectural or engineering activity — as much as thirty to forty percent in some locations. However, whether the work is preservation of historical landmarks, adaptive reuse, structural reinforcement or mechanical/electrical retrofit, these jobs are especially risk-prone.

Because alterations work often calls for special procedures and skills not normally required on new building projects, the architect or engineer needs to tread carefully. Archival research, complex testing, detailed cost estimates, conformance to codes and laws, an increased design professional role during the building phase — all require a different focus from that of new construction.

THE PROBLEM

Most difficulties associated with rehabilitation projects stem from a failure — for whatever reason — to understand the existing structure. In virtually every renovation project, you must make some assumptions about the construction methods and materials originally used in the building. Record drawings of older buildings are rarely accurate, and complete documentation is almost never available. Each column or beam can contain an unpleasant surprise and the very real possibility of the discovery of asbestos or other hazardous materials. Few owners are willing to spend the money necessary for preliminary research and testing, yet you are still expected to work with sketchy information supplied by a variety of outside sources — test results, samplings, property surveys, and the location of buried utilities, for example — for which you are not responsible and cannot, therefore, assume accuracy. Assuring compliance with codes and regulations on alteration projects can be difficult and time-consuming, perhaps because many codes were not written with renovation work in mind. And now there are new liability risks to consider. Failure to conform to the new Americans with Disabilities Act could mean being charged with a civil rights violation. (See *Americans with Disabilities Act* for more information.)

Furthermore, you take on an expanded role when rehabilitating an older building. The design and documentation phase for preservation work, for example, is more extensive than that for similarly sized new construction. Increased involvement during construction and added coordination with the contractor are also commonplace. This can expose you to liability problems if you move beyond the normal scope of services and give in to the temptation to suggest means or methods of construction procedures on the jobsite.

THE SOLUTION

Talk to your client. Make sure he or she understands the uncertainties involved in alterations work and the scope of the project. Explain that hidden conditions will undoubtedly affect the work and can cause costly changes or delays. Find out, up front, how much preliminary research and invasive testing your client is willing to fund. Work with your client to develop and carefully define your workscope, with the understanding that if circumstances change, so will your role and corresponding fees. Insist on an adequate contingency fund in the project budget. (See *Changed Conditions* and *Contingency Fund*.)

No matter how unlikely it seems that you will encounter toxic substances on the site, you must plan for that eventuality. We recommend that you always insert a clause that provides for the possibility of discovering hazardous materials on the jobsite. (Refer to Parts One and Four of *Environmental and Health Hazards* for discussion and sample language.)

As yet, there is no standard form agreement for alterations projects. However, the special risks associated with the work mean you should pay special attention to your contract. When working with your attorney to create the agreement best suited to your situation, be sure to include other important provisions. (Refer to the See Also list at the end of this section and those specific sections elsewhere in this book.) Finally, you will want to address the uncertain nature of renovation work. Consider the following:

Verification of Existing Conditions

Inasmuch as the remodeling and/or rehabilitation of an existing building requires that certain assumptions be made regarding existing conditions, and because some of these assumptions may not be verifiable without expending additional sums of money or destroying otherwise adequate or serviceable portions of the building, the Client agrees, to the fullest extent permitted by law, to indemnify and hold the Design Professional harmless from any claim, liability or cost (including reasonable attorneys' fees and costs of defense) for injury or economic loss arising or allegedly arising out of the professional services provided under this Agreement, excepting only those damages, liabilities or costs attributable to the sole negligence or willful misconduct of the Design Professional.

This clause and all other clauses herein are intended as examples only and should be reviewed and modified by competent legal counsel to reflect variations in applicable local law and the specific circumstances of your contract.

See also:

Americans with Disabilities Act
Changed Conditions
Codes and Standards Compliance
Construction Observation
Contingency Fund
Environmental and Health Hazards
Excluded Services
Information Provided by Others
Jobsite Safety
Scope of Services
Termination

RETAINAGE

In owner-contractor agreements, a retainer is often used in lieu of a performance bond. (See *Performance Bond*.) A retainer is usually a fixed percentage (frequently ten percent) withheld from each payment to a contractor to ensure proper completion of the work. Problems arise, however, when a client attempts to impose such a contractor-oriented provision on a consultant who performs a professional service rather than delivers a physical product.

THE PROBLEM

Some clients try to impose a retainage provision on their design professionals. This makes little sense. Is your client technically qualified to say when your work is satisfactory or not and how the retainer will be used to correct deficiencies?

A contractor's work is — and should be — reviewed by someone else for correctness and degree of completion. In fact, it is usually the engineer or architect who reviews the contractor's work. If that review reveals that significant remedial work is necessary and the contractor fails or refuses to correct problems, the contractor can be dismissed and corrections can be made using the retainage withheld from his or her fee.

Your professional work is not reviewed by anyone else on the project. It may be safe to say that clients who demand a retainage from you have not considered how it could be applied. If the retainage is to help offset costs resulting from your negligent performance, negligence would have to be proved first by a competent judicial forum. And if your clients intend to use the retainage to correct all problems with your work, then the client would be attempting to hold you to a standard of performance far in excess of that required by law, and without the benefit of fair legal process.

THE SOLUTION

Any retainage requirements should be deleted from your contract. If your clients persist, however, insist that they identify typical scenarios indicating specifically when and how the retainage would be applied. If the clients cannot do this, or if their examples are unsatisfactory, it may be best not to undertake the project.

SEE ALSO:

Billing and Payment
Contingency Fund
Performance Bond
Standard of Care

RIGHT OF ENTRY

When clients own the building sites design professionals have been retained to evaluate, right of entry is a simple matter. Sometimes, however, clients might have only an option to purchase the property — and that purchase might hinge on the architect's or engineer's studies or findings. Sometimes, too, it is necessary for the design professional to enter a neighboring parcel of land, and permission is needed from the adjacent owners — not necessarily a foregone conclusion if they are not in favor of the proposed project.

THE PROBLEM

The typical Right of Entry clause used by many clients calls for you to obtain all the permits and licenses necessary for right of entry. But these permits may require that the project or land be restored to its original condition following any testing you deem important. The result: not only could you spend considerable time and energy in obtaining the permits, you also assume additional liability just by being on the property.

THE SOLUTION

The cost and difficulty in obtaining entry permits is more properly borne by the client. The best solution may be a Right of Entry clause similar to the following:

RIGHT OF ENTRY

The Client shall provide for the Design Professional's right to enter the property owned by the Client and/or others in order for the Design Professional to fulfill the Scope of Services included hereunder. The Client understands that use of testing or other equipment may unavoidably cause some damage, the correction of which is not part of this Agreement. The Client agrees, to the fullest extent permitted by law, to indemnify and hold the Design Professional and his or her subconsultants harmless from any claim, liability or cost (including reasonable attorneys' fees and costs of defense) for injury or loss arising or allegedly arising from procedures associated with testing or investigative activities or discovery of hazardous materials or suspected hazardous materials on said property.

This clause and all other clauses herein are intended as examples only and should be reviewed and modified by competent legal counsel to reflect variations in applicable local law and the specific circumstances of your contract.

Your contract should have a broad indemnification regarding the unanticipated discovery of hazardous materials. (See *Environmental and Health Hazards* for suggested language.)

The use of an indemnification is important. If you even suspect the presence of hazardous materials, this suspicion could result in rumors that might lower a property's value. Even if your suspicions are incorrect and no such materials are found, you might face a claim from someone who argues that your "overreaction" resulted in a lowering of property values. (See *Indemnities*.)

SEE ALSO:

Codes and Standards Compliance
Confidentiality
Delays
Environmental and Health Hazards
Indemnities
Permits and Approvals
Public Responsibility

RIGHT TO RETAIN SUBCONSULTANTS

During the course of a complex project, it may become necessary for a design professional to retain additional expertise or consultant services not originally contemplated.

THE PROBLEM

When subcontracting restrictions are too severe, it could affect your ability to hire necessary subconsultants. You may have to contact the client repeatedly to obtain consent and prepare extensive paperwork. This slows progress and could create a technical breach of contract should you have to call in a subconsultant in an emergency without the client's prior consent.

THE SOLUTION

Perhaps the best solution is a provision in your contract that specifically addresses the retention of subconsultants and gives you sufficient license to do so. One such approach is to provide a broad list of subconsultants as a part of, or an exhibit to, the contract, thus eliminating the need for prior consent:

RIGHT TO RETAIN SUBCONSULTANTS

The Design Professional may use the services of subconsultants when, in the Design Professional's sole opinion, it is appropriate and customary to do so. Such persons and entities include, but are not limited to, surveyors, specialized consultants and testing laboratories. The Design Professional's use of other consultants for additional services shall not be unreasonably restricted by the client provided the Design Professional notifies the Client in advance.

This clause and all other clauses herein are intended as examples only and should be reviewed and modified by competent legal counsel to reflect variations in applicable local law and the specific circumstances of your contract.

You also can append a specific list of consultants you believe may be necessary to fulfill your work. They can be listed generically ("shall include a construction cost estimator, testing laboratory...") or you can list by name those you commonly rely on for specific functions, giving your client an opportunity to voice any objection.

. . . may use the services of such subconsultants, listed in Exhibit___ of this contract, when, in the Design Professional's sole opinion, it is appropriate and customary to do so. Such persons . . .

Finally, use terms consistent with other clauses in your contract. For example, if you refer to "subconsultants" in one clause, don't switch to "subcontractor" in another. (For further discussion, refer to *Contractual Reference to the Design Professional* and *Subconsultants*.)

SEE ALSO:

Assignment
Contractual Reference to the Design Professional
Extension of Protection
Multiple Prime Contracts
Subconsultants

SCOPE OF SERVICES

A comprehensive scope of services consists of three separate parts: (1) services that the design professional will perform for a basic fee; (2) services that are available to the client for an additional fee; and (3) services that are specifically excluded because the client has refused them or will arrange to have them performed by another party.

THE PROBLEM

Sometimes client-written contracts attempt to use broad, general language in their workscope provisions. They may require you as the prime, for instance, to "provide any and all architectural and engineering services necessary to the completion of the project." Such language makes your services difficult to quantify. Unless your basic services are carefully defined, you may not be able to recoup adequate compensation for any additional services you are required to perform. Furthermore, even under the best of circumstances, it is impossible to know for a fact all the services that might be needed due to changed or unanticipated conditions or required by new codes or regulations. So be wary of any client-developed contract that asks you to state that the scope agreed upon is "adequate for the project."

THE SOLUTION

Work with your client to develop a comprehensive scope of basic services. Help your client define his or her expectations and explain how these expectations can be met. Not only will this step give your client a better understanding of your role in the construction process, it will also give you the opportunity to outline available services of which he or she may not be aware. You can use the basic services lists in the standard AIA or EJCDC agreements, or you may want to develop your workscope from a matrix or checklist. If your contract does not delineate the workscope, you can append your checklist or matrix to the agreement. Whatever form your negotiation takes, make certain you review with your client those services you will provide, those you can provide for an additional fee and those you will not provide.

You and your attorney might consider language such as:

SCOPE OF SERVICES

The Client and the Design Professional have agreed to a list of Basic Services the Design Professional will provide to the Client, listed on the appended Scope of Services, Exhibit A.

If mutually agreed to in writing by the Client and the Design Professional, the Additional Services listed in Exhibit B, appended hereto, shall be provided by the Design Professional. These Additional Services are not included as part of Basic Services and shall be paid for by the Client in addition to payment for Basic Services, in accordance with the Design Professional's prevailing fee schedule, as provided in Section ____ , Compensation.

This clause and all other clauses herein are intended as examples only and should be reviewed and modified by competent legal counsel to reflect variations in applicable local law and the specific circumstances of your contract.

If you do not have a separate contract article on Excluded Services, you should add the following to the above wording:

Services not set forth above as Basic Services or Additional Services and listed in Exhibits A or B to this Agreement are excluded from the scope of the Design Professional's services and the Design Professional assumes no responsibility to perform such services.

Under some circumstances, you may want more extensive protection from liability arising from not performing excluded services. (See *Excluded Services* for a complete discussion and contract wording.)

In any case, make certain your contract has some form of Excluded Services provision as well as a reasonable Termination clause that gives you the right to terminate your services if you and your client cannot resolve such issues as additional services to be provided and their fees. If your client is unwilling to give you a reasonable escape hatch, you should be wary. Beware, also, of client-drafted clauses which ask you to agree or even certify that the Scope of Services proposed will be "adequate to meet the project needs," or use similar sweeping language. If unexpected conditions are encountered, such a provision could leave you open to providing extensive services beyond those you intended for your basic fee. Delete any such wording from your contract.

SEE ALSO:

Changed Conditions
Excluded Services
Termination

SEVERABILITY AND SURVIVAL

This provision combines two simple but important concepts that, although independent of each other, are often grouped together in a contract.

First, it is important to retain in force all other provisions of a contract even if an individual clause is found to be invalid and is severed from the body of the contract by operation of law (in other words, if a judge or a statute renders a provision invalid).

Second, some protective terms and conditions should *survive* and remain enforceable even after a contract is completed or terminated.

THE PROBLEM

If any element of a contract is found to violate the law (even a law enacted or changed after your contract is signed), such as a clause setting a usurious rate of interest on overdue receivables, or an unconscionably worded indemnity, there is a danger that the entire contract could be declared void in some jurisdictions. This would leave you in an untenable position, with no enforceable contract with your client.

Further, unless your contract explicitly states otherwise, some jurisdictions may construe your contract to be null and void once your work is complete and you have been paid. This would negate any indemnities, limitations of liability or other protections you want to remain enforceable after the completion of the contract.

THE SOLUTION

The best solution is a simple contract paragraph in which you and your client state your mutual intent regarding these issues. Because it benefits both of you, your client should have no objection. With your attorney's help, you might include a provision such as this:

SEVERABILITY AND SURVIVAL

**Any provision of this Agreement later held to be unenforceable
for any reason shall be deemed void, and all remaining provisions shall continue in full force and effect.**

**Articles ___ , ___ and ___ shall survive the termination of this
Agreement and shall remain enforceable between the parties.**

*This clause and all other clauses herein are intended as
examples only and should be reviewed and modified by
competent legal counsel to reflect variations in applicable
local law and the specific circumstances of your contract.*

Be sure to list those articles you wish to survive, such as Limitation of Liability or
any Dispute Resolution provisions. Include indemnities in your favor, too, particularly those pertaining to asbestos or hazardous materials and any other protection
you might wish to rely on in the future. Your clients will likewise want to add any
indemnities or protections that favor them.

An alternative to listing individual Articles would be a blanket clause:

**. . . in full force and effect. All obligations arising prior to the
termination of this Agreement and all provisions of this Agreement allocating responsibility or liability between the Client
and the Design Professional shall survive the completion of the
services hereunder and the termination of this Agreement.**

It should be understood that this latter language is bilateral; that is, it provides that
protective clauses favoring the client (you indemnifying the client) will survive as
well as those that benefit you (such as the client indemnifying you and limiting your
liability).

SEE ALSO:

Arbitration
Dispute Resolution
Indemnities
Limitation of Liability
Statutes of Repose and Limitation

SHOP DRAWING REVIEW

Of all the design professional's duties, the review of shop drawings and submittals is one of the most demanding and tedious. Perhaps that's why it is also a task that is often not performed well — with serious consequences.

THE PROBLEM

Because today's construction process is so complex, shop drawings have become a major source of claims against design professionals. These claims can result from both procedural failures (delays) as well as technical failures (not catching discrepancies or errors in details).

In truth, the fundamental problem is often that none of the parties involved (owner, contractor, as well as the design professional) understand exactly where the responsibility for shop drawings should lie. But many architects and engineers continue to contractually assume levels of responsibility beyond those required, review drawings unneccesarily or perform aspects of drawing review rightly the role of the contractor. The problem is magnified when designers give insufficient attention to the timely processing of shop drawings or assign the job to underqualified people. A lack of precision in contract terms and internal procedures and the failure to treat submittal review as a critically important task can prove costly to a design firm.

THE SOLUTION

One school of thought holds that cautious wording on your shop drawing stamp and in your contract can somehow lessen the risk you face when you review shop drawings. The reality is that no matter how carefully you and your attorney craft your stamp and contract language, you will still be held to the standard of care; you are obligated to use that reasonable degree of skill and judgment in performing the review function that other design professionals would have used under similar circumstances. (See *Standard of Care*.) Conservative language on your shop drawing stamp may not protect you. If you call for a submittal, then review and return it to the contractor without objection, a court may well say you "approved" it — regardless of the language you use on your stamp.

Your best course, therefore, is to define precisely your role in the review process and to establish and follow effective procedures for handling submittals. Consider the following suggestions:

1. Seek to limit your responsibilities by appropriate contract language. Clearly and precisely describe your duties in reviewing submittals. Spell out, too, those items for which you are not responsible but which are instead the contractor's duty, such as dimensions, gauges, quantities, weights, and construction means and methods. This language may need to be customized to your practice and the particular project:

SHOP DRAWING REVIEW

The Design Professional shall review and approve Contractor submittals, such as shop drawings, product data, samples and other data, as required by the Design Professional, but only for the limited purpose of checking for conformance with the design concept and the information expressed in the contract documents. This review shall not include review of the accuracy or completeness of details, such as quantities, dimensions, weights or gauges, fabrication processes, construction means or methods, coordination of the work with other trades or construction safety precautions, all of which are the sole responsibility of the Contractor. The Design Professional's review shall be conducted with reasonable promptness while allowing sufficient time in the Design Professional's judgment to permit adequate review. Review of a specific item shall not indicate that the Design Professional has reviewed the entire assembly of which the item is a component. The Design Professional shall not be responsible for any deviations from the contract documents not brought to the attention of the Design Professional in writing by the Contractor. The Design Professional shall not be required to review partial submissions or those for which submissions of correlated items have not been received.

2. Identify shop drawings by type and direct the contractor as to exactly which ones you will review. It may be contrary to your nature as a design professional, but don't yield to the temptation to review more drawings than necessary to protect the integrity of your design. Of course, this will depend on the type of project and your own professional judgment. If you receive uncalled-for submittals from the contractor, they should be stamped "Not Required for Review" and returned at once.

3. Require a schedule of the submittals you will need from the contractor prior to construction and insist he or she adhere to it. Inform the contractor in writing when any delays in submittal may cause delay in your own processing. But as the contractor is expected to stick to the submittal schedule, you, too, must abide by your promised turnaround time. Allow yourself sufficient leeway to perform your own review, but adhere to your promised schedule.

4. Insist that the contractor do his or her job — that all submittals be reviewed and approved by the contractor before being sent to you. Never accept submittals directly from a subcontractor or vendor. If you believe the contractor has not reviewed a submittal carefully but has just rubber-stamped it, and that it contains obvious errors, return it immediately with a note of explanation and insist the shop drawing be rechecked. Keep a record of the errors or discrepancies you find to facilitate review of the resubmittal.

5. Do your job well. Assign people who are well-qualified to check shop drawings rather than the least experienced in your office. Insist on a thorough review. You are generally responsible for checking for conformance with the overall design concept. Is it compatible with the rest of the design? Does it fit and is it coordinated with the requirements of the overall project, that is, that portion designed by you? If possible, have another well-qualified member of your firm double-check the review prior to returning the shop drawing to the contractor. On the other hand, don't assume responsibility that is not yours. If you have not agreed to check dimensions, don't do so.

6. Establish within your firm an effective logging, tracking and follow-up system for shop drawing and submittal processing — and appoint reliable people to maintain it. Document each step of the process in writing, using standardized logs, transmittals and checklists.

7. Use a shop drawing stamp to indicate you have reviewed the submittals. (Two examples follow in *Exhibit 11.*) Whatever language you choose, be certain it is consistent with your agreement with your client and the General Conditions of the construction contract:

EXHIBIT 11

SHOP DRAWING STAMPS

☐ Reviewed   ☐ Furnish as Corrected

☐ Rejected   ☐ Revise and Resubmit

☐ Submit Specific Item

This review is only for general conformance with the design concept of the project and general compliance with the information given in the Contract Documents. Corrections or comments made on the shop drawings during this review do not relieve contractor from compliance with the requirements of the plans and specifications. Approval of a specific item shall not include approval of an assembly of which the item is a component. Contractor is responsible for: dimensions to be confirmed and correlated at the jobsite; information that pertains solely to the fabrication processes or to the means, methods, techniques, sequences and procedures of construction; coordination of his or her Work with that of all other trades; and for performing all work in a safe and satisfactory manner.

{Name of Design Professional Firm}

Date _____ By _____

☐ Approved   ☐ Furnish as Corrected

☐ Rejected   ☐ Revise and Submit

☐ Submit Specific Item

This review is only for general conformance with the design concept of the project and general compliance with the information given in the Contract Documents. Corrections or comments made on the shop drawings during this review do not relieve contractor from compliance with the requirements of the plans and specifications. Approval of a specific item shall not include approval of an assembly of which the item is a component. Contractor is responsible for: dimensions to be confirmed and correlated at the jobsite; information that pertains solely to the fabrication processes or to the means, methods, techniques, sequences and procedures of construction; coordination of the Work of all trades; and for performing all work in a safe and satisfactory manner.

{Name of Design Professional Firm}

Date_____ By_____

8. Insist on a clause in the General Conditions of the construction contract that requires the contractor to provide you with written notice of deviations of any type from the requirements of the contract or from the Construction Documents. Such a clause should state that the contractor remains liable for any deviations unless you review and acknowledge such changes in writing.

9. Work with your client in advance to ensure the owner-contractor contract is consistent with the language and intent of your own agreement with the owner. Review all logs, correspondence, stamps, transmittals and miscellaneous documentation to make certain the language is consistent with your contract and the intent of all parties.

10. As a general rule, don't review shop drawings or other submittals concerning the proposed implementation of means, methods, procedures, sequences or techniques, or other temporary aspects of the construction process. Those are the responsibility of the contractor, and review of these submittals could subject you to responsibility not normally undertaken by a design professional.

SEE ALSO:

Construction Observation
Delays
Inspection
Jobsite Safety
Standard of Care
Stop Work Authority

SPECIFICATION OF MATERIALS

Some products widely used in the building industry — lead-based paint and asbestos, for example — were eventually determined to be hazardous. In most cases, these discoveries came only after many years of use. Before this, and like everyone else, design professionals were unaware of any risk and confidently called out materials thinking they were safe and effective.

When these products were ultimately deemed hazardous, some claimants and their attorneys tried to hold design professionals at least partially responsible for the damages or injuries these materials caused. These claims were tantamount to insisting that architects and engineers should have practiced to a higher standard of care and possessed knowledge in advance of medical science and current technology.

THE PROBLEM

Although it's unfair to be held accountable for specifying materials widely thought to be safe and later discovered to be hazardous, it happens to design professionals every day. And while a designer may, in time, be absolved of liability, he or she will have spent months or years and thousands of dollars in defense. It is, after all, very easy to get into litigation — and very, very tough to get out.

There are two separate, but related, issues concerning specifying building materials. Chances are, you've run into at least one.

First, let's suppose you and your colleagues have been specifying an insulation product for several years that medical science and the current building industry consider effective and safe. You call for its use in an apartment building. Five years after the building is completed, a new study shows the material to be carcinogenic. Can you be held responsible?

Another scenario finds you in a difficult dilemma: Your client insists that you specify a product you feel may not be safe or reliable. Perhaps it's a product (such as asbestos cement pipe) that, while allowable under current building codes, contains material that is hazardous in other forms or applications. (See Part Four of *Environmental and Health Hazards* for a discussion.) Or it might be new material or equipment that, in your opinion, has yet to undergo the test of time. Or it might be a product that, while in general use, has never been proven in the particular application needed for your client. If, against your better professional judgment, you agree to specify a product that later proves to be flawed or dangerous, could you be liable for damages?

THE SOLUTION

Luckily, there are a few measures you can employ to help avoid claims. First, make it a practice to specify only those products and technologies that you know will do the job, that are time-tested and proven in a particular application. Ask yourself: What would other reasonable design professionals do in these circumstances? (Refer to *Public Responsibility* and *Standard of Care* for related discussions.) What's more, you should try to avoid any product that has even a hint of potential health or safety hazard associated with it.

If your client insists that you specify an item which, although not life-threatening, is a product with which you are not comfortable — a question of quality or ease of maintenance or operation, for instance — put your objections to your client in writing. If he or she overrules you, protect yourself by having the client confirm this in writing. If the item in question involves health or safety issues, however, it is another matter altogether. If you cannot convince your client of the possible risks, you must look to the termination provisions of your contract rather than endanger the life or health of anyone. (See *Termination*.)

If your client wants you to call for a new product or one with which you are unfamiliar, do your research. Your goal is to be able to demonstrate that you made a reasonable professional effort to explore the suitability and reliability of the product. Collect brochures, product specification sheets, warranties, and guarantees from the manufacturer and keep them for your records. Document your conversations with the suppliers and your client regarding the product, including any reservations you might have raised. Require the manufacturers, suppliers, and installers to give you assurances that the product is suitable for the intended application. Ask appropriate field representatives of the manufacturer and supplier to be present during the installation to ensure that their product is installed properly and according to their specifications.

You can address these issues in your contract with a provision that spells out and limits your responsibility. We offer a sample clause:

SPECIFICATION OF MATERIALS

The Client understands and agrees that products or building materials which are permissible under current building codes and ordinances may, at some future date, be banned or limited in use in the construction industry because of presently unknown hazardous characteristics. The Design Professional shall endeavor, during the term of this Agreement, to inform the Client of any product or material specified for this project which the Design Professional becomes aware is a known or suspected health or safety hazard. The Client agrees that if the Client directs the Design Professional to specify any product or material, after the Design Professional has informed the Client that such product or material may not be suitable or may embody characteristics that are suspected of causing or may cause the product or material to be considered a hazardous substance in the future, the Client waives all claims as a result thereof against the Design Professional. The Client further agrees that if any product or material specified for this project by the Design Professional shall, at any future date be suspected or discovered to be a health or safety hazard, then the Client shall waive all claims as a result thereof against the Design Professional.

In addition, the Client agrees, to the fullest extent permitted by law, to indemnify and hold the Design Professional harmless from any damage, liability or cost (including reasonable attorneys' fees and defense costs) arising in any way from the specification or use of any products or materials which, at any future date, become known or suspected health or safety hazards, whether unknown to the Design Professional during the term of this Agreement or of which the Design Professional has warned the Client, excepting only those damages, liabilities or costs attributable to the sole negligence or willful misconduct of the Design Professional.

This clause and all other clauses herein are intended as examples only and should be reviewed and modified by competent legal counsel to reflect variations in applicable local law and the specific circumstances of your contract.

Make sure you coordinate any such provision with your Codes and Standard Compliance clause, as well as with the provision you have concerning asbestos. (See *Environmental and Health Hazards.*)

SEE ALSO:

Codes and Standards Compliance
Environmental and Health Hazards
Public Responsibility
Standard of Care
Termination

STANDARD OF CARE

What was the standard of care? Was it met? These are the first questions asked when a design professional is accused of negligence. The legal interpretation of the professional standard of care, however, may vary widely from the public's perception — and a client's expectations.

All that is expected or required of design professionals is that they render their services with the ordinary degree of skill and care that would be used by other reasonably competent practitioners of the same discipline under similar circumstances — taking into consideration the contemporary state of the art and geographic idiosyncrasies. This concept dates from English Common Law doctrine, which held that the public had the right to expect that those providing services would do so in a reasonably careful and prudent manner, as tested or established by the actions of one's own peers under like circumstances. Nowhere in this doctrine or definition is there any mention of "perfection." Being perfect isn't contemplated or even required for design professionals. The only test is the quality of the design professional's actions: Are his or her actions reasonable, normal and prudent under the given circumstances?

THE PROBLEM

Perhaps because architecture and engineering are perceived as exacting professions or sciences, the public has difficulty acknowledging your potential for human error. Clients, too, have expectations, sometimes unrealistic, of you as a design professional — and these can subject you to liability claims when they are not met.

Some clients will attempt in their contracts to change the standard of care language to require architects or engineers to "perform to the highest standard of practice." If you accept such a clause — or any language that seeks to raise the customary standard — you are agreeing to be judged by far more than the ordinary standard of practice. This increases your risk, and your professional liability insurance will not cover you for that increased exposure.

You also may be leaving yourself open to heightened risk and difficulty in negotiating realistic contract terms with your client if you tend to "puff" your firm's abilities in superior terms ("the best" or "most qualified") in your promotional literature or project marketing proposals.

THE SOLUTION

While it's true that most design professionals strive for perfection in their work, it is also true that perfection is impossible to attain. Nor is it expected of you under the law: you are not required to be perfect. In fact, the perfect set of plans has yet to be produced by a design firm. Your best approach is to ensure that your client has realistic expectations of you and your services. Tell your client that perfection is unattainable at any price.

Another important measure is to have a contract clause that defines the standard of care to which you will perform. If your client drafts a contract clause that purports to raise the standard of care to a higher level, you must delete the offending words and revise the standard back to an "ordinary" or "normal" or "reasonable" level. Consider the following:

STANDARD OF CARE

Services provided by the Design Professional under this Agreement will be performed in a manner consistent with that degree of care and skill ordinarily exercised by members of the same profession currently practicing under similar circumstances.

This clause and all other clauses herein are intended as examples only and should be reviewed and modified by competent legal counsel to reflect variations in applicable local law and the specific circumstances of your contract.

Should you feel it necessary or helpful, you may want to consider offering to correct defective services without an additional fee. Note, however, this offer does not include any of the costs to perform construction or to add items that may have been omitted from the original design. You might add to the previous clause:

> . . . similar circumstances. Upon notice to the Design Professional and by mutual agreement between the parties, the Design Professional will correct those services not meeting such a standard without additional compensation.

And you can go even further. You can attempt to insert language in the General Conditions of the Owner-Contractor contract (the A201, if you are using AIA documents) that sets reasonable expectations of the design professional for both the owner and the contractor, making it clear that the instruments of service may well contain conflicts, errors, omissions and the like. (See *Appendix II* for suggested language.)

You should attempt to add a Contingency Fund provision to your contract or, if there is going to be a contingency fund in the owner-contractor agreement, you might attempt to have included in the list of contingencies those costs resulting from discrepancies in your design documents. (See *Contingency Fund*.)

SEE ALSO:

Appendix II
Codes and Standards Compliance
Contingency Fund
Defects in Service
Non-Negligent Services

Statutes of
Repose or Limitation

Some forty-five states have statutes of limitation or statutes of repose that establish a maximum time period during which lawsuits of a particular kind can be brought against another party. The difference between the two can be important. Both limit the time for making a claim. However, a statute of limitation is triggered by the date of injury or damage. Under a statute of repose, the time begins to run upon a certain event — often "substantial completion." Most of the states that have such statutes applicable to the construction industry have statutes of repose. They vary widely as to what and to whom they apply, what the "trigger" or starting date is, and the time limits applicable to various types of claims.

The Problem

Every design professional confronts a similar dilemma: "How long must I continue to be responsible for my projects? When, if ever, can I rest easy — even retire — without the threat of liability hanging over me?"

Because the wording and interpretation of the statutes may vary, and because most construction-related statutes of repose have been challenged in court (some successfully), simply relying on current legal or legislative whims makes it difficult to manage your liability exposure. For how much and for how long should you insure the risk? What fee should you charge to compensate for that risk? It is difficult to know when you're "off the hook" if you cannot anticipate whether or not a particular statute (if one even exists in your state) may bar a potential claim.

THE SOLUTION

You don't have to accept liability that extends into infinity. Just as you negotiate your scope for a project, so, too, can you negotiate to limit your liability exposure — as to time periods as well as dollar limits. (See *Limitation of Liability*.) It is certainly possible to establish by contract your own time bar to legal action, even if your state legislature has not done so — or has failed to do so satisfactorily. While it will not affect third-party claims, you and your client can set your own ground rules for claims against each other by establishing in your agreement both the period of time in which the claim can be made and when that period begins. A clause that accomplishes both could read as follows:

TIME BAR TO LEGAL ACTION

All legal actions by either party against the other arising out of or in any way connected with the services to be performed hereunder shall be barred and under no circumstances shall any such claim be initiated by either party after _____ (___) years have passed from the date of issuance of the Certificate of Completion, unless the Design Professional's services shall be terminated earlier, in which case the date of termination of this Agreement shall be used.

This clause and all other clauses herein are intended as examples only and should be reviewed and modified by competent legal counsel to reflect variations in applicable local law and the specific circumstances of your contract.

You and your client can select an appropriate point at which the time period begins, such as the date of issue of the final certificate for payment, completion of construction phase services or another date of your choosing. The length of time you select must be reasonable and must not be longer than that established by local law — which could create an insurance problem if you extended your liability. Check with your attorney and your professional liability insurance specialist on this point. If the project is insured by a project policy, you may want to tie the time period to the policy's Extended Discovery Period that begins upon substantial completion of the project. (See *Insurance*.)

It is important to synchronize, if possible, the starting dates of all time periods (contractor's warranty, time bar to legal action and any other notice periods) by using the same trigger date for all parties involved in the project. In particular, make certain that the General Conditions of the construction contract reflect that date. The filing of the Notice of Substantial Completion is the date frequently used for this purpose.

SEE ALSO:

Codes and Standards Compliance
Definitions
Indemnities
Insurance
Limitation of Liability
Severability and Survival
Standard of Care
Third Party Claims

Stop Work Authority

Some clients want to give the design professional contractual authority — and responsibility — to reject the work of a contractor or to stop the work altogether if corrections are not made.

The Problem

If you reject or stop work, you create an immediate exposure for yourself. Having the right to stop work can be and often is construed as having the duty to stop work. Several liability issues arise. For instance, if you have a duty to stop work because of poor construction quality, might you not also have a duty to stop work if jobsite safety is in question? And who is responsible for consequential damages if delays result from your stop-work order?

The economic impact of stopping work on a project can be massive when you take into account all the possible costs of mobilization, equipment expenses and delay claims. A client or contractor who questions the wisdom of your stop-work order could very well sue you for monumental costs associated with such delays.

Perhaps even more important, the contractual right to stop work is a significant factor in determining whether you might be subject to civil, criminal or OSHA penalties if a construction worker is injured.

The Solution

Given everything at stake, the owner — and only the owner — should make the decision to stop work. Delete any client-provided contract clause that gives you such stop-work authority. You can, however, with proper contractual protection, reject portions of the work that do not, based on your observations, conform to your plans and specifications.

Be certain you have a clause in your agreement that clearly states what your responsibilities are. Consider the following example:

REJECTION OF THE WORK

The Design Professional shall have the authority to reject any work of the contractor which is not, in the professional judgment of the Design Professional, in accordance with the plans, specifications and other construction documents. Neither this authority nor the good faith judgment to reject or not reject any such work shall subject the Design Professional to any liability or cause of action on behalf of the contractor, subcontractors or any other suppliers or persons performing portions of the work on this project.

This clause and all other clauses herein are intended as examples only and should be reviewed and modified by competent legal counsel to reflect variations in applicable local law and the specific circumstances of your contract.

If you and your attorney feel you need stronger protection, you can seek an indemnity from your client and require him or her to insert a similar provision in the owner-general contractor agreement. (See *Indemnities*.)

Bear in mind that there is always some risk involved when you reject specific parts of the contractor's work because you believe the work does not conform to your plans and specifications. However, the courts have generally upheld the authority of the design professional to reject work — so long as it is based on a good faith professional opinion.

If you want even more protection — and if you can get your client to agree to it — consider changing "rejection" to "recommend rejection" in the above clause. With this approach, it would be up to the client to reject the work. You can give your client all the input needed along with your recommendations to reject portions of the work. But remember, the right to stop work — and the awesome responsibility it entails — must remain squarely on the owner's shoulders.

SEE ALSO:

Claims Arbiter Service
Confidential Communications
Consequential Damages
Construction Observation

Delays
Indemnities
Inspection
Jobsite Safety

SUBCONSULTANTS

Depending on the size and complexity of a project, it is not unusual to require the services of many experts in a variety of disciplines on the design team. As technologies evolve, in addition to the subconsultants traditionally employed, specialists in fields as diverse as vertical transportation, acoustical engineering, environmental analysis, security, communications, waste handling, lighting and a host of other professions may be required. While there are times when these consultants contract directly with the owner of a project, most often a prime design professional will subcontract with these consultants. (See *Multiple Prime Contracts*.)

THE PROBLEM

It's astonishing how many subconsulting arrangements continue to be performed without written contracts. It is a dangerous practice whether you are the prime or the subconsultant. No matter how competent the other party and no matter how long-standing your working relationship, if you have only a verbal agreement, you are both taking an enormous risk. Should something go wrong, your duties, fees and rights are not spelled out.

A second problem is the cost — in both staff time and direct legal expense — of having to defend yourself if a claim arises and you are named because of something your prime or subconsultant did wrong. As the prime, you have vicarious liability for the negligence of your subconsultants — whom you selected and for whose services you are responsible. As a subconsultant, you could be named in an action against the prime. In either event, if you have done nothing wrong, it is unfair to have to spend large sums to defend yourself because of someone else's error or omission.

THE SOLUTION

Many seasoned prime consultants recommend that you develop a group of experienced specialists in various fields. Your goal is to cultivate a long-term relationship with this circle of consultants upon whom you will call again and again. Look for people who have performed consistently and well, who have standards for design quality and efficiency similar to yours. You want consultants who stay on top of their discipline and are creative in their problem solving approaches.

Likewise, if you are a subconsultant, it is in your best interest to develop a long-term affiliation with a prime design professional with whom you work well and whose work you respect. Both of you will benefit from such an association. You develop a better understanding of each other's requirements and procedures; communication is easier with someone with whom you have worked before.

Such a long-term relationship also helps resolve disputes and encourages better cooperation. If you both hope to work together on future projects — if the prime knows he or she can rely on the quality and productivity of the sub; if the sub knows he or she can expect a steady stream of revenues through the prime — you both have incentive to cooperate and to work out any problems that arise.

Long-term associations also make it easier to obtain fair, written agreements for every job. If you do many projects together, you could develop a single master contract with your prime or subconsultant (annually or longer) and then simply use individual work orders that detail the workscope for each project. It also means the basic terms of your agreement don't change; you always know what to expect of each other.

In any case, whether it's multiple projects involving the same prime and subconsultant or a one-time project, we strongly recommend that you do not undertake a project without a written agreement signed by both of you.

In these contracts, there are two important points you should address. First, you should always include an indemnity that is both fair and insurable. We recommend you use a mutual indemnity that gives both of you equal protection. If there is a lawsuit for negligence arising out of the project, you both will almost certainly be named as defendants. Even if you are exonerated, the expense of defending yourself will likely consume your insurance deductible (if you are insured), as well as your time and staff costs — a considerable sum. By providing for mutual indemnity based on comparative fault, you are saying that you will reimburse the other party to the extent your fault (negligence) exceeds his or her fault. As a practical matter, this will only be determined if the claim eventually is decided by a court. But it is a way to recoup your legal and defense costs if you are comparatively blameless. (Please refer to *Indemnities* for a detailed discussion.) We repeat a suggested provision here:

INDEMNIFICATION

The Design Professional and the Subconsultant mutually agree, to the fullest extent permitted by law, to indemnify and hold each other harmless from any and all damage, liability or cost (including reasonable attorneys' fees and costs of defense) arising from their own negligent acts, errors or omissions in the performance of their services under this Agreement, to the extent that each party is responsible for such damages and losses on a comparative basis of fault.

This clause and all other clauses herein are intended as examples only and should be reviewed and modified by competent legal counsel to reflect variations in applicable local law and the specific circumstances of your contract.

Second, require in your contract that each of you will maintain and furnish proof of appropriate insurance to the other. (Refer to *Insurance* for a discussion, and talk with your professional liability insurance specialist about what coverages and limits to specify.) Whether on an annual or individual project basis, your agreement should require each of you to provide to the other certificates of insurance that show the coverages you carry.

There are several other provisions you will need to discuss and negotiate. For instance, who will retain ownership of the documents? (See *Copyrights* and *Ownership of Instruments of Service* for more discussion.) How will you handle payment? (Refer to *Billing and Payment* and *Pay When Paid*.) Will the subconsultant perform construction observation on his or her designs? (See *Construction Observation* and *Design Without Construction Phase Services*.)

Whether you are a prime or subconsultant, it is worthwhile to develop, with the help of a knowledgeable attorney — and this book — a standard subconsulting contract form with which you are comfortable. You can start with one of the professional association subcontract forms or develop a form of your own. As a starting point for negotiation, it is best to offer your own preferred contract. Remember that your goal — in both your business and contractual relationships — is to arrive at an arrangement that is reasonable and fair and allows each of you to reach your objectives.

One last note: If you are a prime design professional, we recommend you pass through to your subconsultants any liability protections (such as indemnities and limitations of liability) that you are able to obtain from your client. This can be done in one of a variety of ways. First, in your agreement with your client, you can include your subconsultants among the parties to be indemnified or whose liability is be limited. (Refer to *Indemnities* and *Limitation of Liability*.) Second, you can include in your subconsulting agreements protective language similar to that which you obtain in your prime contract with your client. Third, you can have a general provision in your prime contract that extends all protective measures to your subconsultants. (See *Extension of Protection*.)

SEE ALSO:

Billing and Payment
Construction Observation
Copyrights
Design Without Construction Phase Services
Extension of Protection
Indemnities
Insurance
Multiple Prime Contracts
Ownership of Instruments of Service
Pay When Paid
Right to Retain Subconsultants
Scope of Services
Unauthorized Changes to Plans

SUPPLANTING ANOTHER DESIGN PROFESSIONAL

From time to time, one design professional will replace another on a project, either to complete work already started or to take on the next element of service, such as construction observation.

THE PROBLEM

The interruption of a design professional's service can cause serious difficulties and liability exposure for both the architect or engineer who leaves a project and the supplanting designer.

If you are replaced mid-project, you lose control over the future of your own work, leaving someone else to follow through on design decisions you have made. Similarly, if you are the replacement design professional, you, too, are working at a disadvantage: the design professional who preceded you has an understanding of details that cannot be totally conveyed through plans or specifications, whether they are complete or not. Some details are bound to fall through the cracks. Certainly, all of the original design will have to be reviewed and evaluated. Absent a discussion with your predecessor, you will be forced to make numerous assumptions, creating substantial risk. If problems arise, there will be a question as to who is at fault. It is possible, too, that the very fact you are supplanting another architect or engineer could indicate that you are walking into a problem-plagued project.

THE SOLUTION

If you are the original architect or engineer on a project, consider using contract language that protects you if your work is completed by another. Such language could be as follows:

REPLACEMENT OF THE
DESIGN PROFESSIONAL

If the Design Professional for any reason does not complete all the services contemplated by this Agreement, the Design Professional cannot be responsible for the accuracy, completeness or workability of the contract documents prepared by the Design Professional if used, changed or completed by the Client or by another party. Accordingly, the Client agrees, to the fullest extent permitted by law, to indemnify and hold the Design Professional harmless from any claim, liability or cost (including reasonable attorneys' fees and defense costs) for injury or loss arising or allegedly arising from such use, completion or any unauthorized changes made by any party to any contract documents prepared by the Design Professional.

This clause and all other clauses herein are intended as examples only and should be reviewed and modified by competent legal counsel to reflect variations in applicable local law and the specific circumstances of your contract.

Check with your attorney. The above clause could be a separate provision or incorporated into Suspension and/or Termination wording. (See *Suspension* and *Termination*.)

On the other hand, if you are the supplanting architect or engineer, explain to your client the critical liability issues involved. Suggest that you make an evaluation of the partially completed work on a time and materials basis. Seek the client's permission to discuss issues with your predecessor before you accept the work, and insist on an indemnity for claims arising from any services performed by the prior design professional. (See *Indemnities*.) Make certain, too, that your contract has an indemnification for Information Provided by Others. (See that clause for suggested language.)

If your client objects or forbids you to consult with a previously retained design professional, chances are the other design professional knows something the client does not want you to know — or is owed money. No matter what indemnification may be available, you should strongly consider walking away from the project or at least speaking informally with the designer you are replacing, particularly if he or she is an individual you respect as a competent professional.

SEE ALSO:

Assignment
Construction Observation
Extension of Protection
Indemnities
Information Provided by Others
Subconsultants
Suspension
Termination

SUSPENSION OF SERVICES

There are times when a project needs to be suspended or delayed during design or construction — for reasons of client convenience, funding delays, regulatory changes or even natural disasters or strikes. If the interruption lasts for more than a few days, however, the design firm will incur extra expenses in stopping and restarting services. It may become necessary to reassign staff, reschedule other projects and perhaps notify municipal agencies. If the suspension becomes protracted, the owner and designer need a clear understanding: How long should a suspension continue before the design professional is entitled to additional fees? For what costs is the designer entitled to reimbursement? If the suspension is even more lengthy, at what point can the design professional terminate the contract?

On the other hand, the design professional should also have the right to suspend services for cause, especially a client's breach of certain contract terms. Breach of nonessential contract terms may not legally entitle a party to terminate an agreement but, in most states, would be sufficient grounds for suspension until the breach is corrected.

THE PROBLEM

Stop and start projects cause big headaches for design firms. If you must significantly alter your schedules and reassign personnel and facilities, you lose continuity, efficiency and profitability. A suspension could impact other projects for other clients. If the project sits suspended for a long period, memories fade, details may be lost, and it takes more time to get staff back up to speed. Unless your contract provides for it, you may not be compensated for expenses incurred in the interruption and resumption of your services.

Absent some specific contract provision, you might not be legally entitled to terminate if the suspension goes on too long. You must not allow yourself to be "put on hold" indefinitely and then be expected to resume services at the snap of a client's finger, under the original terms, fees and schedule. (See *Termination* for a related discussion.)

Realize, too, that if your contract has a fixed schedule or completion date, you could be held to that schedule if you do not provide for an extension of time based on any suspension of the project. (See *Timeliness of Performance* for a discussion.)

Finally, unless your contract has some "teeth" to help you enforce certain client duties — especially payment provisions — you may have little recourse if your client defaults. Laws vary from state to state as to what constitutes a sufficient breach of contract by your client to entitle you to terminate the contract outright. To allow for these variations, you need the right to at least suspend your services if timely payment is not made — without breaching the contract yourself or incurring liability for delay. If the nonpayment continues for a sufficient time after you have made demand and given proper notice of the breach, you may be entitled to terminate, but, in the meantime, at least you will not have added to your receivables. (Refer to *Billing and Payment* for a related discussion and suggested contract clauses.)

The Solution

Add a provision to your agreement that gives your client the right to suspend the project for a reasonable but defined length of time. After that, you should be entitled to an equitable adjustment in fees to compensate for expenses caused by the interruption and resumption of your services. Also provide for an adjustment to your completion date for any time lost due to a suspension. If the project is suspended for an unreasonable period, you should have the right to terminate your contract.

In addition, give yourself the right to suspend your services without risk or liability for delay in the event of nonpayment of your fees, or for any other breach by your client of terms you consider critical to the progress of your services. Here is a sample Suspension provision:

SUSPENSION OF SERVICES

If the project is suspended for more than thirty (30) calendar days in the aggregate, the Design Professional shall be compensated for services performed and charges incurred prior to receipt of notice to suspend and, upon resumption, an equitable adjustment in fees to accommodate the resulting demobilization and remobilization costs. In addition, there shall be an equitable adjustment in the project schedule based on the delay caused by the suspension. If the project is suspended for more than ninety (90) calendar days in the aggregate, the Design Professional may, at his or her option, terminate this Agreement upon giving notice in writing to the Client.

If the Client fails to make payments when due or otherwise is in breach of this Agreement, the Design Professional may suspend performance of services upon five (5) calendar days' notice to the Client. The Design Professional shall have no liability whatsoever to the Client for any costs or damages as a result of such suspension caused by any breach of this Agreement by the Client.

This clause and all other clauses herein are intended as examples only and should be reviewed and modified by competent legal counsel to reflect variations in applicable local law and the specific circumstances of your contract.

We have chosen thirty, ninety and five days as reasonable periods for this provision. You and your client can negotiate this, if necessary, to arrive at something that is acceptable and reasonable to both of you. Note that we suggest counting calendar — and not working — days of suspension and stipulate days in the aggregate. Otherwise, in theory, your client could suspend for twenty-nine days, order you to resume work on the thirtieth and then suspend for another twenty-nine, leaving you with no recourse.

Be sure to coordinate your Suspension clause with the Billing and Payment, Changed Conditions and Termination provisions in your contract. While some contracts combine Suspension with a Termination clause, we suggest separating them so that if a court rejects one provision, the other might remain in force. (Refer to those sections for suggested contract language.)

Consider this clause a **Deal Maker** — a must-have in every contract. And it is just as important whether you're a prime or a subconsultant. If you are a subconsultant, the prime should include similar language in his or her agreement with the owner.

See also:

Billing and Payment
Changed Conditions
Delays
Severability and Survival
Termination
Timeliness of Performance

TERMINATION

When a design professional and client sign a contract, the designer is promising to employ his or her professional skills, knowledge, capital and reputation for the benefit of the client under certain conditions in exchange for a stipulated fee. Should these conditions change, or should serious conflicts arise, both the design professional and client need the right to terminate their agreement. While the client may argue he or she should be entitled to more freedom to terminate than the design professional, the designer can and should insist on a broad range of reasons for termination, including breach of any material condition, nonpayment of fees, inability to reach agreement on additional services, changes in the parties or substantially changed conditions. Under these circumstances, the architect or engineer should have the absolute right to terminate the contract upon appropriate notice. (Refer to *Assignment*, *Billing and Payment*, *Changed Conditions* and *Pay When Paid* for related discussions.)

THE PROBLEM

Beware of client-written contracts with one-sided language that permits only your client to terminate the contract. Any agreement that gives just one party the capability of termination is not fair or equitable — and may be unenforceable in some jurisdictions. Beware, too, of a transfer of ownership provision hidden in a termination clause. This would allow the client to terminate you early from the project and yet obtain ownership of your plans. (See *Ownership of Instruments of Service* for more information.) Recognize also that your office could incur substantial shutdown costs if you are terminated prematurely from a project in which you are deeply involved.

THE SOLUTION

Under no circumstances should a contract be silent on the subject of termination. This is a **Deal Maker** clause — a must-have. Every contract should contain a provision that defines the terms under which either party may end their legal relationship. Perhaps the best solution is a clause that permits either party to terminate the contract for "convenience" for any reason upon providing reasonable written notice to the other, and provides for payment of fees and expenses due. Consider the following:

TERMINATION

Either the Client or the Design Professional may terminate this Agreement at any time with or without cause upon giving the other party _____(__) calendar days prior written notice. The Client shall within _____(__) calendar days of termination pay the Design Professional for all services rendered and all costs incurred up to the date of termination, in accordance with the compensation provisions of this contract.

This clause and all other clauses herein are intended as examples only and should be reviewed and modified by competent legal counsel to reflect variations in applicable local law and the specific circumstances of your contract.

If the client insists on a more limited range of reasons for which you may terminate, you could substitute for the first sentence above language similar to the following:

The Client may terminate this Agreement at any time with or without cause upon giving the Design Professional _____(___) calendar days prior written notice. The Design Professional may terminate this Agreement upon giving the Client _____(___) calendar days prior written notice for any of the following reasons:

{List of specific circumstances, such as:

1. Breach by the Client of any material term of this Agreement, including but not limited to Payment Terms.
2. Transfer of ownership of the project by the Client to any other persons or entities not a party to this Agreement without the prior written agreement of the Design Professional.
3. Material changes in the conditions under which this Agreement was entered into, coupled with the failure of the parties hereto to reach accord on the fees and charges for any Additional Services required because of such changes.}

In some states, nonpayment of your fees may not be sufficient cause for termination. For this reason, we also recommend a Suspension of Services provision. If your jurisdiction does permit it, termination is a much stronger method to ensure your client's compliance with the terms of your agreement. (See *Suspension of Services*.)

A less desirable third alternative might be to include well-defined termination procedures in any clauses that might necessitate termination, such as Changed Conditions or Billing and Payment. However, this solution may simply lengthen and complicate your contract.

Because termination by your client could leave you with significant costs associated with stopping the project, you can add language to attempt to address this in your clause:

> **The Client shall reimburse the Design Professional for all expenses reasonably incurred by the Design Professional in connection with termination of this Agreement, including but not limited to demobilization, reassignment of personnel, and space and equipment costs.**

The issue of how much you are owed can become complex depending on the type of payment provision in your contract. For this reason, some consultants add a sentence such as, "When a 'lump sum' agreement has been entered into, the Design Professional's termination charges shall include an allowance for profit lost as a result of termination."

Your client also may ask for language that requires your future cooperation with any design professional who might supplant you and the freedom to use those designs and documents you have thus far created. This may or may not be acceptable to you. If you accept such a provision, you should do so only with adequate contractual protection. Agree to turn over only completed documents, not all your preliminary sketches, notes or drafts. You also will want to include Supplanting Another Design Professional and Unauthorized Changes to Plans provisions in your contract, as well as one for Ownership of Instruments of Service. (Refer to those sections for discussion and suggested clauses.) Check with your attorney; he or she may suggest you incorporate such language into your Termination provision. In any case, make certain your client indemnifies you for any changes made to your design without your consent after your termination.

SEE ALSO:

Assignment
Billing and Payment
Changed Conditions
Codes and Standards Compliance
Consequential Damages
Delays
Environmental and Health Hazards
Ownership of Instruments of Service
Pay When Paid
Public Responsibility
Supplanting Another Design Professional
Suspension of Services
Unauthorized Changes to Plans

TESTING LABORATORIES

A testing laboratory is used to perform field and laboratory tests to determine the characteristics and quality of building materials or site and soil conditions. These services may be required during any phase of a project — the planning, design or construction of a building — or in the event of a failure that occurs years after a structure's completion. There are several reasons to call for testing. Sometimes independent testing of structural components is required by local building codes. Certainly, many Preliminary Site Assessments (PSAs) may require sampling and testing to be performed. When remodeling an existing structure, a design professional may specify testing to determine construction techniques and even search for asbestos or other hazardous materials. Very often, forensic testing is employed to discover the causes for a failure.

THE PROBLEM

Although laboratory testing is a service that is normally out of the range of capability and experience of most design professionals, your client may want you to retain the testing laboratory as your subconsultant. But by accepting this responsibility, you would also be accepting inordinate vicarious liability.

Regardless of the reasons for the testing, it usually involves critical issues of quality and safety and might entail the handling of hazardous materials. If you are performing a PSA, for instance, and have a testing lab take samples, those samples may be contaminated. Without adequate contractual protection, you may assume some liability for the handling, proper testing and disposal of those samples. You can also assume liability for any invasive testing by the lab that requires some destruction of your client's property or the property of others. And, finally, if the testing is done improperly, and important decisions are based on the incorrect findings of the laboratory, you will almost certainly be brought into the resulting lawsuit if the lab is your subcontractor.

THE SOLUTION

The best solution is to have the owner contract directly with the testing laboratory. If your client insists, however, and you are forced to subcontract with the testing lab, proceed with extreme caution. Because there is a special set of liability and workscope issues to be addressed, it is best to use a standard agreement for contracting for laboratory services. (The ASFE Standard Form Agreement for

Subcontract Laboratory Services is one such model contract. Please refer to the *Bibliography* for details on contacting ASFE.) In any case, you will want to make certain the lab is adequately insured and will fully indemnify you for its negligent acts, errors or omissions.

Your own contract with the owner should reflect the fact that you are subcontracting the testing services only as a convenience to the owner. Architects and engineers aren't generally trained to determine the quality or results of laboratory tests and may not be able to determine whether the work was done properly. Because you may be in no position to determine the accuracy of the reports furnished to you by the testing lab, you need some kind of contractual absolution from the owner. Here is a sample contract provision:

TESTING LABORATORY SERVICES

It is recognized that the Design Professional has been asked by the Client to subcontract certain laboratory testing services on behalf of the Client to   {name of lab}   , an independent testing laboratory. The Design Professional agrees to do so only as an accommodation to the Client and in reliance upon the Client's assurance that the Client will make no claim nor bring any action at law or in equity against the Design Professional as a result of this subcontracted service. The Client understands that the Design Professional is neither trained nor knowledgeable in the procedures or results of the testing laboratory's services and the Client shall not rely upon the Design Professional to check the quality or accuracy of the testing laboratory's reports. In addition, the Client agrees to the fullest extent permitted by law to indemnify and hold the Design Professional harmless from any damage, liability or cost (including reasonable attorneys' fees and costs of defense) arising from the services performed by {name of lab} except only those damages, liabilities or costs caused by the sole negligence or willful misconduct of the Design Professional.

This clause and all other clauses herein are intended as examples only and should be reviewed and modified by competent legal counsel to reflect variations in applicable local law and the specific circumstances of your contract.

Some design professional firms have their own in-house laboratories. If you have such a facility, and because this work represents extreme liability hazards, it is important that your workscopes and reports be explicit on what you test for, what you do not test for and why. (See *Scope of Services*.) If the owner puts restrictions or limitations on the kinds of samplings you take or the tests you run, your report should reflect that fact. (See *Excluded Services*.) Finally, it is critical to have good quality assurance procedures, properly trained personnel, and an adequate health and safety plan in effect. If you are working with chemical or toxic materials, investigate the availability of environmental impairment insurance.

Whether you have your own lab or you are contracting with one, there are two additional issues that may need to be addressed. First, determine in advance and specify in your contracts who is to be responsible for restoration of any property damaged by the testing activity. Second, state in your contract who is responsible for the disposal of contaminated equipment and samples. If you can, arrange to return all samples to the owner for disposal. It is, after all, his or her property; any contaminants present were not generated by you and you should not have to be responsible for their disposal. If there are contaminants, you (as the lab or the prime consultant) could be held responsible as a transporter or storer of hazardous materials. If the owner refuses to accept the samples, the lab must use the services of a reputable hazardous waste disposal firm. It is critical that the lab keep impeccable records of any contaminants, whether returned to the owner or transferred to a disposal firm.

As always, your contract should include an Environmental and Health Hazards provision as well as Limitation of Liability and Dispute Resolution clauses. You will need to decide who will retain ownership of the reports and related data. (See *Ownership of Instruments of Service*.) You and your attorney may need to include other clauses too, such as Confidentiality, Buried Utilities, Information Provided by Others, Public Responsibility, and Subconsultants. (Refer to those sections for further discussion and sample clauses.)

SEE ALSO:

Buried Utilities
Confidentiality
Dispute Resolution
Environmental and Health Hazards
Excluded Services
Indemnities
Information Provided by Others

Limitation of Liability
Ownership of Instruments of Service
Public Responsibility
Scope of Services
Subconsultants
Termination

THIRD PARTY CLAIMS

The legal obligations of architects and engineers to others are sometimes difficult to
interpret. The concept of privity once held that design professionals owed a duty of
care only to those with whom they had a contract. However, that duty has been
extended by court decisions to all those who predictably could be harmed by the
actions of design professionals, even if no contract exists. Certainly, those who
suffer bodily injury and/or property damage because of a designer's negligence can
demand compensation. But what about those who claim an architect's negligence
caused them economic loss? Does the law feel that a third party is entitled to
damages if an engineer's negligence deprives him or her of a profit? Frankly, the
jury is still out. Some states hold that a design professional owes no duty of care to a
third party for economic loss, since no contract exists between them. Other jurisdictions have ruled that a contract is not a prerequisite to claiming damages for
economic loss because of negligence. In still other states, courts have decided in
both directions, further muddying the legal waters.

THE PROBLEM

With so much variance in the courts, it is difficult to know where your responsibilities lie. Virtually anyone — from the general contractor, to vendors, to future
owners — can claim that you knew or should have known that they could have
been economically harmed by your negligence and sue you for damages. Their
chances of prevailing depend on several factors, including the jurisdiction in which
the claim is filed and, perhaps, any preventive steps you and your client may have
taken to avoid third party claims. If your contract is silent on the matter, a court
may well interpret that silence against you.

THE SOLUTION

You and your client can — and should — address the issue of third party claims in
your contract. At the very least, such a provision will clearly define your intentions
and responsibilities and may help defeat claims in some jurisdictions where the
case law is not settled or compelling on this issue. Consider:

THIRD PARTY BENEFICIARIES

Nothing contained in this Agreement shall create a contractual relationship with or a cause of action in favor of a third party against either the Client or the Design Professional. The Design Professional's services under this Agreement are being performed solely for the Client's benefit, and no other entity shall have any claim against the Design Professional because of this Agreement or the performance or nonperformance of services hereunder. The Client agrees to include a provision in all contracts with contractors and other entitles involved in this project to carry out the intent of this paragraph.

This clause and all other clauses herein are intended as examples only and should be reviewed and modified by competent legal counsel to reflect variations in applicable local law and the specific circumstances of your contract.

Your client should have no objection to such a clause, since it does not compromise either party's position and may be of some benefit to both of you.

The final sentence of the provision requires the owner (your client) to include a similar third party provision in his or her agreements with each individual in the project. If your client is hesitant to agree to this, you could omit the requirement.

SEE ALSO:

Public Responsibility
Statutes of Repose or Limitation

TIMELINESS OF PERFORMANCE

Perhaps because they do not appreciate the nature of a design professional's services, clients (or, more accurately, their attorneys) often attempt to insert a phrase into contracts that states, "time is of the essence...." Such imprecise, boilerplate language is the sort of thing that is drilled into aspiring attorneys in law school as appropriate when more specificity is impossible. This seemingly innocuous phrase can do the design professional serious harm, however. In fact, it might be interpreted to mean that his or her services must be completed according to a strict schedule. Even a minor delay could become cause for a client to terminate the contract or make a claim for damages.

THE PROBLEM

Just as no one would tell a surgeon how quickly to complete a delicate operation, you, too, must be given adequate time to do a competent, professional job. In the contract formation stage, it is impossible to tell with certainty how long you will need to complete the various phases of the project. Unanticipated problems, site conditions, client delays, uncertainty in the scope and scale of the client's program, acts of God — all these variables and more can render any estimation of a schedule for your services pure guesswork.

Fuzzy language, such as "time is of the essence," could lead to claims that even minor deviations from the client's unstated expectations meant that you either breached the contract (which could result in a refusal by the client to pay your fees) or resulted in delay damages (for which you could be liable since you had acknowledged the importance of timeliness in your agreement).

There is also a possibility that your professional liability insurance does not cover you for claims arising from late delivery of plans and specifications, even absent any allegation of negligence. While DPIC Companies does provide such coverage in their policies, many insurers do not.

THE SOLUTION

Delete any "time is of the essence" language in client-drawn contracts. Your best approach is either to remain silent on the issue of timeliness of performance or to address the problem with language that is somewhat general in nature, such as the following:

TIMELINESS OF PERFORMANCE

The Design Professional will perform his or her services with due and reasonable diligence consistent with sound professional practices.

This clause and all other clauses herein are intended as examples only and should be reviewed and modified by competent legal counsel to reflect variations in applicable local law and the specific circumstances of your contract.

If the client demands a definitive project schedule in the contract, you need a different approach. You must be sure that any appended schedule has plenty of leeway, that you are certain you can meet its deadlines with room to spare before you commit to it. Such a clause might read:

The Design Professional acknowledges the importance to the Client of the Client's project schedule and agrees to put forth reasonable efforts in performing the services with due diligence under this Agreement in a manner consistent with that schedule, as provided in Exhibit ___ hereto. The Client understands, however, that the Design Professional's performance must be governed by sound professional practices.

Your contract also should contain a good, no-responsibility-for-delays provision. (See *Delays* for sample language and a related discussion.)

One last option: If your client wants notice of impending slippage in the schedule, you might agree to add some notification language such as:

Should the Design Professional discern that the schedule will not be met for any reason, he or she shall so notify the Client as soon as practically possible.

Bear in mind, however, that this provision creates an additional obligation. If you fail to notify, you could be in breach of contract.

SEE ALSO:

Billing and Payment
Consequential Damages
Delays
Liquidated Damages
Public Responsibility

TITLES

In most contracts, each clause is given a title for ease of reference.

THE PROBLEM

If a clause's title addresses a single issue but the clause actually encompasses more than one, or if the title is not interpreted in the same way by both parties, it could be argued that there were provisions hidden by misleading or incomplete titles. As lame as this argument may sound, it has been upheld in court. For this reason, it is sometimes necessary to call special attention to certain provisions, by underlining or the use of capital letters. (One such example is a Limitation of Liability provision. Refer to that section for more discussion.)

THE SOLUTION

Claims of misleading titles can be avoided by simply stating in your agreement that there is no legal significance to these titles. Such a provision is usually one of the last paragraphs of the agreement, near the signature line:

TITLES

The titles used in this Agreement are for general reference only and are not part of the Agreement.

This clause and all other clauses herein are intended as examples only and should be reviewed and modified by competent legal counsel to reflect variations in applicable local law and the specific circumstances of your contract.

Regardless of whether you include such a provision, always advise your client to read the contract thoroughly before signing it and to have it reviewed by his or her attorney.

SEE ALSO:

Definitions
Limitation of Liability

UNAUTHORIZED CHANGES TO PLANS

Sometimes changes are made to construction documents by the owner, a contractor or even a building department official without the knowledge and approval of the architect or engineer.

In a few states, if an architect's or engineer's design is changed without his or her knowledge by the contractor or owner, and those changes result in damages, the law gives the designer protection from liability. This is not true in many jurisdictions, however. In most states, absent some contractual safeguards, the design professional may well become liable — or at least have to mount a defense — because of someone else's mistakes.

THE PROBLEM

It is so easy for someone else to make changes to your design. A contractor who is having difficulty making a detail in the plans work might make a minor (and what he or she thinks is a harmless) field change without consulting you. The danger here increases if you are performing only limited construction phase services or none at all. (See *Construction Observation* and *Design Without Construction Phase Services*.) Perhaps your contract is terminated after the construction documents are complete, leaving the construction phase to another design professional — who makes modifications to your design. (Refer to *Supplanting Another Design Professional*.) Consider the building inspector who, being a helpful sort of chap, makes an offhand suggestion to a contractor about an alternate approach to a problem. If you aren't there to intercede, the contractor probably will defer to the building inspector. Then there is the owner who asks for a copy of your plans on computer disk and has his or her own in-house designers make modifications without your knowledge. (See *CADD*.) Or think about the developer of a residential project who asks you to design five models and then makes changes to accommodate site differences when building the rest of the development. (See *Prototype Designs*.) Unless you have adequate protection from liability, you are subject to claims in all these instances — and many more.

THE SOLUTION

Your best bet is to add a provision in your contract that absolves you of responsibility for changes that are made without your authorization. You would also want the owner to include a provision in the contractor's contract (and to be passed on to the contractor's subcontractors) prohibiting any changes without your knowledge and consent.

UNAUTHORIZED CHANGES

In the event the Client consents to, allows, authorizes or approves of changes to any plans, specifications or other construction documents, and these changes are not approved in writing by the Design Professional, the Client recognizes that such changes and the results thereof are not the responsibility of the Design Professional. Therefore, the Client agrees to release the Design Professional from any liability arising from the construction, use or result of such changes. In addition, the Client agrees, to the fullest extent permitted by law, to indemnify and hold the Design Professional harmless from any damage, liability or cost (including reasonable attorneys' fees and costs of defense) arising from such changes, except only those damages, liabilities and costs arising from the sole negligence or willful misconduct of the Design Professional.

This clause and all other clauses herein are intended as examples only and should be reviewed and modified by competent legal counsel to reflect variations in applicable local law and the specific circumstances of your contract.

As always, you should work closely with your attorney to ensure this provision is coordinated with any other clauses in your contract that address CADD, Copyrights, Design Without Construction Phase Services, Ownership of Instruments of Service, Prototype Designs, Supplanting Another Design Professional and Termination. (Please see those sections for suggested language and discussions.)

SEE ALSO:

CADD
Construction Observation
Copyrights
Design Without Construction Phase Services
Ownership of Instruments of Service
Prototype Designs
Supplanting Another Design Professional
Termination

VALUE ENGINEERING

Value engineering is the detailed, systematic review of a project in an attempt to obtain optimum value for every dollar spent. The goal is to eliminate or modify features that add cost to a building but in no way add to its quality, life, utility or appearance. By using a nonadversarial, problem-solving approach, value engineers (VEs) look at trade-offs between design concepts, construction techniques, materials, building types, and up-front versus life-cycle costs to arrive at the best overall value for the structure. Often the value engineering team works closely with the architect or engineer of record; in fact, many value engineers prefer to include the original designers on the evaluation team.

But value engineering can also be a term used to describe quite a different process, usually marketed to project owners who feel their budgets are imperiled and who want a second opinion. All too often, this evaluation is performed by design professionals who are not certified VEs. The procedure can sometimes deteriorate into what amounts to second-guessing of the original designer by an architect or engineer hired to cut the up-front costs of a project. In fact, some of these "VEs" even base their compensation on how much they save. This sort of value engineering undermines the professional status and credibility of the designer of record and can reduce the quality and safety of the project or perhaps even endanger the public.

THE PROBLEM

In contract and liability issues, value engineering raises as many questions as it answers. If you are the original designer whose work is being evaluated, what is the extent of your responsibility? Unless your contract and/or workscope state otherwise, you could be expected to perform substantial redesign work — with no compensation. Do you have the right to disagree with the VE's recommendations? It is quite possible that reasonable yet alternative design solutions will produce a similar result. Do you have a responsibility to make changes that you don't believe are appropriate? What if a lawsuit results from the changes you didn't accept? Are you liable?

On the other hand, if you are the value engineer, how much liability will you incur for mistakes made by the building's original designer? If you must make assumptions based on information provided to you by the designer of record, are you protected if that information is flawed? How much responsibility is yours should the owner elect not to implement your recommendations?

THE SOLUTION

In any project where value engineering is contemplated, it should be directed by certified, qualified VE specialists. (Many government projects require the presence of a certified value engineer on the design team. See the *Bibliography* for details on how to contact the Society of American Value Engineers regarding certification requirements.)

Furthermore, compensation for value engineers should never be based on savings carved out of the original design. Such an arrangement creates a clear conflict of interest.

If you are the design professional of record and you know or believe value engineering will be performed on your project, you should anticipate it in your contract. Develop a clear understanding with your client as to the extent of your obligations to redesign to accommodate any decisions based on the value engineering. Your contract should include a clause to limit responsibility for redesign and to give you the ability to object to the recommendations of the value engineer. In addition, make certain any redesign you provide will be performed as an additional service and compensated for accordingly. Here is a sample clause:

VALUE ENGINEERING

If the Client retains the services of a Value Engineer (VE) to review the Construction Documents prepared for this project by the Design Professional, it shall be at the Client's sole expense and shall be performed in a timely manner so as not to delay the orderly progress of the Design Professional's services. All recommendations of the VE shall be given to the Design Professional for his or her review, and adequate time will be provided for the Design Professional to respond to these recommendations. The Design Professional shall be compensated as Additional Service, as provided for herein, for all time spent to review the recommendations of the VE and to incorporate those accepted by both the Client and the Design Professional. If the Design Professional objects to any recommendations made by the VE, he or she shall so state in writing to the Client, along with his or her reasons for objecting. If the Client insists on incorporating in the Construction Documents any changes to which the Design Professional has objected in writing, the Client agrees, to the fullest extent permitted by law, to indemnify and hold the Design Professional harmless from any damage, liability or cost (including reasonable attorneys' fees and costs of defense) which arise in connection with or as a result of the incorporation of such design changes insisted upon by the Client.

Of course, if you feel there is a threat to public health and safety if certain recommendations are implemented, you must document your concerns thoroughly and follow up with both the VE and your client to reach a resolution. In addition, you may have a duty to notify appropriate building safety agencies in accordance with your obligations under your license. (See *Public Responsibility* for more information and sample contract wording.)

If your firm is performing the value engineering, you will want contractual protection for liability arising out of the design or construction phase services provided by the original design team of record. You will want a waiver and an indemnity from your client, if permitted in your jurisdiction. In addition, we recommend that you include a Limitation of Liability provision as well as a clause to protect you from flawed information given to you by the original designer. (Refer to *Indemnities, Information Provided by Others* and *Limitation of Liability* for more information.) Here is a starting point:

In consideration of the Consultant performing a Value Engineering (VE) review of this project, the Client warrants that the Consultant shall be entitled to rely upon the completeness and accuracy of all information provided to the Consultant. The Client agrees that all recommendations made by the Consultant as a result of the VE review shall be furnished by the Client to the appropriate designer(s) of record for review and comment. Based on that review and comment, the Client shall decide whether to implement the VE's recommendations. The Client agrees to waive all claims against the Consultant arising from the services to be provided under this Agreement.

In addition, the Client agrees, to the fullest extent permitted by law, to indemnify and hold the Consultant harmless from all damage, liability or cost (including reasonable attorneys' fees and costs of defense) arising from the services provided under this Agreement, except for the sole negligence or willful misconduct of the Consultant.

Remember, as the value engineer, it is not your role to make the design changes; your charter is to furnish recommendations. It is important that the original design professional review those recommendations and have an opportunity to respond. All final decisions about redesign must be made by the owner and agreed to by the original designer of record — and only after all alternatives have been discussed and the impact of any changes carefully considered. Talk to your attorney. Your contract must make clear that the responsibility and liability for those decisions remain where they belong — with the owner.

SEE ALSO:

Bibliography
Indemnities
Information Provided by Others
Limitation of Liability
Public Responsibility

APPENDIX I

STANDARD CONTRACTS CHECKLIST

Following is a quick-reference checklist you will find helpful if you use either of the most popular standard association contracts: the *AIA B141* (and the *B511, Guide for Amendments to AIA Document B141*) or the *EJCDC 1910-1*. Keeping in mind the nature of your practice and the risks of a particular project, you can check the list to determine if and where your concerns are addressed in the standard contract you plan to use. You can then review the discussions and sample clauses offered in this Guide, compare them with the standard forms and, with your attorney's help, strengthen or amend the contract as needed.

Keep in mind that the standard association contracts have been thoroughly researched, have long been subject to interpretation by the courts and have both association and industry approval. Furthermore, they are interrelated and coordinated with other documents (the General Conditions and subcontracts, for instance). If you plan to amend them in any way, use the services of an attorney.

The checklist covers all of the sections in this Guide. If, under a contract heading, there is no entry on a given subject, then the subject is not addressed in that standard contract or its amendments. In some instances, neither of the standard contracts address the subject. If that subject is of concern to you, you may want to review the appropriate section in the Guide to see if you should add such a provision to your contract. In other instances, topics have multiple entries, meaning that a standard contract addresses some portion of that topic in more than one section of the contract.

Checklist for use with AIA and EJCDC Standard Forms of Agreement

The Contract Guide from DPIC Companies, Inc.	AIA Document B141-1987 Ed.	B511-1990	EJCDC 1910-1 1992 Ed.
Americans with Disabilities Act			
Arbitration	Article 7	7.1	8.6 & Exhibit G
Assignment	9.5	9.10	8.5.2
Attorneys' Fees			
Authorized Representatives	4.4		1.3.8 & 4.1
Betterment			
Billing and Payment	4.3 & Articles 10 & 11		Section 6 & Exhibit B
Buried Utilities			
CADD		6.1	
Certifications, Guarantees and Warranties	4.11		3.1.18 & 4.12 & Exhibit D
Changed Conditions	3.3.1 & 3.3.2		3.1.4 & 3.1.5
Claims Arbiter Service	2.6.15 - .19		2.5.9
Codes and Standards Compliance	3.3.1.2		
Condominiums			
Confidential Communications			
Confidentiality	9.9		
Consequential Damages			Exhibit H8.7.4.2
Construction Observation	2.6 & 3.2	2.6.5.1	2.5.2 & Exhibit C
Contingency Fund	5.1.2		Exhibits E7.2.2 & H8.7.4.4
Contractual Reference to the Design Professional	Throughout	Throughout	Throughout
Copyrights	6.1	6.1.1	

The Contract Guide from DPIC Companies, Inc.	AIA Document B141-1987 Ed.	B511-1990	EJCDC 1910-1 1992 Ed.
Corporate Protection			
Defects in Service	4.10		4.16
Definitions	9.2		1.3
Delays	1.1.2 & 2.6.18 & 3.3.1.3 & 11.5.1		3.2.3.3 & 3.2.3.4 & 5.2 & 5.4
Design Without Construction Phase Services		2.6.1	4.11
Dispute Resolution		7.5.1	8.6 & Exhibit G
Environmental and Health Hazards			
If You Don't Expect to Encounter Pollutants	9.8		8.7.3
If You Know or Suspect You Will Encounter Pollutants	9.8	9.8.1	
Preliminary Site Assessments			
Asbestos	9.8		8.7.3
Excluded Services	Article 3		
Extension of Protection			
Fast Track Projects	3.3.9	2.7	5.5
Foreign Projects			
Governing Law	9.1		8.4
Incorporation by Reference			
Indemnities		1.2.2 & 2.6.20 & 4.12.1& 6.1.2 & 9.8.1	8.2 & 8.7 & Exhibit H8.7.4.3
Information Provided by Others	3.4.7 & 4.9	1.2.1 & 1.2.2 & 4.12.1	3.1.2 & 4.3 & 4.4
Inspection			2.5.8 & 4.10

The Contract Guide from DPIC Companies, Inc.	AIA Document B141-1987 Ed.	B511-1990	EJCDC 1910-1 1992 Ed.
Insurance	9.4	10.2.1.7	8.3 & Exhibit F
Integration	9.6		9.2
Interpretation			
Jobsite Safety	2.6.6		2.5.2.2 & 2.5.10.2
Lenders' Requirements			4.12
Limitation of Liability		12.2	Exhibit H
Liquidated Damages			
Multiple Prime Contracts	3.4.9	4.12	4.11
Non-Negligent Services			
Notices			8.8
Opinion of Probable Construction Costs	2.2.5 & 2.3.2 & 2.4.3 & 3.4.10 & 5.2		2.1.5 & & 4.14 & Section 7 & Exhibit E
Ownership of Instruments of Service	Article 6	6.1	8.2
Pay When Paid			
Performance Bonds			
Permits and Approvals	2.4.4		4.8
Prototype Designs			
Public Responsibility			
Quality Control			
Record Documents	3.4.16		2.6.4
Renovation/Remodeling		1.2	
Retainage			
Right of Entry	2.6.7		4.6

The Contract Guide from DPIC Companies, Inc.	AIA Document B141-1987 Ed.	B511-1990	EJCDC 1910-1 1992 Ed.
Right to Retain Subconsultants			1.1
Scope of Services	1.1.1 & Articles 2 & 3		Section 2 & Exhibit A
Severability and Survival			8.9 & 8.10
Shop Drawing Review	2.6.12	2.6.12	2.5.6
Specification of Materials			
Standard of Care			1.1
Statutes of Repose or Limitation	9.3		
Stop Work Authority	2.6.11		
Subconsultants	2.1.1 & 3.4.19		1.1
Supplanting Another Design Professional			
Suspension of Services	8.2 & 8.5	8.8.1	5.3 & 5.4
Termination	8.1 & 8.3 & 8.4 & 8.6 & 8.7		6.2.3 & 8.1
Testing Laboratories	4.7		4.4.2
Third Party Claims	9.7		8.5.3
Timeliness of Performance	1.1.2 & 11.5.1		Section 5
Titles			
Unauthorized Changes to Plans		2.6.20	
Value Engineering			3.1.12 & 4.11

APPENDIX II

THE TEAMWORK ETHIC

In times past, owners, contractors, subcontractors and design professionals cooperated to solve problems as they arose on a construction project. Over the years, however, the industry has changed. Gone is the approach of working together to get the job done — on time and within budget. Extras, delays, problems, disputes, claims and lawyers are now the rule rather than the exception. Unfortunately, we've all heard of at least one contractor who fails to report problems promptly, withholding information with the intent of magnifying the cost of extras and thereby enlarging his or her profit. This certainly violates the spirit, and in many instances, the letter of the construction contract (see Article 3.2.1, *AIA Document A201*, 1987 ed.) and increases the risk for the design professional. If the underlying defects are in the plans or specifications, the client will no doubt look to the design professional to pay to correct any problems — problems that might have been eliminated or at least mitigated if the contractor had reported them early.

Many in the construction process deplore the waste and frustration of the current system and are looking for a better way — a return to the teamwork ethic. Dispute resolution methods other than litigation are taking root, alternative project delivery systems are being employed, and processes that foster a team spirit — such as *partnering* — are being introduced.

This kind of teamwork means that the owner and contractors need to acknowledge their own responsibilities for the success of the project. For example, they have an obligation to report promptly to the design professional any defects they observe in the contract documents. To foster the spirit of partnership — the idea that "we're all in this together" — and to set up realistic expectations for both the client and the contractor, some design professionals ask their client to insert language similar to the following into the General Conditions:

The Contractor acknowledges and understands that the Contract Documents may represent imperfect data and may contain errors, omissions, conflicts, inconsistencies, code violations and improper use of materials. Such deficiencies will be corrected when identified. The Contractor agrees to carefully study and compare the individual Contract Documents and report at once in writing to the Owner any deficiencies the Contractor may discover. The Contractor further agrees to require each subcontractor to likewise study the documents and report at once any deficiencies discovered.

The Contractor shall resolve all reported deficiencies with the Design Professional prior to awarding any subcontracts or starting any work with the Contractor's own employees. If any deficiencies cannot be resolved by the Contractor without additional time or additional expense, the Contractor shall so inform the Owner in writing. Any work performed prior to receipt of instructions from the Owner will be done at the Contractor's risk.

This clause and all other clauses herein are intended as examples only and should be reviewed and modified by competent legal counsel to reflect variations in applicable local law and the specific circumstances of your contract.

Such a clause acknowledges the obvious but sometimes unspoken truth that the plans will not be perfect. Some architects and engineers may be reluctant to admit this lack of perfection, but such a realistic statement may help diffuse a later claim from an owner or contractor that he or she expected perfection from the design professional. This provision — coupled with a reasonable Standard of Care clause in the designer's contract — should go far in establishing proper expectations for all parties.

BIBLIOGRAPHY

ACEC Guidelines to Practice: Alternative Dispute Resolution for Design Professionals. Vol. 1, No. 7. Washington, DC: American Consulting Engineers Council, 1991.

ACEC Guidelines to Practice: Professional Liability Risk Management. Vol. 1, No. 3. Washington, DC: American Consulting Engineers Council, 1990.

ADA: A Resource Guide. Washington, DC: The American Institute of Architects, 1992.

ADR: Alternative Dispute Resolution for the Construction Industry. Silver Spring, Md.: The Association of Engineering Firms Practicing in the Geosciences, 1988.

ADR by Covenant. Silver Spring, Md.: The Association of Engineering Firms Practicing in the Geosciences, 1989.

AIA Practice Management Programs: Total Quality Management for Architects. Washington, DC: The American Institute of Architects, 1992.

Architect's Handbook of Professional Practice. 11th ed. Washington, DC: The American Institute of Architects, 1988.

Ashcraft, Howard W. Jr. "Drafting and Managing Limitation of Liability Clauses." Report prepared for Hanson, Bridgett, Marcus, Vlahos and Rudy, San Francisco, Ca., March 1993.

Avoiding and Resolving Disputes During Construction: Successful Practices and Guidelines. Rev. ed. New York: American Society of Civil Engineers, 1991.

Carr, Frank; Creighton, James; Edelman, Lester; and Lancaster, Charles. *Nonbinding Arbitration.* U. S. Army Corps of Engineers (Institute for Water Resources), Pamphlet 90-ADR-P-2, 1990.

Carr, Frank; Creighton, James; and Edelman, Lester. *Partnering.* U. S. Army Corps of Engineers (Institute for Water Resources), Pamphlet 91-ADR-P-4, 1991.

Construction Industry Arbitration Rules. New York: The American Arbitration Association, 1992.

Construction Industry Mediation Rules. New York: The American Arbitration Association, 1992.

Fisher, Roger and Ury, William. *Getting to Yes*. Boston: Houghton Mifflin, 1981.

Hatem, David J. "Liability Risks and Concerns of Environmental Professionals." *Pitfalls for Real Estate Professionals*. Book 92-1914. Boston: Massachusetts Continuing Legal Education, April 1992.

Huber, Peter W. *Liability: The Legal Revolution and its Consequences*. New York: Basic Books, Inc., 1988.

Ingardia, Michael P. and Hill, John F. *CADD Contracting Guidelines for Design Firms*. Washington, DC: American Consulting Engineers Council, 1992.

An Introduction to Total Quality Management. Washington, DC: The Associated General Contractors of America, 1992.

Lessons in Professional Liability: A Notebook for Design Professionals. Rev. ed. Monterey, Ca.: Design Professionals Insurance Company, 1988.

The LOL Handbook: A Guide to the Use of Limitation of Liability for Design Professionals. Monterey, Ca.: DPIC Companies, Inc., 1993.

Olson, Walter K. *Galileo's Revenge: Junk Science in the Courtroom*. New York: Harper Collins, 1991.

Olson, Walter K. *The Litigation Explosion: What Happened When America Unleashed the Lawsuit*. New York: Truman Talley Books-Dutton, 1991.

Owner's Guide to Saving Money by Risk Allocation. Washington, DC: The Associated General Contractors of America, 1990.

Partnering: A Concept for Success. Washington, DC: The Associated General Contractors of America, 1991.

PLAN Project Representative's Manual. Silver Spring, Md.: Professional Liability Agents Network, 1990.

Preventing and Resolving Construction Disputes. New York: Center for Public Resources, 1991.

Understanding and Purchasing Professional Liability Insurance. Washington, DC: American Consulting Engineers Council, 1991.

WHERE TO FIND ADDITIONAL INFORMATION

American Arbitration Association, 140 West 51st Street, New York, NY 10020-1203, (212) 484-4000/Fax 307-4387.

American Consulting Engineers Council, 1015 Fifteenth Street N.W., Washington, DC 20005, (202) 347-7474.

American Institute of Architects, 1735 New York Avenue N.W., Washington, DC 20006, (202) 626-7300.

American Society of Civil Engineers, 345 East 47th Street, New York, NY 10017-2398, (212) 705-7496.

ASFE: Professional Firms Practicing in the Geosciences, 8811 Colesville Road, Suite G106, Silver Spring, MD 20910, (301) 565-2733.

Associated General Contractors of America, 1957 E Street N.W., Washington, DC 20006, (202) 393-2040.

Center for Public Resources, 366 Madison Avenue, New York, NY 10017, (212) 949-6490.

Coalition of American Structural Engineers, 1015 Fifteenth Street N.W., Suite 802, Washington, DC, 20005, (202) 347-7474.

Copyright Office, Information Section, Library of Congress, Washington, DC 20559, (202) 707-3000.

Professional Liability Agents Network, 8811 Colesville Road, Suite G106, Silver Spring, MD 20910, (301) 589-5642.

Society of American Value Engineers, 60 Revere Drive, Suite 500, Northbrook, IL 60062, (708) 480-9282.

INDEX

PARTNERING

Considering all the fanfare that project partnering has been receiving recently, one might be tempted to dismiss the process as just the latest fad to come along in the construction industry. But a closer look reveals an intriguing trend. Hundreds of construction project participants are successfully creating a positive dispute prevention atmosphere by implementing partnering.

Partnering is hardly a new idea. Rather, it is an old precept restated — the affirmation of good faith and fair dealing that somehow has been lost in too many construction contracts. It is the pledge to work together to enhance quality, efficiency, on-time performance and to improve relationships and communications with a fair profit for all participants. In short, it is a promise to work towards the best of all forms of dispute resolution: dispute *avoidance*.

The concept is simple: to dispel the adversarial "us-versus-them" approach all too commonly found on today's construction projects and to promote instead a "let's-all-pull-together" attitude. While the actual steps may vary, they usually involve team-building activities led by a third party partnering facilitator who helps define common goals, improve communication and cultivate a problem-solving attitude among key representatives of the design and construction team *before* work on a project begins. Most often, the participants decide on specific steps for resolving disputes and draft a pledge stating their commitment to deal fairly with one another. They may then meet regularly to weigh their progress. Many partnering arrangements make it a point to reaffirm their commitment once the project has been under way for some time.

The benefits realized by architects and engineers who participate in partnering can be significant. Their role in the decision-making process may be enhanced, for example. Design professionals' liability and thus exposure to litigation is reduced. Designer participation in construction phase services is more likely. (See *Construction Observation* and *Design Without Construction Phase Services* in *The Contract Guide* for more information.) What's more, the process may help reduce cost overruns as well as help avoid project delays and resulting delay claims. The process should also enhance project profitability by minimizing time-consuming conflicts and negative behavior that occur when relationships sour. As a bonus, design professionals who suggest partnering to their clients may also find it an effective sales tool because it sets them apart from other firms.

THE PROBLEM

Given all the benefits, why aren't owners, designers and contractors rushing to implement partnering on all their projects? Many clients — and design professionals — don't yet understand the process and its potential benefits. Some owners may believe that a partnering arrangement may require more energy and up-front costs than they are willing to invest and regard it as nothing more than a '90s "touchy-feely" waste of time. What's more, although many public entities and large firms are beginning to incorporate partnering into larger projects, thus far the process has not been widely used on smaller projects. Often, architects and engineers do not realize that the precepts of partnering can be successfully applied to projects of all sizes and descriptions.

There is also the concern, held by some cautious design professionals and a few insurance companies, that entering into a partnering arrangement might constitute a contractual relationship between the contractor and the design professional and would, in those few states where privity of contract is required in order to sue somebody, give the contractor a legal basis to sue the designer. (See *Third Party Claims*.) Other design professionals wonder if partnering puts the design professional at a two-against-one disadvantage, in which a contractor sides with an owner to try to get unmerited advantage over the architect or engineer. Some also worry that partnering might increase their liability for construction related and jobsite safety problems.

There is one more difficulty. Often, projects that do employ partnering include only the owner and the contractors and exclude the design professionals from the process. This makes little sense. To exclude the very parties who can best interpret design documents and suggest ways to mitigate problems would seem contrary to the partnering idea.

THE SOLUTION

Learn the fundamentals of partnering. Although it is not a panacea for all construction problems, partnering has been shown to be well worth the effort. The American Consulting Engineers Council, Army Corps of Engineers, The American Institute of Architects, Arizona Department of Transportation, Associated General Contractors of America, the Construction Industry Institute — and DPIC — believe partnering represents an important cost-effective method to help manage projects more efficiently and achieve the highest quality results. The difficulties mentioned previously may be real or based on misconceptions, but they all have practical solutions.

For instance, if you or your client think that the costs associated with partnering (a one or two-day facilitated workshop, tailored to the size and complexity of the project, and follow-up meetings) might be too high, take a moment to consider the cost of giving a one-day deposition in a lawsuit — not to mention the loss of good working relationships. Even most smaller projects can effectively and inexpensively implement partnering. If necessary, a properly run, half-day workshop held in your lunchroom can use the same team-building techniques and generate the same spirit as a full-blown, two-day retreat.

In spite of your best efforts to avoid them, you will occasionally come up against bad projects, unethical owners, problem construction managers and contractors who have bid too low. The presence of partnering won't make matters worse. If anything, the better communication cultivated by partnering may serve to identify a problem sooner rather than later.

As for increased liability for jobsite safety and construction claims, we believe — partnered project or not — that every design professional should perform construction phase services. While this may increase the chances of involvement in site issues, that possible increase in risk should be more than offset by better project results. In any case, your contract should have a strong jobsite safety provision — we consider it a **Deal Maker** — that makes clear that responsibility for site safety and construction means and methods remains with the contractor. (See *Jobsite Safety* in *The Contract Guide*.) You can also insist the client add to its agreement with the contractor a provision that states that partnering in no way relieves the contractor of his or her safety responsibilities.

How do you ensure that partnering is implemented on a project — and that you are included? The best solution is the most straightforward. Explain to your client your commitment to the partnering ideals and ask for a similar resolve on his or her part. This is important. In order for partnering to work, it must be owner-driven. The owner must be committed to the concept, be willing to incorporate the concept of partnering into the bid solicitations and take the necessary steps to ensure that the process takes place.

The process begins with a commitment by all parties — owner, design professional and contractor alike — to deal fairly with one another. Negotiate a solid, *fair* contract. You must have an agreement in which the risk is shared equitably; an agreement that gives one party an undue portion of the risk will surely undermine the essence of partnering.

Then you and your client should set forth your mutual expectations in your agreement. Whether or not partnering is anticipated, we think every contract should contain in the preamble — the "whereas" section — an affirmation of your mutual commitment to deal with one another in good faith. One public entity regularly uses the following wording:

> **This contract imposes an obligation of good faith and fair dealing in its performance and enforcement. Accordingly, the Client and the Design Professional, with a positive commitment to honesty and integrity, agree to the following: that each will function within the laws and statutes that apply to their duties and responsibilities; that each will assist in the other's performance; that each will avoid hindering the other's performance; that each will work diligently to fulfill its obligations; and that each will cooperate in the common endeavor of the contract.**

This clause and all other clauses herein are intended as examples only and should be reviewed and modified by competent legal counsel to reflect variations in applicable local law and the specific circumstances of your contract.

This is a good start — and establishes an atmosphere of trust and cooperation in which problems are likely to get solved. But don't stop there. We suggest you go on to include a clause in your agreement with your client that states that partnering will be employed on the project and that you will be included in the process. This accomplishes several things. First, it can serve to introduce the concept of partnering and educate a client who may not be familiar with it — or give a little push to an undecided client. It tells your client and the world that you embrace the concepts of fair dealing and teamwork that partnering fosters. It is a mechanism by which you can make certain that partnering is addressed in the client/contractor contract. Finally, it ensures you will be part of the partnering process.

VOLUNTARY PARTNERING

The Client will encourage participation in a formalized partnering process that involves the Client, the Design Professional and his or her subconsultants, the Construction Manager and the Contractor and his or her principal subcontractors and suppliers. This partnering relationship will be structured to draw on the strengths of each organization to identify and achieve reciprocal goals. The objectives are effective and efficient contract performance and completion of the project within budget, on schedule, in accordance with the plans and specifications, and without litigation. Participation in partnering will be totally voluntary and all participants will have equal status. Any cost associated with implementing partnering will be agreed to in advance by all parties and will be shared equally.

This clause and all other clauses herein are intended as examples only and should be reviewed and modified by competent legal counsel to reflect variations in applicable local law and the specific circumstances of your contract.

Does placing a partnering clause in your contract undermine the spirit of volunteerism necessary to successful partnering? We think not. Participation in an active partnering procedure is, after all, still voluntary. But such a clause also says to your client that you are first and foremost interested in working in a non-adversarial atmosphere that is dedicated to dispute avoidance — and asks your client to retain contractors who are like-minded. Finally, it may be an effective device by which to introduce mediation provisions into your agreement. (Refer to *Dispute Resolution* in *The Contract Guide* for more information.)

We do not believe that signing a partnering charter or participating in a partnering workshop establishes a contractual relationship between you and the contractor(s). But even if one day it is construed to be a contract and even in those states where privity of contract is necessary for a contractor to sue a design professional, we feel the benefits of partnering far outweigh the possible loss of the privity defense.

Of course, a partnering charter in no way supersedes or negates your contract with your client. Just because your project is partnered does not mean you and your client are not obligated to adhere to the terms of your contract. On most jobs, once you stagger home from contract negotiations, you will put your agreement away and may never have to look at it again. If you *do* need it, though, it is right there in its file, setting forth your legal rights and duties, as well as those of your client. Your partnering arrangement in no way undermines that agreement. If you are concerned, however — and it is true that no court of law has yet tested the issue — you and your attorney may want to add an additional sentence to the preceding clause (and perhaps to your partnering charter as well) making clear your intent:

> **By engaging in partnering, the parties do not intend to create a legal partnership, to create additional contractual relationships, or to in any way alter the legal relationship which otherwise exists between the Client and the Design Professional.**

Participants to a partnering workshop typically determine how they will resolve problems that arise. They may create a step-by-step process that encourages resolution at the lowest possible level of management. They may also decide to establish a dispute review board, if the project is large enough to warrant it, or some other mechanism. Mediation or another formal dispute resolution process may be decided upon for conflicts that cannot be solved by the participants. We offer a caveat here, however. You will want to be sure that any reference to *formal* dispute resolution in the partnering pledge does not conflict with but instead complements your contractual dispute resolution provision.

You have nothing to lose. By introducing the concept of partnering to your clients and by placing it in your agreement and in the General Conditions, you are creating an opportunity to educate your client about the process and to set reasonable expectations of all participants to the project. If nothing else, you may be able to ferret out an owner (or contractor) whose value system is different from yours. After all, if they balk at the concepts of good faith and fair dealing of partnering, are they really your kind of client?

REFER TO THESE SECTIONS OF *THE CONTRACT GUIDE*:

Bibliography
Construction Observation
Delays
Design Without Construction Phase Services
Dispute Resolution
Jobsite Safety
Third Party Claims

ADDITIONAL RESOURCES:

A Project Partnering Guide for Design Professionals, Washington, DC: American Consulting Engineers Council and The American Institute of Architects. 1993.

Groton, James P., *Dispute Review Boards — Back-Door Partnering*, Sutherland, Asbill & Brennan.

In Search of Partnering Excellence, Austin, TX: Construction Industry Institute, University of Texas. 1991.

ORDER FORM

Please send me _____ additional copies of *The Contract Guide* at $49.95 per book. This price includes postage and handling. I enclose my check in the amount of $_____ , payable to DPIC Companies, Inc.

Name _____

Firm _____

Address (no P. O. Box) _____

City _____

State _____ Zip _____ Phone _____

DPIC Companies, Inc., P. O. Box DPIC, Monterey, CA 93942
(800) 227-4284

ORDER FORM

Please send me _____ additional copies of *The Contract Guide* at $49.95 per book. This price includes postage and handling. I enclose my check in the amount of $_____ , payable to DPIC Companies, Inc.

Name _____

Firm _____

Address (no P. O. Box) _____

City _____

State _____ Zip _____ Phone _____

DPIC Companies, Inc., P. O. Box DPIC, Monterey, CA 93942
(800) 227-4284